ṢŪFĪ COMMENTARIES ON THE QUR'ĀN IN CLASSICAL ISLAM

The Classical period of Islam, from the tenth to the fifteenth centuries, was the period in which the most influential commentaries on the Qur'ān were written. *Ṣūfī Commentaries on the Qur'ān in Classical Islam* looks at the unique contributions of Ṣūfīs to this genre and how these contributions fit into the theological and exegetical discussions of the time.

The study begins with an examination of several key hermeneutical assumptions of Ṣūfīs, including their understanding of the ambiguous and multivalent nature of the Qur'ānic text, the role that both the intellect and spiritual disciplines play in acquiring knowledge of its meanings, and the ever-changing nature of the self which seeks this kind of knowledge. The second half of the study is an analysis and comparison of the themes and styles of several different commentaries on the Qur'ānic story of Mūsā (Moses) and al-Khaḍir; the figure of Maryam (The Virgin Mary); and the Light Verse. It demonstrates that, while Ṣūfī interpretation has often been characterized as allegorical, these writings are more notable for their variety of philosophical, visionary, literary, and homiletic styles.

Ṣūfī Commentaries on the Qur'ān in Classical Islam is the first comprehensive study of the contributions of Ṣūfīs to the genre of commentaries on the Qur'ān and is essential reading for those with research interests in Ṣūfīsm, Qur'ānic exegesis and Islam.

Kristin Zahra Sands is a Mellon Fellow and Assistant Professor of Islamic Studies at Sarah Lawrence College. Her research interests include Ṣūfīsm, Qur'ānic exegesis, and Islam and media.

ROUTLEDGE STUDIES IN THE QURAN
Series Editor: Andrew Rippin
University of Victoria, Canada

In its examination of critical issues in the scholarly study of the Quran and its commentaries, this series targets the disciplines of archaeology, history, textual history, anthropology, theology, and literary criticism. The contemporary relevance of the Quran in the Muslim world, its role in politics and in legal debates are also dealt with, as are debates surrounding Quranic studies in the Muslim world.

LITERARY STRUCTURES OF RELIGIOUS MEANING IN THE QUR'ĀN
Edited by Issa J. Boullata

THE DEVELOPMENT OF EXEGESIS IN EARLY ISLAM
The authenticity of Muslim literature from the Formative Period
Herbert Berg

BIBLICAL PROPHETS IN THE QUR'ĀN AND MUSLIM LITERATURE
Robert Tottoli

MOSES IN THE QURAN AND ISLAMIC EXEGESIS
Brannon M. Wheeler

LOGIC, RHETORIC AND LEGAL REASONING IN THE QUR'ĀN
God's arguments
Rosalind Ward Gwynne

TEXTUAL RELATIONS IN THE QUR'ĀN
Relevance, coherence and structure
Salwa M.S. El-Awa

ṢŪFĪ COMMENTARIES ON THE QUR'ĀN IN CLASSICAL ISLAM
Kristin Zahra Sands

ṢŪFĪ COMMENTARIES ON THE QUR'ĀN IN CLASSICAL ISLAM

Kristin Zahra Sands

Routledge
Taylor & Francis Group
LONDON AND NEW YORK

First published 2006
by Routledge
2 Park Square, Milton Park, Abingdon, Oxon OX14 4RN

Simultaneously published in the USA and Canada
by Routledge
270 Madison Ave, New York, NY 10016

Routledge is an imprint of the Taylor & Francis Group

Transferred to Digital Printing 2008

Typeset in Times New Roman by
Newgen Imaging Systems (P) Ltd, Chennai, India

British Library Cataloguing in Publication Data
A catalogue record for this book is available
from the British Library

Library of Congress Cataloging in Publication Data
A catalog record for this book has been requested

ISBN10: 0–415–36685–2 (hbk)
ISBN10: 0–415–48314–X (pbk)

ISBN13: 9–78–0–415–36685–4 (hbk)
ISBN13: 9–78–0–415–48314–8 (hbk)

CONTENTS

ACKNOWLEDGMENTS

I am very grateful to have had so many people help and support me in the writing of this book. In its beginning draft as a PhD dissertation at New York University, I benefited greatly from the thorough and thoughtful comments of my advisor, Philip F. Kennedy. Other key readers of the manuscript at this stage were Peter J. Chelkowski and Alfred L. Ivry, teachers whose encouragement and generosity toward me has been unfailing. I would also like to thank several people outside of New York University who carefully read and commented on the entire manuscript in this early stage: Ali Campbell, Ruqiyya Hutton, and Omar Trezise. My primary debt for the book in hand is to Andrew Rippin, the editor of this Routledge Studies in the Quran series, for his astute suggestions and detailed comments. Abd al-Rahman Tayyara was kind enough to check the Arabic transliterations. Any errors that remain, however, are my own. My thanks to David M. Buchman and Brigham Young University Press for allowing me to include excerpts from Dr Buchman's translation of al-Ghazālī's *Niche of Lights*. Finally, I thank my husband Michael for the generosity of spirit he has shown in never complaining about the seemingly endless hours, days, and years spent on this project.

INTRODUCTION

The Qur'ān, for Muslims, represents the word of God revealed to Muḥammad. Its interpretation, then, requires a certain audacity. How can one begin to say what God "meant" by His revelation? How does one balance the praiseworthy desire to understand the meanings of the Qur'ān with the realistic fear of reducing it to the merely human and individualistic? Is interpretation an art, a science, an inspired act, or all of the these? Ṣūfī commentators living in the classical time period of Islam from the tenth to the fifteenth centuries answered these questions in their own unique way, based on their assumptions regarding the nature of the Qur'ānic text, the sources of knowledge considered necessary for its interpretation, and the nature of the self seeking this knowledge. The commentaries they wrote are distinct from other types of Qur'ānic commentaries both in terms of content, which reflects Ṣūfī ideas and concepts, and the variety of styles ranging from philosophical musings to popular preaching to literary narrative and poetry.

Early Western scholarship on Ṣūfī Qur'ānic interpretation focused on the origins of Ṣūfī thought. In his *Die Richtungen der islamischen Koranauslegung*, Ignaz Goldziher characterized the Ṣūfī approach as eisegesis, the reading of one's own ideas into a text.[1] Goldziher firmly believed that Ṣūfī thought is radically different from "original, traditional Islam,"[2] finding little basis for their beliefs in the Qur'ān. Not surprisingly then, he viewed Ṣūfī Qur'ānic commentary as an attempt to reconcile these different belief systems and to justify the Ṣūfī worldview within an Islamic framework through the method of allegoresis. According to Goldziher, the Ṣūfīs were influenced in this by Platonic thought which contrasts the world of appearances with the world of Ideas, just as Ṣūfī exegetes distinguish the exoteric (*ẓāhir*) from the esoteric (*bāṭin*) levels of meaning of the Qur'ān. Although Ṣūfīs insisted that they were uncovering deeper meanings of the Qur'ān, Goldziher found them reading ideas into a text essentially alien or even hostile to their system of thought.

The conclusions of Goldziher regarding the sources of Ṣūfī thought were debated by Louis Massignon, who attempted to show through an analysis of early Ṣūfī vocabulary that it was the Qur'ān itself, constantly recited, meditated upon, and practiced which was the origin and genuine source for the development of Ṣūfism.[3] Paul Nwyia continued Massignon's research, focusing particularly on the mystical commentary attributed to Jaʿfar al-Ṣādiq (d. 765). Nwyia concluded that Jaʿfar al-Ṣādiq's commentary was the result of a dialogue between personal, mystic experience, and the text of the Qur'ān. The vocabulary found in this commentary marks the beginning of the development of specific Ṣūfī terminology that was not derived from foreign ideas and concepts but rather was created to describe the dialogue originating from and remaining within a Qur'ānic context.[4] Both Massignon and Nwyia insisted that the Qur'ānic text remains primary for the Ṣūfī; that is to say, the Muslim mystic does not impose his own ideas on the Qur'ānic text, but rather discovers ideas in the course of his experiential dialogue with the text.[5]

The term allegoresis used by Goldziher does not adequately convey the complex and varied use of metaphorical language in Ṣūfī Qur'ānic commentaries. Studies by such scholars as Henry Corbin,[6] Toshihiko Izutsu[7] and William Chittick[8] on the use of language in other types of Ṣūfī writings have shown the relationship between symbolic and metaphorical language and the concept of imagination, understood not as fantasy, but as an objective reality of the mind and cosmos. In his study of the *Dhakhā'ir al-aʿlāq* of Ibn ʿArabī (d. 1240), Chittick identifies imagination as a concept referring to three different things: a faculty by which humans may obtain knowledge, just as they obtain knowledge from prophetic revelations and rational thought; an intermediate realm between the world of pure spirit and the world of bodies, sometimes called the "world of images" (*ʿālam al-mithāl*); and something that reflects the nature of the cosmos as a whole.[9] The kind of language and discourse used in Ṣūfī writings may, then, appear to be metaphorical while in fact being descriptive of experience in this intermediate realm, or it may be truly metaphorical since language using imagery is considered to be a better indicator of the nature of reality than abstract, rational thought.

The issue of language is related to the problem of defining the nature and objective of Ṣūfī writings. The possibility that Ṣūfīs are merely describing the reality that they see is rejected by those who consider their experiences a form of fantasy and their writings fictive compositions. In an article on the concept of the "world of images" (*ālam al-mithāl*) Fazlur Rahman rejects the ontological existence of this realm and therefore criticizes the claim of some Ṣūfīs to mystical experience within it; instead of descriptions of theophanies, he sees only an artistic impulse struggling to express itself.

> Once the flood of imagination is let loose, the world of figures goes beyond the specifically religious motivation that historically brought it into existence in the first place and develops into the poetic, the mythical, and the grotesque: it seeks to satisfy the relatively suppressed and starved artistic urge. Much of the contents of the *ʿālam al-mithāl* [the world of images], as it develops later, has, therefore, nothing to do with religion but indirectly with theater.[10]

Leonard Lewisohn, on the other hand, suggests that reading Ṣūfī literature without accepting the reality of mystical experience results in a distortion of their writings. If one approaches Ṣūfī works from an aesthetic and literary perspective alone, one will see only allegories instead of metaphysical referents which can only be grasped experientially. While the aesthetic and literary element of Ṣūfī writings is undeniable, Lewisohn states that there is no "art for art's sake in Ṣūfī literature."[11]

Hamid Dabashi has looked at the political dynamics behind Persian Ṣūfī poetry, describing its development within the context of a competition for authority among jurists, philosophers, court politicians, and the Ṣūfīs. As Ṣūfīs began writing poetry, or when poets became Ṣūfīs, they became propagandists for their mystical doctrines rather than poets first and foremost, subordinating the artistic impulse to a mystical worldview. Like Lewisohn, he agrees that the artistic impulse is secondary, but describes the phenomenon as an appropriation of art for other purposes.[12] Michael Sells views the interaction between these groups in a different way, as a creative clash of cultures. He suggests that the use of different language contexts by Ṣūfīs demonstrates a central aspect of classical Islamic culture, "the interpermeability and interfusion of discursive and cultural worlds."[13] J.C. Bürgel notes the major role that Ṣūfism played in allowing the arts to flourish in the Islamic world and suggests that this is because Ṣūfī theories made acts of creativity "licit magic," while more orthodox Islam criticized and sometimes condemned poetry, representational art and music, seeing in their power an attempt to rival the creativity and power of God.[14]

The objective of this book is to add to these previous discussions by studying the relationship of Ṣūfīs to the Qur'ān more comprehensively. Understanding the nature of this relationship provides insight into the use of creative composition in other genres adopted by the Ṣūfīs as well. Part I of the study concerns Ṣūfī hermeneutics, a word used here to refer to the way in which Ṣūfīs described the nature of the Qur'ānic text and the types of knowledge and methods needed to understand it. The unique characteristics of Ṣūfī interpretation are further highlighted by means of an analysis of the writings of those who criticized and defended it. Part II begins with a brief overview of the lives and exegetical works of the Ṣūfī commentators studied for this work. Selections from their commentaries on the story of Mūsā and al-Khaḍir, the figure of Maryam, and the Light Verse will be presented in order to demonstrate common themes and different compositional styles.

The most basic question addressed in these works, and the question from which all other questions are derived, is how to best approach the Qur'ān in order to discover its richness and transforming possibilities. It is a question asked directly in the hermeneutical writings and addressed indirectly in the commentaries themselves. Because interpretation is seen as an unending process which will be different for each individual, Ṣūfī interpretations are more suggestive than declarative; they are "allusions" (*ishārāt*) rather than explanations (*tafāsīr*), to use the Arabic terms. They therefore indicate possibilities as much as they demonstrate the insights of each writer. The concept of imagination which plays such a prominent role in Ibn 'Arabī's thought is less pronounced in the writings studied here. There is instead an emphasis on the connection between knowledge granted directly from God (*'ilm ladunī*) and the ethics and spiritual practice of the individuals seeking this knowledge. The language and type of discourse chosen to express this knowledge varies with the different commentators, and demonstrates the individuality of each. The interplay of language worlds and discourses in classical Islam which Sells notes is very much apparent here; many of these commentaries can only be understood within the context of discussions occurring within other areas of Islamic thought.

The role of creativity in these writings is not a question that is addressed, probably because the self is not viewed as the origin of this knowledge. This is not to say, however, that the writers studied here are unaware of issues of style and composition. On the contrary, these aesthetic matters are considered important because the primary function of these works is didactic. The question of creativity is addressed somewhat indirectly through the justifications made for the highly individualistic nature of these interpretations, especially in the apologetic writings of Abū Ḥāmid al-Ghazālī (d. 1111).

Much of the subject matter in this book could be productively compared to studies on the interpretation of books considered sacred in other traditions as well as contemporary hermeneutical and literary theories on reading texts. I have, however, deliberately avoided making these comparisons in order to keep the focus on the complexity of the classical Islamic and Ṣūfī discussions on Qur'ānic interpretation. Western scholarship has only just begun to scratch the surface of the vast literature included within the genre of Qur'ānic commentary; this study represents only a small contribution towards what will hopefully be a greater appreciation of the enormous variety of Islamic thought.

A word should be said about the use of the terms Ṣūfī and Ṣūfism throughout this work. As Carl Ernst has pointed out, the Arabic equivalents to these words are terms used relatively infrequently in the writings we now label as Ṣūfī. When they are used in classical works, it is in a prescriptive rather this descriptive sense.[15] In the works studied here, the authors do not refer to themselves as Ṣūfīs but rather as "the people of allusion and understanding" (*ahl al-ishāra wa'l-fahm*), "the people of meanings" (*ahl al-maʿānī*), "the people of love" (*ahl al-ʿishq*), "gnostics" (*ʿārifūn*), "verifiers" (*muḥaqqiqūn*), and "the people of states" (*ahl al-mawājid*), to give just a few examples. However, despite the different terminology and writing styles employed, these works share common hermeneutical assumptions and elements. The use of unifying terms to describe their approach, then, seems appropriate and the words "Ṣūfī" and "Ṣūfism" are the logical choice in English, despite the problems outlined by Ernst.

The translations in this work are my own unless otherwise noted. I have benefited greatly from the work of previous translators and the choice to use my own translation in many places is due to a concern for consistency in terminology rather than a criticism of the translations of my predecessors. The translations of the Qur'ān have been made after consulting the translations of Arberry, Ali, and Asad. I have taken the liberty of omitting the frequent phrases of blessings that occur in these texts for the sake of brevity and clarity. The transliteration system used is that of *The Encyclopedia of Islam* with the exception of *j* for *jīm* and *q* for *qāf*.

Part I

HERMENEUTICS

1

THE QUR'ĀN AS THE OCEAN OF ALL KNOWLEDGE

Ṣūfī interpretation begins with several basic premises: that the Qur'ān contains many levels of meaning, that man has the potential to uncover these meanings, and that the task of interpretation is endless. In their exegetical writings, Ṣūfīs quote such Qur'ānic verses as *We have left nothing out from the Book* (6:38), *We have counted everything in a clear register* (36:12), *There is nothing whose treasures are not with Us and We only send it down in a known measure* (15:21),[1] and, *If all the trees on the earth were pens and the sea seven seas after it to replenish it, the words of God would not be depleted* (31:27).[2] The image of the Qur'ān as an ocean is a particularly popular one, as in this quote from the *Jawāhir al-Qur'ān* of Abū Ḥāmid al-Ghazālī.

> I will rouse you from your sleep, you who have given yourself up to recitation, who have taken the study of the Qur'ān as a practice, who have seized upon some of its outward meanings and sentences. How long will you wander about the shore of the sea with your eyes closed to its wonders? Was it not for you to sail through its depths in order to see its amazing things, to travel to its islands to pick its delicacies, to dive to its bottom and become rich from obtaining its jewels? Don't you despise yourself for losing out on its pearls and jewels as you continue to look only to its shores and exoteric aspects?
>
> Haven't you heard that the Qur'ān is an ocean from which the knowledge of all ages branches out just as rivers and streams branch out from the shores of the ocean? Don't you envy the happiness of people who have plunged into its overflowing waves and seized red sulfur,[3] who have dived into its depths and taken out red rubies, shining pearls and green chrysolite, who have roamed its shores and gathered gray ambergris and fresh blooming aloes wood, who have clung to its islands and found an abundance in their animals of the greatest antidote and pungent musk?[4]

A similar passage can be found in the introduction to the Qur'ānic commentary of 'Abd al-Razzāq al-Kāshānī (d. 1329):

> Their souls are purified by [the Qur'ān's] exoteric sense (*ẓāhir*) because it is water which flows copiously and the thirst of their hearts is quenched by its inner sense (*bāṭin*) because it is a surging sea. When they wish to dive in order to extract the pearls of its secrets the water crashes over them and they are submerged in its current. The riverbeds of insights (*fuhūm*) flow from this deluge according to their capacities, while the streams of realizations (*'uqūl*) proceed from its rivers. The riverbeds bring forth piercing jewels and pearls upon the shores and the streams cause flowers and fruit to bloom upon the banks. Hearts take from the overflow as much as they can, filling their laps and sleeves, while souls set out to harvest the fruits and lights, grateful for finding them, their desires fulfilled by them.[5]

The idea that there are exoteric (*ẓāhir*) and inner (*bāṭin*) senses of the Qur'ān was well developed by Ṣūfīs before al-Kāshānī. Although the division of the exoteric and the inner has its basis in the Qur'ān,[6] its importance in hermeneutical discussions is more closely tied to a *ḥadīth* attributed to 'Abd Allāh b. Mas'ūd (d. 652).

The *ḥadīth* of Ibn Mas'ūd

The *ḥadīth* of Ibn Mas'ūd is the *ḥadīth* most frequently quoted by the Ṣūfīs as proof of the many dimensions of the Qur'ān open to interpretation. Commentators who were not Ṣūfīs, such as Abū Ja'far al-Ṭabarī (d. 923),[7] quoted it as well but they understood it in a different way. Here is al-Ṭabarī's version of the *ḥadīth* from the introduction to his Qur'ānic commentary, *Jāmi' al-bayān*:

> The messenger of God said, "The Qur'ān was sent down in seven *aḥruf*. Each *ḥarf* has a back (*ẓahr*) and and belly (*baṭn*). Each *ḥarf* has a border (*ḥadd*) and each border has a lookout point (*muṭṭala'*)."[8]

Al-Ṭabarī includes this *ḥadith* among several other *aḥādīth* about the seven *aḥruf*, devoting several pages to the controversy over the meaning of the word "*ḥarf* (pl. *aḥruf*)" and concluding that the seven *aḥruf* refer to both dialects (*alsun*) of the Arabs and aspects (*awjuh*) of the revelation.[9] The meaning of this particular Tradition, according to al-Ṭabarī is as follows:

> "Each *ḥarf* has a border (*ḥadd*)" means that each of the seven aspects (*awjuh*) has a border delimited by God which no one may go past. As for his words "and each *ḥarf* has a back (*ẓahr*) and a belly (*baṭn*)," its back (*ẓahr*) is that which becomes apparent (*ẓāhir*) in recitation and its belly (*baṭn*) is its interpretation (*ta'wīl*) which is hidden (*baṭana*). His words,

> "and each of the borders has a lookout point (*muṭṭala'*)" means that each of the borders in which God has delineated the permitted and prohibited and the rest of His revealed laws has a measure of the rewards and punishments of God which will be seen and beheld in the Hereafter and met at the Resurrection, just as 'Umar b. al-Khaṭṭāb[10] said, "If everything in the world belonged to me, assuredly I would ransom myself with it against the terror of the lookout point (*muṭṭala'*)."[11]

For al-Ṭabarī, the inner sense (*bāṭin*) refers to events in the future, knowledge of which is not given to man until the Day of Resurrection. The word *ta'wīl* has different meanings in the Qur'ān; al-Ṭabarī seems to use it here in its sense of the unfolding of events, not interpretation.[12]

Roughly contemporary with al-Ṭabarī, the Ṣūfī interpretation of Sahl al-Tustarī (d. 896) gives us a reading of this *ḥadīth* that is different in two important respects. The first is in its designating knowledge of the external sense (*ẓāhir*) as public (*'āmm*) and knowledge of the inner sense (*bāṭin*) as private (*khāṣṣ*). The second difference is in the interpretation of the lookout point (*muṭṭala'*). Using the tradition from 'Umar, al-Ṭabarī understands this as a terrifying vantage point on the Day of Resurrection. Al-Tustarī, on the other hand, understands the *muṭṭala'* as a vantage point of the heart, an overview from which one can understand what God meant by certain verses of the Qur'ān while still in this life.

> Every verse of the Qur'an has four kinds of meanings: an exoteric sense (*ẓāhir*), an inner sense (*bāṭin*), a limit (*ḥadd*), and a lookout point (*muṭṭala'*). The exoteric sense is the recitation, the inner sense is understanding (*fahm*), the limit is what [the verse] permits and prohibits, and the lookout point is the elevated places of the heart (*qalb*) [beholding] what was intended by it as understood from God Almighty. The knowledge of the exoteric sense is public knowledge (*'ilm 'āmm*) and the understanding of its inner sense and what was intended by it is private (*khāṣṣ*).[13]

Al-Tustarī does not specify in this passage as to exactly who possesses this public and private knowledge. Throughout his *tafsīr*, he uses the terms "elect" (*khuṣūṣ*) and common people (*'umūm*) without saying what he means by this distinction.[14]

Abū Ṭālib al-Makkī (d. 998), writing about a hundred years after al-Tustarī in his *Qūt al-qulūb*, interprets the *ḥadīth* in much the same way as al-Tustarī, adding details regarding exoteric and esoteric knowledge, and confirming the view that the lookout point (*muṭṭala'*) refers to a vantage point attainable in this life. He seems to reference the saying of 'Umar found in al-Ṭabarī, but manages to soften its frightening aspect by a play on words:

> Its back (*ẓahr*) is for experts in the Arabic language (*ahl al-'arabiyya*), its inner sense (*bāṭin*) is for the people of certainty (*ahl al-yaqīn*), its limit (*ḥadd*) is for the exotericists (*ahl al-ẓāhir*), and its lookout point

> (*muṭṭala*ʿ) is for the people of elevated places (*ahl al-ashrāf*) who are the gnostics (*ʿārifūn*), loving and fearing; they have beheld (*iṭṭalaʿū*) the kindness of the One who looks down (*muṭṭali*ʿ) after having feared the terror of the lookout point (*muṭṭala*ʿ).[15]

Al-Ghazālī mentions the Ibn Masʿūd *ḥadīth* in his defense of Ṣūfī exegesis in his *Iḥyāʾ ʿulūm al-dīn*. His use of the *ḥadīth* is part of a more combative style intended to rebut religious scholars who believe that Qurʾānic commentary should be based entirely on the transmitted traditions of the Companions and the Followers of the Prophet. Al-Ghazālī's challenges them to explain the meaning of the Ibn Masʿūd *ḥadīth* if exegesis is to be so restricted. He bluntly states that "the one who claims that the Qurʾān has no other meaning than what exoteric exegesis (*ẓāhir al-tafsīr*) has explained (*tarjama*), should know that he has acknowledged his own limitations and therefore is right with regards to himself, but is wrong in an opinion which brings everyone else down to his level."[16]

But al-Ghazālī is rather unique in his desire to engage with the opponents of Ṣūfism head-on. The approach of Rūzbihān al-Baqlī (d. 1209) in his Qurʾānic commentary *ʿArāʾis al-bayān* is more typical. He writes for his fellow Ṣūfīs alone, describing the division between exotericists and Ṣūfīs as part of God's plan in Creation:

> Then he gave the external reins of [the Qurʾān] to the hands of the exotericists (*ahl al-ẓāhir*) among the scholars (*ʿulamāʾ*) and the wise (*ḥukamāʾ*) so that they introduce its precepts, limits, regulations, and laws, and He reserved the unseen of the secrets of His speech and the hidden subtleties of His signs for the best of His people. He disclosed Himself in His words by the attribute of unveiling (*kashf*), eyewitnessing (*ʿiyān*), and explanation (*bayān*) to their hearts (*qulūb*), spirits (*arwāḥ*), intellects (*ʿuqūl*), and innermost secrets (*asrār*).
>
> He taught them the sciences of His realities (*ḥaqāʾiq)* and the phenomena of His intricacies (*daqāʾiq*). He purified the degrees of their intellects by the unveiling of the lights of his Beauty. He sanctified their understandings by the splendor of His Majesty. He made them the places for the hidden deposits of the symbols (*rumūz*) of His speech, the obscurities of His secrets deposited in His Book, the subtlety of His allusions (*ishārāt*) to the sciences of the ambiguous verses (*mutashābihāt*) and [other] difficulties of the verses. He Himself informed them of the meanings of that which He hid in the Qurʾān so that they would come to know by means of His causing them to know. He anointed their eyes by the light of His nearness and communion. He showed them the unseen mysteries of the brides of different kinds of wisdom and knowledge, and the meanings of the innermost understanding and innermost secret, the exoteric sense (*ẓāhir)* of which is a fundamental principle (*ḥukm*) in the Qurʾān and inner sense (*bāṭin*) of which is an allusion (*ishāra*) and

> unveiling (*kashf*) which God (*al-ḥaqq*) reserves for His purified ones and His greater friends (*awliyā'*) and His exiled beloved among the sincere and close companions (*muqarrabūn*).
>
> He veiled these secrets and marvels from others, those among the scholars of the external sense (*'ulamā' al-ẓāhir*) and the exotericists (*ahl-rusūm*) who have an abundant portion of the abrogating and the abrogated, and the comprehension and knowledge of the permitted and prohibited, the limits and rules.[17]

Although Ṣūfīs in this time period used the term "exotericists" (*ahl al-ẓāhir* or *ahl al-rusūm*), they did not call themselves "esotericists" (*bāṭiniyya*) since this was a derogatory term applied to those who rejected the literal sense of the Qur'ān and the exoteric practices of Islam, especially the Ismā'īlīs. None of the Ṣūfīs studied here rejected the external aspects of practice and knowledge, but rather considered these the necessary prerequisites for proceeding with the inward aspects.

Niẓām al-Dīn al Nīsābūrī (d. 1327) echoes the thoughts of Rūzbihān in his interpretation of the Ibn Mas'ūd *ḥadīth*, found in the introduction to his Qur'ānic commentary entitled *Gharā'ib al-Qur'ān wa raghā'ib al-furqān*. He writes that the exoteric sense (*ẓāhir*) of the Qur'ān is what scholars (*'ulamā'*) know, and the inner sense (*bāṭin*) is what is hidden from them, and he adds, "and we speak of it as we have been commanded and entrust the knowledge of it to God most High."[18] Al-Nīsābūrī provides both exoteric and esoteric definitions for the word *muṭṭala'*. The first repeats the tradition of 'Umar found in al-Ṭabarī regarding the lookout point on the Day of Resurrection. The second definition confirms the Ṣūfī belief in the possibility of acquiring this vision in the here and now. The *muṭṭala'* is "the point of ascent (*maṣ'ad*), a place to which one arrives where one understands [a thing] as it is (*yafhamu kamā huwa*)."[19]

Al-Kāshānī's commentary on the *ḥadīth* interprets the back (*ẓahr)* and the belly (*baṭn*) as exoteric exegesis (*tafsīr*) and esoteric interpretation (*ta'wīl*). He understands the limit (*ḥadd*) as the place "where understandings of the meaning of the words end" and the lookout point (*muṭṭala'*) as the place to which one rises up from the limit and "beholds (*yaṭṭali'u*) the witnessing of the all-knowing King."[20]

In all of these interpretations of the Ibn Mas'ūd *ḥadīth*, the division of the Qur'ān is basically twofold, exoteric and esoteric. The exoteric is the external sense (*ẓahr*) and the commands and prohibitions that constitute the limit (*ḥadd*). The esoteric is the inner sense (*baṭn)* and the gnostic's lookout point (*muṭṭala'*). In 'Alā' al-Dawla al-Simnānī (d. 1336), this twofold sense is expanded into a four-fold hierarchical interpretative process:

> O seeker of the inner meaning of the Qur'ān! You should first study the literal level of the Qur'ān and bring your body into harmony with its commands and prohibitions. Secondly, you should occupy yourself with

> purifying your inner being so that you may comprehend the hidden meaning (*baṭn*) of the Qur'ān according to the instruction of the Merciful One and the inspiration of the Holy Angel. Thirdly, you should contemplate the gnosis of its limit (*ḥadd*) in the realm of hearts. [Only then] will you be distinguished with witnessing its point of ascent (*muṭṭala*ʿ) without thought or reckoning.[21]

According to al-Simnānī, the source of interpretation varies according to these four different levels of the Qur'ān:

> The commentator on the exoteric dimension of the Qur'ān should rely exclusively upon his external sense of hearing through which he learned the verses himself. The mystic should rely on inspiration (*ilhām*) to comment on the esoteric dimension, while the accomplished Sufi who has truly declared the unity of God should only comment on the limit with divine permission. The individual who has attained the secret of the essence should not comment at all, but proceed in a faltering manner into the point of ascent of the Qur'ān.[22]

Al-Simnānī relates the four levels of meaning to four realms of existence: the Human Realm (*nāsūt*), the Kingdom (*malakūt*), the Omnipotence (*jabarūt*), and the Divinity (*lāhūt*).[23]

Sayings from ʿAlī and Jaʿfar al-Ṣādiq

In addition to the Ibn Masʿūd *ḥadīth*, the Ṣūfīs found validation for their belief in the existence of deeper, discoverable meanings in the Qur'ān in sayings attributed to ʿAlī (d.661) and Jaʿfar al-Ṣādiq (d. 765), important figures for both Ṣūfīs and Shīʿīs.[24] The first of the sayings attributed to ʿAlī quoted below echoes the *ḥadīth* of Ibn Masʿūd:

> Every verse of the Qur'ān has four kinds of meaning: an exoteric sense (*ẓāhir*), an inner sense (*bāṭin*), a limit (*ḥadd*), and a lookout point (*muṭṭala*ʿ). The exoteric sense is the recitation (*tilāwa*), the inner sense is understanding (*fahm*), the limit (*ḥadd)* is the rulings of what is permitted and prohibited, and the lookout point (*muṭṭala*ʿ) is what is meant by God for the servant by [the verse]. It is said that the Qur'ān is a clear expression (*ʿibāra*), an allusion (*ishāra*), subtleties (*laṭā'if*) and realities (*ḥaqā'iq*), so that the clear expression is for hearing, the allusion is for the intellect (*ʿaql*), the subtleties are for witnessing (*mushāhada*) and the realities are for self-surrender (*istislām*).[25]
>
> There is no good in an act of worship without comprehension, nor in a recitation without pondering.[26]

> The Messenger of God (peace and blessings of God be upon him), did not confide anything in me which he concealed from people, except that God most High gives a servant understanding of His Book.[27]
>
> If I had wished, I could have loaded seventy camels with commentary (*tafsīr*) on the *Fātiḥa* of the Book (the opening *sūra*).[28]
>
> For the one who understands (*yafhamu*) the Qur'ān, thereby whole bodies of knowledge are explained (*fussira*).[29]

Those attributed to Ja'far al-Ṣādiq are:

> The Qur'ān is recited with nine aspects (*awjuh*): the Truth (*ḥaqq*), truth (*ḥaqīqa*), realization (*taḥqīq*), realities (*ḥaqā'iq*), oaths, contracts, limits, the cutting off of attachments, and the exaltation of the One who is worshipped.[30]
>
> The Qur'ān was sent down in seven modes (*anwā'*): to inform, entrust, awaken affection, ennoble, unite, frighten and restrain. Moreover, it was revealed as a command, a prohibition, a promise, a threat, an indulgence, a foundation, and a test. Moreover, it was revealed as an inviter, a guardian, a witness, a preserver, an intercessor, a defender, and a protector.[31]
>
> The Book of God has four things: the clear expression (*'ibāra*), the allusion (*ishāra*), subtleties (*laṭā'if*) and realities (*ḥaqā'iq*). The clear expression is for the common people (*'awāmm*), the allusion is for the elite (*khawāṣṣ*), the subtleties are for the friends (*awliyā'*), and the realities are for the prophets (*anbiyā'*).[32]

2

THE QUR'ĀNIC TEXT AND AMBIGUITY

Verse 3:7

The Ṣūfīs' insistence upon the multivalent nature of the Qur'ānic text is related to their understanding of its ambiguity. A key verse here is Qur'ān 3:7 because it addresses the problems in interpreting a text that is both clear and ambiguous.

> *He it is who sent down to you the book containing clear verses* (ayāt muḥkamāt) *which are the mother of the Book and others that are ambiguous or similar* (mutashābihāt). *As for those in whose hearts is a turning away, they follow what is ambiguous or similar* (mutashābih) *in it, seeking discord and seeking its interpretation* (ta'wīl) *but none knows its interpretation except God. Those who are firmly rooted in knowledge* (al-rāsikhūn fīl-'ilm) *say, "We believe in it; the whole is from our Lord," and no one remembers except those who possess understanding* (ūlū al-albāb).

An alternative translation of the last part of this verse is possible, which makes *those who are firmly rooted in knowledge* a continuation of the phrase *except God*, resulting in the statement *but none knows its interpretation except God and those who are firmly rooted in knowledge who say, "We believe in it; the whole is from our Lord."* Most classical commentaries on this verse attempt to define what is meant by the clear and ambiguous verses of the Qur'ān and those *seeking discord* and those *firmly rooted in knowledge.* As is often the case in Ṣūfī commentaries, Ṣūfī interpretations are best understood within the context of exoteric commentaries such as al-Ṭabarī's that cite the interpretative traditions transmitted from the Companions and Followers of the Prophet.

The clear and ambiguous verses (*muḥkamāt wa mutashābihāt*)

In his commentary on the Qur'ān, al-Ṭabarī mentions five early interpretations for what constitutes the clear and ambiguous verses (*muḥkamāt wa mutashābihāt*).[1] Among these five, al-Ṭabarī's preferred interpretation is that the *muḥkamāt* are those verses that may be interpreted and understood by religious scholars (*'ulamā'*) whereas the *mutashābihāt* are those verses that may be interpreted only by God – the disconnected letters occurring at the beginning of several chapters of the Qur'ān or verses pertaining to future eschatological events.[2] Although this interpretation is often referred to in later commentaries, the interpretation more widely preferred after al-Ṭabarī is the one attributed to Muḥammad ibn al-Zubayr (d. 728–38), which states that the *muḥkamāt* are verses that can only be interpreted in one way, while the *mutashābihāt* are verses that allow for various interpretations.[3] As we shall see, this interpretation was used to develop a methodology for dealing with the difficult theological issues raised by verses concerning God's attributes and actions.

Ṣūfī interpretations of Qur'ān 3:7 understand the Ibn al-Zubayr tradition as additional confirmation of different levels of meaning in the Qur'ān. The *muḥkamāt* verses constitute the basic message necessary for salvation addressed to all mankind while the *mutashābihāt* are addressed to an elect group of individuals; the Qur'ānic text is designed both to reveal and conceal, to communicate both simply and profoundly. This concept is described in the Qur'ānic commentary of the Ṣūfī Abū'l-Qāsim al-Qushayrī (d. 1074). Al-Qushayrī, always liberal in the use of metaphor in his writing, appears here to be using the literal meanings of the words "revelation" (*tanzīl*) and "interpretation" (*ta'wīl*) to evoke an image of something that descends with ease but is brought back up with great difficulty.

> He has classified the discourse for them. From its apparent sense (*ẓāhir*), there is the clarity of its revelation (lit., "its being sent down," *tanzīlihi*) and from its obscure sense (*ghāmiḍ*), there is the problem of its interpretation (lit., "its being brought back," *ta'wīlihi*). The first kind is for the purpose of unfolding the law and guiding the people of the outwardly manifest (*ahl al-ẓāhir*). The second kind is for the purpose of protecting secrets (*asrār*) from the examination of outsiders.[4]

The Persian Qur'ānic commentator Rashīd al-Dīn al-Maybudī (fl. 1135) used al-Qushayrī's commentary as a source for his own, incorporating and expanding on his work in a decidedly literary manner. In this section of his *Kashf al-asrār*, al-Maybudī develops al-Qushayrī's suggestion that the obscurity in the Qur'ān is intentional, adding a short poem that taunts those who would undertake the search for deeper meanings casually:

> There are two exalted parts to the Qur'ān. One of them is the clear apparent sense (*ẓāhir-i rawshan*) and one is the difficult obscure sense (*ghāmiḍ-i mushkil*). This apparent sense is the majesty of the law (*sharī'at*) and that obscure sense is the beauty of reality (*ḥaqīqat*). This apparent sense is so that the masses (*'āmma*) of mankind might understand and practice this in order to reach the comfort (*nāz*) and blessing. That obscure sense is so that the elite (*khawāṣṣ*) of mankind might submit to and accept that, in order to reach the blessing of the secret (*rāz*) of the friend. How great is the distance (lit., descent and ascent)

between the place of the comfort and blessing and the place of intimacy and the secret! Because of the grandeur of that state and the nobility of that work, the veil of obscurity (*ghumūḍ*) and ambiguity (*tashābuh*) is not removed, so that not just any stranger could set foot in that quarter, since not everyone is worthy of the tale of the secrets of kings.

Do not stroll around the royal curtain of secrets!
  What can you do since you are not a man?
A real man ought to be peerless in each of the two worlds
  since he drinks the last drops of the draught of friends.[5]

By creating a series of corresponding polarities here, the *muḥkamāt* and the *mutashābihāt* of the Qur'ānic text, the masses (*'āmma*) and the elite (*khawāṣṣ*), the law (*sharī'a*) and the reality (*ḥaqīqa*), God's Majesty and Beauty; al-Maybudī connects the structure of the Qur'ān to that of mankind and the cosmos.

This linking of the structure of the Qur'ānic text to the nature of existence can also be seen in the commentary of Rūzbihān al-Baqlī. For Rūzbihān, the *muḥkamāt* are those verses that cannot be altered from how they were in pre-eternity. These are verses for believers that contain the practical application of the commandments, functioning like medicine for the sick in healing mankind and strengthening faith. They provide all that is necessary for man's salvation. The *mutashābihāt*, on the other hand, give information, to the few who are prepared to receive it, about the mysterious way in which God manifests Himself in His creation.

> The *mutashābihāt* are descriptions of the ambiguous wrapping (*iltibās*) of the Attributes (*ṣifāt*) and the manifestation (*ẓuhūr*) of the Essence (*dhāt*) in the mirror of witnessings (*shawāhid*) and signs (*ayāt*).[6]

Iltibās is a term found frequently in Rūzbihān's writings. It is a verbal noun derived from the Arabic root *lbs*. Two first form verbs from this root occur in the Qur'ān: *labisa*, which means to wear something or to clothe someone, and *labasa*, which means to confuse. The eighth form of the verb, *iltabasa* (verbal noun: *iltibās*), means "to become entangled" or "to become confused."[7] Rūzbihān uses the word to refer to the process by which God "clothes" His messages in forms that can be confusing or ambiguous to people.[8] The *mutashābihāt* are examples of these kinds of messages.

Another way to express the concept of *iltibās* is to speak of unity and multiplicity, the terminology that 'Abd al-Razzāq al-Kāshānī uses in his comments on Qur'ān 3:7. Without specifically identifying it, al-Kāshānī refers to Ibn al-Zubayr's interpretation before expanding it to include Ṣūfī metaphysical ideas and terminology:

> Potentiality of meaning and ambiguity cannot touch [the *muḥkamāt*]; they convey only one meaning. *They are the mother*, i.e. the root (*aṣl*) of

> the Book. *And others that are mutashābihāt.* They convey two meanings or more, and the truth and falsehood are ambiguous (*yashtabihu*) in them. That is because the Truth (*ḥaqq*) has one face, which is the absolute abiding face after the annihilation of creation, not admitting multiplicity or plurality. He also has multiple additional faces in accordance with the mirrors of the loci of manifestation (*maẓāhir*). [These faces] are what become manifest from that one face according to the preparedness (*isti'dād*) of each locus of manifestation. The truth and falsehood are ambiguous in them. The revelation appeared in this manner so that the *mutashābihāt* would turn towards the faces of the different forms of preparedness (*isti'dādāt*). So everyone clings to that which is appropriate to it, and the test and trial thereby become manifest.[9]

When al-Kāshānī speaks of loci of manifestation (*maẓāhir*), he is employing one of the terms initiated by Ibn 'Arabī to explain the nature of existence. God is One both in His Essence and His attribute as the Manifest, while the loci within which He manifests are qualified by multiplicity. "Preparedness" (*isti'dād*) is the term he uses to describe the receptivity of individually created things and beings to the manifestation of God, each becoming a locus of manifestation according to its innate capacity.[10] Although the terminology of al-Kāshānī and Rūzbihān are different, the basic concept is the same, that God created the world in such a way that truth and falsehood intermingle in an ambiguous way. Like al-Qushayrī and al-Maybudī, they distinguish between the *muḥkamāt* verses that send a message to all mankind and the *mutashābihāt* verses that are addressed to a few. The elitism here is not unique to Ṣūfīs but how the elite are defined is, as we shall see in the following section.

Those in whose hearts is a turning away and those who are firmly rooted in knowledge (*al-rāsikhūn fī'l-'ilm*)

Qur'ān 3:7 describes two ways in which mankind responds to the ambiguous verses (*mutashābihāt*) in the Qur'ān. Those *in whose hearts there is a turning away* try to create discord by means of these verses, whereas *those who are firmly rooted in knowledge* (*al-rāsikhūn fī'l-'ilm*) have faith in God's message as a unified whole. This part of the verse provoked extensive discussions in Qur'ānic exegesis concerning what constitutes sound interpretative methodology. The answer depends on how the *mutashābihāt* are defined. If the *mutashābihāt* are taken to refer to those events known only to God, such as future events, then *those firmly rooted in knowledge* (*al-rāsikhūn fī'l-'ilm*) leave their interpretation to God.[11] This is al-Ṭabarī's preferred interpretation and the one which produces the clearest statement regarding the role of the interpreter. By narrowing the definition of the *mutashābihāt* to the verses of disconnected letters and the verses having to do with future events, al-Ṭabarī narrows the area of the unknowable in the Qur'ān, thereby emphasizing its clarity.

> all of the verses of the Qur'ān that God revealed to His Messenger were revealed as a clear explanation (*bayān*) to him and his community and guidance to the worlds. It is not possible that anything could be included in it that they did not need, or anything that they did need but had no way of knowing by interpretation.
>
> Since this is so, mankind has a need for everything in the Qur'ān even though there are some meanings they can do without and many meanings that they very much need. This is like when God says, *on a day when some of the signs of your Lord will come, no soul will benefit if it has not already believed or earned something good by means of its faith* (6:158). The prophet taught his community that the sign that God speaks of in this verse... is the rising of the sun from the west. What the worshippers needed to know was the time period in which repentance would benefit them without restricting it to years, months, or days. God explained this for them by means of the Book and clarified it for them by means of His messenger acting as an exegete (*mufassir*). They did not need to know the length of time between the revelation of this verse and the appearance of this sign. They had no need of knowing it for their religion or present life. It is knowledge that God has reserved for Himself exclusively and not His creation, and He has veiled it from them.[12]

The *muḥkamāt* consist of everything except the verses having to do with the future events and disconnected letters. Although these *mukḥamāt* verses could be interpreted in various ways, their intended meaning has been made clear elsewhere in the Qur'ān or in the explanations of the Prophet. The role of the religious scholar (*'ālim*) is merely to present this intended meaning.

> If the *mutashābihāt* are as we have described, everything else is *muḥkam* by virtue of its having only one meaning and one interpretation. No one hearing it would need any explanations for it. Or, it is clear despite its possessing many aspects and interpretations and the possibility of many meanings because there exists an indication to its intended meaning either through an explanation by God Himself or an explanation by His Messenger to his community. The knowledge of the religious scholars (*'ulamā'*) in the community will not go beyond that because of what we have explained here.[13]

In keeping with his narrow definition of what constitutes the *mutashābihāt*, al-Ṭabarī prefers the reading of the verse that limits knowledge of the interpretation (*ta'wīl*) of the *mutashābihāt* to God alone, although he presents views from the Companions and Followers of the Prophet supporting the other reading as well. Because the verses with disconnected letters and those relating to future events make up a relatively small portion of the Qur'ānic text, al-Ṭabarī's preferred interpretation retains a broad role for the religious scholar in interpretation, since in this definition the *muḥkamāt* constitute the majority of the Qur'ān.

However, if the *mutashābihāt* are taken to refer to verses that can be interpreted in more than one way, then *those who are firmly rooted in knowledge (al-rāsikhūn fī'l-'ilm)* are those who know how to interpret them in light of the *muḥkamāt*. Al-Ṭabarī quotes Ibn al-Zubayr as saying,

> Then they refer the interpretation of the *mutashābiha* to what they know of the interpretation of the *muḥkama* that admit only one interpretation. The book is thereby harmonized by what they say, one part confirming another. By means of it, the proof (*ḥujja*) is established, victory appears, falsehood departs and infidelity is refuted.[14]

As for *those in whose hearts is a turning away*, they do the opposite, finding the meaning they want in the ambiguous verses, even when this meaning contradicts the clear verses.[15]

The Mu'tazilī commentator al-Zamakhsharī (d. 1144)[16] gives examples of how this methodology works in his *Kashshāf 'an ḥaqā'iq al-tanzīl*, applying it to support Mu'tazilī views denying the possibility of seeing God and affirming man's absolute free will. According to al-Zamakhsharī, the Qur'ānic verse *Vision cannot encompass Him* (6:103) is the *muḥkam* verse to which the *mutashābih* verse *gazing at their Lord* (75:23) must be referred. The first verse is to be understood literally while the second must be interpreted in light of the literal truth of the first. Likewise, the *muḥkam* verse *God does not command what is shameful* (7:28) makes sense of the *mutashābih* verse *When We intend to destroy a town, We command those who live easy lives in it, and they act sinfully* (17:16), which otherwise would seem to suggest that God commands some people to sin.[17]

The problem with this interpretative methodology is that one person's *muḥkam* verse is easily another's *mutashābih* and vice versa. In the process, the potential exists for undermining the very message of the Qur'ān, a danger noted by the theologian Fakhr al-Dīn al-Rāzī (d. 1210)[18] in his *Al-Tafsīr al-kabīr*:

> Know that among the apostates there is one who has attacked the Qur'ān because of its inclusion of the *mutashābihāt*. He said, "You say that the duties which mankind has been charged with are connected to this Qur'ān until the Coming of the Hour. Yet we see that [the disagreement over the *mutashābihāt*] reaches the point where each follower of a school of thought clings to it according to his own school, so that the Jabarite [determinist] clings to the verses of compulsion such as *We have placed veils upon their hearts lest they understand it, and heaviness in their ears* (6:25, 17:46, 18:57). The Qadarite [proponent of free will] says, "no, this is the school of infidels," indicating that God related this about the infidels when blaming them, saying, *They say our hearts are veiled from what you call us to and in our ears is a heaviness* (41:5) and in another place, *they say, "our hearts are enclosed in a covering"* (2:88, 4:155).

> Similarly, the one who affirms the beatific vision clings to His words *on that day faces will be radiant, gazing towards their Lord* (75:22–3) and the denier clings to *Vision cannot encompass Him* (6:103). The one who affirms that God has direction clings to His words *they fear their Lord above them* (16:50) and His words *the Merciful sat upon the throne* (20:5), while the denier clings to His words *there is nothing like Him* (42:11).
>
> Then each one calls the verse that agrees with his school *muḥkam* and the verses which disagree with his school *mutashābih*. Maybe the situation of preferring one verse over another derives from covert preference and weak positions. So how can it be fitting for the Wise to have made the Book that is the reference point for all of the religion until the Coming of the Hour thus? Wouldn't the objective be more likely attained if He had made it conspicuously evident and free of these *mutashābihāt*?[19]

After quoting this provocative question al-Rāzī provides several possible answers. He tells us that there are many religious scholars who believe that the difficulties of the *mutashābihāt* increase the reward for those who struggle to discover the truth, forcing them to exercise their minds, and freeing them from ignorance and uncritical faith (*taqlīd*). These verses also cause one to learn the methods of interpretation (*ta'wīlāt*) and preferring one (verse) over another (*tarjīḥ ba'ḍihā 'alā ba'ḍ*). The strongest benefit, according to al-Rāzī, is that these verses facilitate comprehension of the more difficult aspects of God's attributes and actions for those with the capacity for such comprehension, while at the same time not confusing those for whom simple explanations are best.[20]

Despite the dangers al-Rāzī outlines for the interpretative method of preferring one (verse) over another (*tarjīḥ ba'ḍihā 'alā ba'ḍ*), he nonetheless accepts its validity and necessity, and attempts to establish guidelines for how this is to be done. Simply put, any expression in the Qur'ān that can be interpreted in more than one way must be interpreted by its more probable meaning (*rājiḥ*) unless there is a clear-cut indicator (*dalīl munfaṣil*) that demonstrates the absurdity of the apparent sense (*ẓāhir*). According to al-Rāzī, this clear-cut indicator (*dalīl munfaṣil*) can be either linguistic (*lafẓī*) or rational (*'aqlī*). However, even though a definitive rational indicator can demonstrate the absurdity of the probable meaning, the intended meaning remains a matter of conjecture (*ẓann*). Guessing is permissible only for legal matters where action is required, not for the fundamentals of faith.[21]

An example of the kinds of expressions al-Rāzī means here are the anthropomorphic descriptions of God in the Qur'ān in verses such as *The Merciful sat upon His throne* (20:5). According to al-Rāzī, anthropomorphists (*mushabbiha*) seek to validate their beliefs with the apparent sense (*ẓāhir*) of this verse, even though it has been clearly established by reason (*thabata bi ṣarīḥ al-'aql*) that God cannot be characterized as confined in space. The anthropomorphists, then, are among *those in whose hearts there is a turning away* because they try to support their false ideas by claiming that an ambiguous verse is a clear verse.[22]

The interpreter's task, in al-Rāzī's opinion, is to correctly identify which verses are the clear verses and which are the ambiguous verses, working as "impartial verifiers" (*muḥaqqiqūn munṣifūn*) rather than proclaiming the verses that agree with their school of thought *muḥkamāt* and the verses which disagree with the same *mutashābihāt*. When it can be shown definitively that the apparent sense of a verse is impossible, the sound interpreter knows that what is intended is a figurative expression (*majāz*) for its reality (*ḥaqīqa*). However, figurative expressions are capable of many meanings and the preference of one over another can only be a linguistic preference. Since this is not definitive proof, it is not permissible. Accordingly, when *those who are firmly rooted in knowledge* (*al-rāsikhūn fī 'l-'ilm*) and *those who possess understanding* (*ūlū al-albāb*) see something ambiguous in the Qur'ān, they accept that it has a sound meaning with God and believe in it without knowing its exact meaning. Al-Rāzī, then, prefers the reading of this verse that stops after *and no one knows its interpretation except God*.[23] However, far from belittling the role of the commentator, al-Rāzī understands this verse as praise for those who do exegesis correctly.

> This verse indicates the grandeur of the situation of the theologians (*mutakallimūn*) who search for rational indicators (*al-dalā'il al-'aqliyya*) and by means of them seek knowledge of the essence, qualities, and acts of God.[24]

Al-Rāzī is following the views of his fellow Ash'arī al-Ghazālī here, who makes three recommendations in his *Qānūn al-ta'wīl* for dealing with verses whose literal meaning seems to contradict knowledge obtained by the intellect (*ma'qūl*). The first is not to aspire to fully know the meaning of these verses. The second is to accept that interpretation is unavoidable because reason does not lie. The third recommendation is to refrain from specifying an interpretation when the [various] possibilities [of interpretation] are incompatible.[25] The best recourse is to say,

> I know that its literal meaning is not what is intended, because it contains what is contrary to reason. What exactly is intended, however, I do not know, nor do I have a need to know, since it is not related to any action, and there is no way truly to uncover [its meaning] with certainty. Moreover, I do not believe in making judgements by guessing... This means that one should say, "We believe therein; the whole is from our Lord" (3:7).[26]

Others, such as Ibn Taymiyya (d. 1328),[27] a fierce critic of the writings of al-Ghazālī and al-Rāzī, asserted that the literal sense of the Qur'ānic text must never be abandoned, whether that abandonment is through interpretation (*ta'wīl*) or through entrusting its meaning to God (*tafwīḍ*). Ibn Taymiyya's insistence upon staying with the literal sense was not a rejection of the use of reason, but rather was based on the claim that true reason will never be in contradiction with the Qur'ān and sound *aḥādīth*.[28] He defines his own methodology of sound interpretation based entirely on these sources, a methodology which we will examine in Chapter 5.

Although al-Ghazālī limits the role of reason in his *Qanūn al-ta'wīl* and the permissibility of interpreting the *mutashābihāt*, he makes a significant exception to this rule in a book written towards the end of his life, *Iljām al-ʿawāmm ʿan ʿilm al-kalām*.The book addresses the problem of traditions attributed to the first generations of Muslims (*salaf*) that appear to interpret anthropomorphic descriptions of God in the Qur'ān literally. Al-Ghazālī not only denies that the *salaf* ever interpreted these passages literally, but also claims that they established guidelines detailing how the general public (*ʿawāmm*) should understand them. According to al-Ghazālī, the general public should avoid literal interpretations of anthropomorphic verses of the Qur'ān while, at the same time, avoiding any attempt to understand their true, non-literal meanings. They should avoid paraphrasing the text or engaging in theological proofs and arguments regarding them. Instead, they should accept that these verses do have a meaning that is fitting to God, but a meaning that can only be understood by the Prophet, his leading Companions, saints (*awliyā'*), and *those firmly rooted in knowledge* (*al-rāsihkūn fī 'l-ʿilm*). The *mutashābihāt*, then, are primarily addressed to an elite.

> If you were to say, "What is the benefit in speaking to mankind about something which they do not understand?" Your answer is that the goal of this speaking is to facilitate the understanding of those who are worthy of it: the saints (*awliyā'*) and those firmly rooted in knowledge (*al-rāsihkūn fī 'l-ʿilm*).[29]

Important here is the definition that al-Ghazālī provides for what he means by the general public (*ʿawāmm*) on the one hand, and the saints and *those firmly rooted in knowledge* on the other. He includes in the first category the litterateur (*adīb*), the grammarian, the *ḥadīth* specialist (*muḥaddith*), the exegete (*mufassir*), the jurist, and the theologian (*mutakallim*). None of these people should attempt interpretations (*ta'wīlāt*), nor act freely with the external sense of the words (*al-taṣarruf fī khilāl al-ẓawāhir*) of the Qur'ān or traditions. Al-Ghazālī warns that it is prohibited (*ḥarām*) to plunge into the sea if you are not a good swimmer, and the sea of gnosis (*maʿrifa*) of God is far more dangerous than the sea of water. Those who are permitted to interpret the difficult passages of the Qur'ān are

> those who devote themselves exclusively to learning to swim in the seas of religious gnosis (*maʿrifa*); who restrict their lives to Him alone; who turn their faces from this world and the appetites; who turn their backs on money and fame, mankind, and all other pleasures; who devote themselves to God in the different types of knowledge and actions; who act

> in accordance with all the ordinances of the religious law and its courtesies (*ādāb*) in performing the obediences and avoiding the objectionable; who have emptied out their hearts from everything except God; who despise the world and even the Hereafter and the Highest Paradise next to love of God. They are the divers in the sea of gnosis.[30]

In shifting to metaphorical language, al-Ghazālī signals his shift from theologian to Ṣūfī. The only people qualified to interpret the *mutashābihāt*, after the Prophet and some of his immediate followers, are the Ṣūfīs, and their methodology is that of Ṣūfī practice.

Al-Ghazālī frequently functions, as he does here, as an apologist for Ṣufism, and we will examine some of his many attempts to defend Ṣūfī Qur'ānic interpretation in more detail later. For now, however, we will move on to what other Ṣūfīs have to say in less apologetic works about how *those firmly rooted in knowledge* approach the *mutashābihāt* of the Qur'ān. The echoes of the discussions we have seen so far regarding verse 3:7 can be heard in these works, but take second place to the claim that there are some who receive knowledge directly from God concerning the ambiguous passages of the Qur'ān. Here is what al-Qushayrī has to say about those firmly rooted in knowledge (*al-rāsikhūn fī 'l-'ilm*):

> The way of those whose knowledge is firmly rooted (*al-'ulamā' al-rasūkh*) in seeking its meaning is in accordance with the fundamentals (*uṣūl*). Whatever their investigation obtains is acceptable and whatever resists the effect of their reflection (*fikr*) they surrender to the World of the Unseen.
>
> The way of the people of allusion and understanding (*ahl al-ishāra wa'l-fahm*) is listening with the presence of the heart (*ḥuḍūr al-qalb*), so that the object of their levels of understanding (*fuhūm*), appearing from the things that are made known, is based upon the allusions of unveiling (*ishārāt al-kashf*).[31]

Again making a distinction between public and private interpretation, al-Qushayrī notes that those who receive this knowledge should not share it with others without being commanded to do so.

> If they have been asked to maintain the veil and conceal the secret, they feign dumbness. If they have been commanded to reveal and proclaim, they freely release the elucidation of the Truth and speak from knowledge received from the Unseen.[32]

Al-Qushayrī uses metaphors to describe those who understand these deeper meanings and those who do not.

> Those who have been confirmed with the lights of insights (*anwār al-baṣā'ir*) are illuminated by the rays of the suns of understanding

> (*fahm*). Those who have been clothed in a covering of doubt have been denied the subtleties of actualization, so that states (*aḥwāl*) divide them and mere conjectures (*ẓunūn*) plague them, and they are swept away in the wadis of doubt and deception. They only become more and more ignorant, more and more estranged through their uncertainty.[33]

Rūzbihān al-Baqlī gives one possible explanation for why some can legitimately interpret the ambiguous verses while others should not. He writes that those who understand the meanings of the *mutashābihāt* see God in everything without falling into the trap of believing that God is incarnated in the world, while those who do not understand this mystery create chaos when they try to interpret them.

> *As for those in whose hearts is a turning away, they follow what is mutashābih in it.* The people of blind imitation (*taqlīd*) plunge into the *mutashābihāt*, seeking unity (*tawḥīd*), but are cut off from witnessing it because they are the victims of illusion (*aṣḥāb al-wahm*), and the victim of illusion does not recognize the truth of temporally originated things (*al-ashyā' al-muḥdatha*). How can he recognize the existence of the Truth (*ḥaqq*) by the mark (*rasm*) of illusion? If he tries to seek the different kinds of knowledge of the *mutashābihāt*, he will not reach the truth regarding them and may create discord (*fitna*). It is because of this that the Prophet said, "Reflect upon the bounties of God, not His Essence." One who has not traversed the seas of the realities of certainty has not seen the mirror of realization. The distinguishing mark (*rasm*) of the *mutashābihāt* falls short of that which has been marked for his faith. He does not grasp their meanings because this is the station of the lovers (*ahl al-ʿishq*) who see the Truth (*ḥaqq*) in everything. As one of the people of meanings (*ahl al-maʿānī*) said, "I do not see anything without seeing God in it." This is the description of the manifestation of the Divine self-disclosure (*tajallī*) in the mirror of engendered existence (*kawn*). But this does not mean that God is in things because He is free from all forms of incarnation (*ḥulūl*).[34]

Because *those firmly rooted in knowledge* are inwardly rooted in the knowledge of how things really are, they are outwardly calm, courageous, and self-effacing before life's vicissitudes.

> *Those firmly rooted in knowledge* are those who witness the quality of spirits (*arwāḥ*) [existing] prior to the bodies (*ashbāḥ*) in the court of pre-eternity, who have seen with their own eyes the concealed secrets of the particulars of the eternal types of knowledge. They have understood from them the end results of their situation in the pathways of subsistence (*baqā'*). They are firmly rooted in the sea of the source of certainty (*ʿayn al-yaqīn*) and are not agitated by the appearance of worldly authorities

> who are characterized by change, transformation, deceit and treachery. They are not overwhelmed by acts of force and the fear they arouse; they stand firm before the blows of God, standing firm with God in that which appears from Him bearing the mark of effacement (*maḥw*) and obliteration (*ṭams*). They know that all of it is a trial and a test, so they remain tranquil in servanthood (*'ubūdiyya*) as their outward distinguishing mark and are firmly rooted in the witnessing of lordliness (*rubūbiyya*) in their inward absolute reality.[35]

Once again al-Kāshānī expresses a similar idea using different terminology. *Those who are firmly rooted in knowledge* are those who see unity and not multiplicity, the abiding face and not the appearance of multiplicity in the mirrors of created things. Al-Kāshānī understands the scholarly tradition of interpretation of referring the *mutashābihāt* to the *muḥkamāt* as interpretation through this mode of perception.

> The gnostic verifiers (*al-'ārifūn al-muḥaqqiqūn*),[36] who recognize the abiding face in whatever form or outward appearance it takes, recognize the true face among the various faces which the *mutashābihāt* take and they refer them to the *muḥkamāt*, following the example of the poet:
>
> There is only one face yet
> when you count the qualities there is multiplicity.
>
> Those who are veiled, *those in whose hearts is a turning away* from the Truth, *seek what is mutashābih* because of their being veiled by multiplicity from unity. The verifiers follow the *muḥkam*, subordinating the *mutashābih* to it and choosing from its possible aspects what conforms to their religion (*dīn*) and school of thought (*madhhab*). *Seeking discord*, i.e. seeking to mislead themselves and others. *And seeking its interpretation (ta'wīl)* according to what conforms to their state (*ḥāl*) and method (*ṭarīq*). When the knife is crooked, its scabbard becomes crooked. Because they do not recognize the one abiding face among the other faces, it necessarily follows that they do not recognize the true meaning among the other [possible] meanings.[37]

According to the Ṣūfīs, the knowledge of *those who are firmly rooted in knowledge* is not like the knowledge of religious scholars, but neither does it contradict it. One of the earliest writers on this topic, al-Tustarī, explains that their knowledge comes from their detachment from ordinary passion – a detachment which opens up the possibility of being granted profound knowledge directly from God of the many levels of meaning in the Qur'ān.

> *Those firmly rooted in knowledge*. It has been related from 'Alī that they are those whom knowledge protects from the intrusion of passion

> (*hawā*) and arguments presented without [knowledge of] hidden things (*al-ghuyūb*), because God has guided them and given them power over his hidden secrets in the treasuries of the different kinds of knowledge (*'ulūm*). They say, "*We believe in it*," and God is thankful to them and has made them the people of firmrootedness (*ahl al-rusūkh*) and extraordinary accomplishment in knowledge, an increase from Him, just as He said, *Say, "Lord, increase me in knowledge"* (20:114).
>
> God made an exception for *those firmly rooted in knowledge* in their saying, "*all of it is from our Lord*," meaning the abrogating and the abrogated, the *muḥkam* and the *mutashābih*. They are those who have uncovered (*kāshifūn*) three kinds of knowledge, since those who know (*'ulamā'*) are of three kinds: those who devote themselves exclusively to knowledge of their Lord (*rabbāniyyūn*), those who devote themselves exclusively to knowing the Light (*nurāniyyūn*), and those who devote themselves exclusively to knowing the Essence (*dhātiyyūn*).[38] Additionally, there are four kinds of knowledge: revelation (*waḥy*), God's self-disclosure (*tajallī*), [knowledge] from what is near [to Him] (*'indī*) and [knowledge] from [His very presence] (*ladunī*), as in His words *We gave him mercy from Us* (*alaynāhu raḥmat*^{an} *min 'indinā*) *and taught knowledge to him from Our very presence* (*'allamnāhu min ladunnā 'ilm*^{an}) (18:65).[39]

In his comments on *but no one remembers except those who possess understanding*, al-Kāshānī adds detachment from habit (*'āda*) as another prerequisite for receiving deeper understanding. He also uses the etymology of the word *albāb* from the phrase *those who possess understanding* (*ūlū al-albāb*)[40] to create a metaphor for the transformation that is necessary to become wise. *Lubb* (pl. *lubūb*) means the choicest part or the kernel of foods such as nuts or wheat and *lubāb* (pl. *albāb*), from the same root, is the choicest part of anything. When said of a man, it means his intellect or understanding.[41] Referring implicitly to this dual meaning, al-Kāshānī compares the "kernels" of the wise to the "husks" of the more ordinary human characteristics.

> *And no one* remembers that singular and decisive knowledge (*al-'ilm al-wāḥid al-faṣl*) within the ambiguous and manifold particulars (*al-tafāṣīl al-mutashābiha al-mutakaththira*) *except* those whose intellects (*'uqūl*) have been purified by the light of guidance and freed from the husk (*qishr*)[42] of passion (*hawā*) and habit (*'āda*).[43]

Al-Nīsābūrī uses the metaphor of husks and kernels somewhat differently in his commentary on this verse. For al-Kāshānī, the contrast is between those who perceive unity and those who perceive multiplicity. For al-Nīsābūrī, the contrasts are between ego existence and spiritual existence, the knowledge acquired in this life (*'ulūm kasbiyya*) and knowledge given directly to man by God (*'ilm ladunī*) on the Day of the Covenant.[44]

> *And no one remembers except those possessing understanding (ūlū al-albāb)*, those who follow the example of the Prophet, leaving the darkness of the husks (*qushūr*) of their ego existence (*wujūduhum al-nafsānī*) for the light of the kernel (*lubāb*) of their spiritual existence (*wujūduhum al-rūḥānī*). They are those who are firmly rooted in the husks of the acquired types of knowledge (*al-'ulūm al-kasbiyya*) and who have reached the realities of the kernel (*lubāb*) of types of knowledge received from His very presence (*al-'ulūm al-laduniyya*) *from the very presence of one who is Wise, Knowing (min ladun ḥakīm khabīr)* (11:1).
>
> In the verse there is an allusion (*ishāra*) to the fact that the types of knowledge of *those who are firmly rooted* were all taught to them on the Day of the Covenant (*al-mithāq*), since He disclosed the attribute of lordship to the seeds of future humanity *and He made them testify regarding themselves* (7:172) by the evidence of lordship, *Am I not your Lord?* (7:172). Through the witnessing of this evidence, the knowledge of unity (*tawḥīd*) was firmly embedded in the natural disposition (*jibla*) of the seeds of future humanity and *they said, "Yes."* All of the different types of knowledge are included in the knowledge of unity, just as He said, *and He taught Adam all of the names* (2:31).
>
> The seeds were sent back to the loins and were veiled by the attributes of humanity (*ṣifāt al-bashariyya*), and were transferred to wombs and wandered through the ages from one state and place to another, from the most remote places to the process of birth. The speaking soul, which knew the knowledge of unity, was sent back to the lowest of the low forms, veiled in the veil of humanity, forgetful of these different types of knowledge and the speech regarding them.
>
> But then his parents remind him of this knowledge by means of symbols (*rumūz*) and analogies (*qarā'in*) until he remembers some of them from beneath the veils of human nature and stages of development. He speaks in the language of his parents, not the language with which he answered his Lord, saying, "*Yes*." For that language was the kernel (*lubb*) of this language that is the husk (*qishr*). In a similar way, the entire outer and inner existence of man are husks of the kernel (*lubāb*) of that existence which heard and answered on the Day of the Covenant. His hearing is the husk of that hearing which listened to the speech of the Truth. His sight is the husk of that sight which saw the beauty of the Truth. His heart is the husk of that heart which understood the speech of the Truth. All of his different types of knowledge are the husk of those types of knowledge which were learned from the Truth.

> Thus, the Prophet was only sent to remind him of the truth of these different types of knowledge, the husk of which his parents had reminded him, just as He said, *Remind! You are only a reminder!* (88:21). So the reminding is for everyone (*al-tadhkīru ʿāmm*) but only a few remember (*al-tadhakkuru khāṣṣ*). Because of this, He said, *and no one remembers except those who possess understanding (ūlū al-albāb)*.[45]

What distinguishes the Ṣūfī understanding of *those who are firmly rooted in knowledge* from other viewpoints is primarily their understanding of what type of knowledge is involved. Most Muslim thinkers accepted some combination of reason, authoritative tradition, and linguistic expertise as valid tools for interpreting the Qur'ān. For the Ṣūfīs, the sciences based on these tools are part of what al-Nīsābūrī calls acquired knowledge (*ʿulūm kasbiyya*). The sciences that lead to deeper knowledge of the Qur'ān's meaning, however, are received directly from God (*ʿilm ladunī*). In Chapter 3, we will see the relationship between this type of knowledge and spiritual practice.

3

UNCOVERING MEANING

Knowledge and spiritual practice

For the Ṣūfīs, knowledge cannot be separated from spiritual practice. Abū Naṣr al-Sarrāj (d. 988)[1] explains this view in his *Kitāb al-luma'*, one of the earliest books to discuss the methodology of Ṣūfī Qur'ānic interpretation. According to Abū Naṣr al-Sarrāj, the Ṣūfīs are characterized by their practical application (*isti'māl*) of the verses of the Qur'ān and the Traditions of the Prophet, which produces noble qualities, virtuous actions, and higher states, all of which are implied in the word *adab*. Although this manner of acting in imitation of the Prophet is also discussed in the books of scholars (*'ulamā'*) and jurists (*fuqahā'*), al-Sarrāj claims that their understanding of these behaviors and attitudes is not as deep as their understanding of other sciences. He states that it is the Ṣūfīs who alone understand the various realities and attributes of states such as repentance (*tawba*), piety (*wara'*), trust in God (*tawakkul*), contentment (*riḍā'*), to name just a few. The people who experience these states attain them in various degrees according to what God has apportioned to them.[2]

In addition to their experience of states, the Ṣūfīs are also characterized by their knowledge of the soul (*nafs*), its characteristics and inclinations, the subtleties of hypocrisy (*riyā'*), hidden lust (*al-shahwāt al-khafiyya*), and hidden polytheism (*al-shirk al-khafī*). They know how to rid themselves of these vices by turning to God and giving up any sense of one's own ability and power.[3]

The Ṣūfīs are distinguished as well by what they have discovered (*mustanbaṭāt*) in sciences that are difficult for jurists and scholars to understand. Their ability to loosen the knots and understand what is difficult comes from their sacrificing the very core of their beings (*badhl al-muhaj*), so that when they speak of these discoveries, they speak from direct experience of them.[4] Because of what they have discovered, the people of understanding (*fahm*) among the actualized (*muḥaqqiqūn*) conform to the Qur'ān and the practice of the Prophet externally (*ẓāhir*[an]) and internally (*bāṭin*[an]). When they act in this manner, God grants knowledge to them of the deeper meanings of the Qur'ān and Traditions of the Prophet.[5]

This last passage from Abū Naṣr al-Sarrāj alludes to a *ḥadīth* that is cited in full by al-Ghazālī in his discussion of the relationship between certain kinds of knowledge and behavior in his *Jawāhir al-Qur'ān*.

> Maybe you will say, "So demonstrate the purpose of the relationship between the two worlds, and why visions are by similitude (*al-mithāl*) and not the unambiguous (*al-ṣarīḥ*), and why the Prophet used to see Gabriel often in a form other than his own but only saw him twice in his own form."
>
> Know that you have become arrogant and have reached quite a height if you think that the knowledge of this can come to you all at once without your undertaking the task of preparing yourself to receive it by discipline (*riyāḍa*), effort (*mujāhada*), complete renunciation of the world, disengagement from the tumult of creation, utter immersion in love of the Creator, and the search for Truth. Knowledge like this will be withheld from the likes of you and it will be said,
>
> You have come
> in order to learn the secret of my happiness
> but you will find me stingy with it.

Let go of your greed to attain this knowledge by means of exchanging treatises. Seek it only through the door of effort (*mujāhada*) and piety (*taqwā*). Then guidance will follow and strengthen your effort, just as God said, *We will surely guide to Our paths those who have struggled* (*jāhadū*) *for Us* (29:69). And the Prophet said, "For anyone who practically applies what he knows, God will bequeath knowledge of what he does not know."[6]

Linking the bestowal of knowledge to practice and behavior was not unique to the Ṣūfīs but the emphasis they placed on it was. Abū ʿAbd al-Raḥmān al-Sulamī (d. 1021) quotes a ninth century Ṣūfī as saying, "The whole of Sufism is ways of behavior (*al-taṣawwuf kulluhu ādāb*)."[7]

Reading the Qur'ān with presence of the heart (*ḥuḍūr al-qalb*)

Among the manners (*ādāb*) that the Ṣūfīs tried to cultivate was a respectful and thoughtful way of reciting or listening to the Qur'ān, intended to facilitate the understanding of its deeper meanings. Abū Naṣr al-Sarrāj writes that

> The people of understanding (*fahm*) among the people of knowledge (*ʿilm*) know that the only way to correctly connect to that to which the Qur'ān guides us is by pondering (*tadabbur*), reflecting (*tafakkur*), being wakeful (*tayaqquẓ*), recollecting (*tadhakkur*) and being present with the heart (*ḥuḍūr al-qalb*) when reciting the Qur'an. They know this as well from His words, *A book which We have sent down to you as a blessing so that they might ponder its verses and so that those who possess understanding might recollect* (38:29). Pondering, reflecting and recollecting are only possible through the heart being present because God said,

> *surely in that there is a remembrance for one who has a heart* (*qalb*) *or will lend an ear with presence* (*aw alqā al-samʿa wa huwa shahīd*) (50:37), that is to say, one who is present with the heart (*ḥāḍir al-qalb*).[8]

There were several different ways in which Ṣūfīs tried to awaken themselves to the task of listening with presence of the heart. One way was to remind themselves of the awesome nature of the revelation and its transcendent origins. An oft-repeated quote is attributed to Jaʿfar al-Ṣādiq saying, "I swear by God that God has disclosed himself (*tajallā*) to His creation in His speech but they do not see."[9] Abū Ṭālib al-Makkī writes in his *Qūt al-qulūb* of a man from the first generations (*salaf*) who used to read a *sūra* and, if his heart wasn't in it, he would repeat it a second time.[10] Another method is recorded in Abū Naṣr al-Sarrāj's *Kitāb al-lumaʿ* and attributed to Abū Saʿīd al-Kharrāz (d. 899):

> There are three ways to listen and to be present while listening. The first is to listen to the Qur'ān as if you were hearing the Messenger of God recite it to you.
>
> Then you should rise from this and hear it as if Gabriel was reciting it to the Prophet, because Allah said, *and surely it is the revelation of the Lord of the worlds. The trustworthy spirit descends with it upon your heart* (26:192–4).
>
> Then you should rise from this so that it is as if you were hearing it from God (*al-ḥaqq*). That is God saying, *We revealed the Qur'ān which is a healing and a mercy to the believers* (17:84), and His words, *the revelation of the Book is from God, the exalted, the wise* (39:1) and it is as if you were hearing it from God most High. Likewise, *Ḥā. Mīm. The revelation of the Book is from God, the exalted, the knowing* (40:1).
>
> In your listening [as if you were hearing it] from God, understanding (*fahm*) is brought out by the presence of your heart (*ḥuḍūr al-qalb*) and your being devoid of any preoccupation with the world and your self by the power of witnessing (*mushāhada*), the purity of remembrance (*dhikr*), focused attention (*jamʿ al-hamm*), good manners (*ḥusn al-adab*), purity of the innermost secret (*sirr*) and sincerity of realization (*ṣidq al-taḥqīq*).[11]

The result of this approach is described as both sweet and awesome. Abū Ṭālib al-Makkī tells us that a scholar said:

> I used to read the Qur'ān but found no sweetness in it until I recited it as if I was hearing the Messenger of God reciting it to his Companions. Then I rose to a station above it and I recited it as if I was hearing Gabriel presenting it to the Messenger of God. Then God brought me to another way station and now I hear it from the Speaker. Here I found from it a blessing and delight I could not resist![12]

He then tells the story of Ja'far al-Ṣādiq who was overcome by something during prayers and fainted. When he came, he was asked about it and said, "I kept repeating the verse in my heart until I heard it from its Speaker and my body was unable to stand firm when I saw His power."[13] Al-Kāshānī quotes this tradition from Ja'far al-Ṣādiq and then relates his own experience:

> Frequently, I used to engage in reciting the Qur'ān and pondering its meanings by means of the faculty of faith. In spite of diligence in devotions, my breast was tight and my heart was agitated, my heart neither opening because of these meanings, nor my Lord turning me away from them, until finally I became familiar and intimate with them. I tasted the sweetness of their cup and their drink. Then my soul was animated, my breast opened, my mind broadened, my heart expanded, my innermost secret made spacious, the moment (*waqt*) and the state (*ḥāl*) made pleasant, and my spirit delighted by that opening. It was as if continually, morning and evening, meanings were being unveiled to me in every verse such as would fatigue my tongue to describe. There could be no power adequate to contain them, nor enumerate them, nor any strength patient enough to divulge and disclose them.[14]

As in many other aspects of Ṣūfī piety, the various methods towards mindful reading were systematized by al-Ghazālī in his *Iḥya'*, drawing upon much of the material found in Abū Ṭālib al-Makkī's *Qūt al-qulūb*,[15] expanding it and arranging it neatly into ten categories regarding the external courtesies of recitation (*ẓāhir ādāb al-tilāwa*) and ten categories regarding inner practices in the recitation of the Qur'ān (*a'māl al-bāṭin fī tilāwat al-Qur'ān*).[16] The external courtesies, which will not be discussed here, have to do with the ritual state of the reciter, where and when he recites, the quantity, speed, volume and beauty with which he recites, the advisability of weeping while reciting, the ritual prostrations and supplications in reciting, and how the Qur'ān is to be written down.[17] The inner practices are as follows:

1. Understanding the exaltedness and grandeur of the speech of the Qur'ān, and God's grace and kindness to His creation in His descending from his exalted throne to the level of their understanding. One of the examples used to explain this is a story of a wise man (*ḥakīm*) who preached to a king. The King asks him how it is that man is able to bear the speech of God. The wise man tells him that God's speaking to man is similar to man's speaking to the animals, descending to their level through the use of sounds and whistles. It is also like the Sun, the full gaze of which man is unable to bear, and yet he is able to attain what he needs from it.[18]
2. Exaltation of the Speaker. The reciter must be mindful[19] of the majesty of the Speaker, knowing that what he reads is not the speech of man, and that there is an extreme danger in reciting the speech of God. Just as only the ritually pure may touch the Qur'ān, only the inward part of the heart that is pure and illuminated by the light of exaltation and reverence will be able to understand

its inner meaning. The act of exaltation of the Speaker will come about only when the reciter reflects upon the attributes, majesty, and acts of God.[20]

3 Presence of the heart (*ḥuḍūr al-qalb*) and abandonment of the talk of the soul (*ḥadīth al-nafs*). Al-Ghazālī seems to be talking here about distracting thoughts. He says that a gnostic was asked, "When you read the Qur'ān does your soul talk about anything?" He said, "What would be more beloved to me than the Qur'ān so that my soul would talk of it?" This kind of mindfulness follows from the previously mentioned exaltation that creates an intimacy without any inattentiveness, as the reciter finds unending delights in the Qur'ān.[21]

4 Pondering (*tadabbur*). Pondering goes beyond being present with the heart (*ḥuḍūr al-qalb*), for one might not be reflecting on anything but the Qur'ān yet nevertheless be merely hearing it without pondering it. Al-Ghazālī tells us that this is the purpose of reciting the Qur'ān and it is why it is recommended to read it in a slow and distinct manner (*tartīl*). He quotes 'Alī b. Abū Ṭālib as saying, "There is no good in an act of worship without comprehension, nor in a recitation without pondering."[22] Al-Ghazālī's distinction here between the presence of the heart (*ḥuḍūr al-qalb*) and pondering (*tadabbur*) is not one made by other Ṣūfī authors, who seem to use *ḥuḍūr al-qalb* as shorthand for all of the methods used in listening attentively. For example, Al-Qushayrī writes, "the method (*sabīl*) of the people of allusion (*ishāra*) and understanding (*fahm*) is listening with the presence of the heart (*ḥuḍūr al-qalb*)."[23]

5 Trying to understand (*tafahhum*). This is to seek to clarify each verse in a suitable manner by contemplating the meanings of the attributes and works of God, and the circumstances of the prophets and the people to which they were sent.[24]

6 The abandonment of the obstacles to understanding (*fahm*). Al-Ghazālī says that the veils to understanding are four: too much concern for the correct articulation of letters; rigidity and zealotry in following (*taqlīd*) a school of thought (*madhhab*) instead of allowing for insight (*baṣīra*) and witnessing (*mushāhada*); persistence in sin, being prideful, or being afflicted in general with a passion for the world with which one complies; belief that there are no meanings of the Qur'ān other than those transmitted from Ibn 'Abbās,[25] Mujāhid[26] and others, and that all other commentary is that from prohibited personal opinion (*tafsīr bi'l-ra'y*).[27]

7 Personal application (*takhṣīṣ*). The reader should assume that every message in the Qur'ān is meant for him. Since God's message is intended for all people, it is intended for each individual. Al-Ghazālī here is inviting people to contextualize the text to their own experience, for if the reader assumes that he himself is being spoken to by God, he will not consider the study of the Qur'ān as work but, rather, will meditate upon it and act in accordance with it.[28]

8 Affectivity (*ta'aththur*). His heart should be affected by the tenor of different verses, so that for everything which he understands, his heart will be connected to a state (*ḥāl*) or strong emotion (*wajd*) such as grief (*ḥuzn*), fear (*khawf*), hope (*rajā'*), and so on. When his knowledge is perfected, the

predominant state of his heart will be awe (*khashya*), for constriction (*taḍyīq*) predominates in the verses of the Qur'ān. Therefore, he will notice that the mention of forgiveness and mercy is connected to conditions that he has yet to fulfill. The Qur'ān is meant to attract these states and to cause one to act on it; otherwise, the trouble of moving the tongue with its letters is insignificant.[29]

9 Ascent (*taraqqī*). Al-Ghazālī repeats the three stations of reciting the Qur'ān from Abū Ṭālib al-Makkī's *Qūt al-qulūb* and elaborates. The first station is the servant who assumes he is reading to God, standing before him, and He sees him and hears him. His state is one of petitioning, adulation, imploring, and supplicating. The second station is when he witnesses with his heart that God sees him and speaks to him with His kindnesses and whispers to him with His blessings and beneficence. Therefore, his state is one of modesty, exaltation, attentiveness (*iṣghā'*) and understanding (*fahm*). The third station is when he sees the Speaker in the speech and the Attributes in the words. Therefore, he does not look to himself, nor to his reading, nor to his blessings but rather, his attention is confined to the Speaker, his reflection devoted to him as he is immersed in witnessing the Speaker to the exclusion of anything else.[30]

10 Disavowal (*tabrī'*). This is the disavowal of one's own ability and power, and of considering oneself with approval and self-validation. The reciter will not consider himself among those who are pious, although he hopes to join them. Instead, he should view himself as one among those who are disobedient and negligent.[31]

4

METHODS OF INTERPRETATION

Beyond describing how to prepare oneself for reading the Qur'ān, Ṣūfīs also wrote more specifically about their exegetical methodologies, referred to by a variety of different words or phrases. Most avoided using the term *tafsīr*, reserving this instead for what they called exoteric Qur'ānic interpretation.

Abū Naṣr al-Sarrāj and the methods of understanding (*fahm*) and allusion (*ishāra*)

Abū Naṣr al-Sarrāj tells us that there are three things that the sound interpreter will never do: change the word order of the Qur'ān; forget his basic servanthood by contesting the divinity; and distort words. Although he gives no examples of the first two errors, he illustrates word distortion (*taḥrīf*) with several examples. Here are two of them:

> This is like what is related about someone who, when asked about His words, *When Job cried to his Lord, "Truly I have been touched by distress (massanī al-ḍurr)"* (21:83), said that its meaning was, "I have *not* been touched by distress (*mā sā'anī al-ḍurr*)." We have heard that someone else, when asked about His words, *Did He not find you an orphan (yatīm) and give (you) shelter?* (93:6), said that the meaning of *yatīm* was understood [not as an orphan but] as the singular, incomparable pearl (*al-durra al-yatīma allatī lā yūjadu mithlahā*).[1]

In contrast to these interpretative errors, Abū Naṣr al-Sarrāj gives examples from two methods he deems to be correct Ṣūfī exegesis, the method of understanding (*ṭarīq al-fahm*) and the method of allusion (*ṭarīq al-ishāra*). One of several examples he gives to illustrate the method of understanding is from Abū Bakr al-Kattānī (d. 934) on Qur'ān 26:89, *only the one who brings to God a sound heart.*

> According to the method of understanding (*fahm*), the sound heart is of three types: One of them is the one who comes to God with a heart in which there is no partner to God; the second is the one who comes to

God with a heart uninterested in anything but God, not desiring anything but God; and the third is the one who comes to God, existing only in Him, having been annihilated from all things in God, and then annihilated from God in God.[2]

Another example is from al-Shiblī (d. 945), who was asked about Qur'ān 50:37:

Truly in this is a remembrance for the one who has a heart or will lend an ear with presence, and he said, "For the one for whom God is his heart," and then he recited, "From me to You, a heart has no meaning. From me to You, every one of my limbs is a heart."[3]

These interpretations do not radically change the topic of the verses but rather meditate upon the meaning of the phrases "sound heart" or "listening with presence." The controversial aspect of the interpretations has more to do with the fact of the inclusion of such Ṣūfī concepts as the annihilation of the self which was strenuously opposed by some Muslims.

The examples Abū Naṣr al-Sarrāj gives for the allusive method of interpretation (*ṭarīq al-ishāra*), on the other hand, demonstrate far-reaching interpretative analogies which constitute a far more problematic kind of exegetical methodology. He quotes Abū Yazīd al-Bisṭamī (d. 874) who, when asked about gnosis (*maʿrifa*), replied with an allegorical interpretation of a Qur'ānic verse from the story of the prophet Sulaymān and the queen Bilqīs.

He said, *Truly, when kings enter a village, they destroy it and debase the exalted among its inhabitants. This is the way they behave* (27:34). What is meant by that is that it is the custom of kings, when they descend upon a village, to enslave its people and make them submissive to them, so that they can do nothing without the command of the king. Likewise, when gnosis (*maʿrifa*) enters the heart (*qalb*), nothing remains in it that it does not uproot, and nothing moves in it that it does not burn.[4]

In the story of Bilqīs and Sulaymān, these words are spoken by Bilqīs, demonstrating her political sagacity in trying to avoid a violent confrontation with Sulaymān's forces. Al-Bisṭamī creates an analogy between the force of an invading king and a powerful knowledge that seizes the heart completely.

Another example Abū Naṣr al-Sarrāj gives of this method is attributed to al-Junayd (d. 910). Considered a more "sober" Ṣūfī than al-Bisṭamī, his allusive interpretation demonstrates the acceptability of this kind of interpretation for most Ṣūfīs.

When asked about his silence and lack of movement during the spiritual concert (*samāʿ*), al-Junayd alluded to His words, *and you see the mountains, thinking them to be firmly fixed, but they will pass as the clouds pass: the artistry of God who perfects everything* (27:88).[5]

The verse is part of a passage describing the events of the Day of Judgment, but al-Junayd applies it here to his spiritual state in the present world.

This method of allusion (*ṭarīq al-ishāra*) is the more problematic of the two methods that Abū Naṣr al-Sarrāj describes because it goes beyond the literal sense of the text. The controversial nature of this kind of interpretation is addressed some 200 years later in the writings of al-Ghazālī, who attempts to distinguish the method from that of the *bāṭiniyya* and philosophers.

Al-Ghazālī and the method of striking similitudes (*ḍarb al-mithāl*)

Al-Ghazālī's *Mishkāt al-anwār* is a book that includes both a methodology for Qur'ānic interpretation and al-Ghazālī's interpretation of the Light Verse of the Qur'an. Al-Ghazālī calls the methodology "the secret and method of creating similitudes (*sirr al-tamthīl wa minhājihi*)"[6] or "the method of striking similitudes (*minhāj ḍarb al-mithāl*)."[7] The phrase *ḍarb al-mathal* or *ḍarb al-amthāl* is used twenty-seven times in various forms in the Qur'ān – mostly to describe the analogies and parables created by God to explain things to mankind.

Al-Ghazālī connects the method of "striking similitudes" to the existence of two worlds, worlds which he describes using both philosophical and Qur'ānic terminology. The one world is spiritual (*rūḥānī*), intellectual (*'aqlī*), and supernal (*'ulwī*); it is the world of Sovereignty (*malakūt*) and the Unseen (*ghayb*). The other world is physical (*jismānī*), sensory (*ḥissī*), and lower (*suflī*); it is the world of Dominance (*mulk*) and the Visible (*shahāda*).[8]

The World of the Visible (*'ālam al-shahāda*) is the place from which one rises up to the World of Sovereignty (*'ālam al-malakūt*), an ascension made possible by the interrelationship (*munāsaba*) and connection (*ittiṣāl*) between the two. To help man's ascent, God has made the World of the Visible parallel to the World of Sovereignty. There is nothing in this world that does not have a likeness (*mithāl*) or several likenesses in that world, and there is nothing in that world which does not have a likeness or likenesses in this world.[9] To illustrate this, al-Ghazālī uses the example of the viewing the celestial bodies by Ibrāhīm (Abraham).[10]

> Indeed, there are high and noble luminous substances (*jawāhir nūrāniyya sharīfa 'āliyya*) in the World of Sovereignty (*'ālam al-malakūt*) that are called angels. Because lights emanate from them to human spirits, they are called "lords" (*arbāb*) and God is the "Lord of lords." They have varying degrees of luminosity that have similitudes (*amthāl*) in the World of the Visible (*'ālam al-shahāda*): the sun, the moon and the stars.
>
> At first, the traveler on the way (*al-sālik lil-ṭarīq*) reaches a degree that is the degree of the stars, and the radiance of [the star's] light becomes clear to him. The fact becomes unveiled to him that the lowest world is entirely under its authority and the radiance of its light. Suddenly, from [the star's] beauty and sublimity, it becomes clear to him,

> and he says, *"This is my lord!"* (6:76). Then, when what is above [this star] becomes clear to him, the degree of the moon, he sees that the former has set in relationship to the latter, so he says, "*I do not love that which sets*" (6:76).
>
> Likewise, he continues to ascend until he reaches that which has its similitude in the sun, and he sees that it is greater and more sublime. Yet he sees that it also has its similitude in its interrelationship (*munāsaba*) to the others, and whatever has a relationship with something imperfect is imperfect itself and "sets." From this, he says, "*I have turned my face to the one who created the heavens and the earth in pure faith* (*ḥanīf^{an}*)" (6:79).[11]

The method of striking similitudes (*ḍarb al-mithāl*) is to find the connections between the physical and the spiritual world. Another example al-Ghazālī gives of this interpretative method in the *Mishkāt al-anwār* concerns God's speech to Mūsā (Moses) in which Mūsā is asked to remove his shoes in the holy valley where he has seen a fire.[12]

> If the first waystation of the prophets is the ascent to the world sanctified from the turbulence of sense perception and imagination, then the similitude (*mithāl*) of that waystation is the *holy valley* (20:12). And if it is not possible to tread that holy valley without removing the two worlds, meaning the present world and the hereafter, turning towards the One, God (*al-ḥaqq*)..., then the similitude of that removal is the *taking off of the shoes* at the time of switching to the pilgrims' garments in order to turn towards the holy Kaʿba.[13]

Al-Ghazālī finds two parallel meanings for the removal of Mūsā's shoes here. In the first, he compares the removal of the shoes to a spiritual state in which one distances oneself from concern for this world or the next. In the second, he compares it to the ritual enacted during the preparation for the pilgrimage. Al-Ghazālī explains that the method of striking similitudes (*ḍarb al-mithāl*) is like the science of dream or vision interpretation (*taʿbīr*).[14]

Accepting the literal and the symbolic meaning simultaneously is like accepting two different kinds of language acts. In his *Jawāhir al-Qurʾān*, al-Ghazālī suggests that knowledge of the deeper meanings of the Qurʾān requires knowledge of the language of similitudes:

> I do not think that you will be successful (in seeking out the secrets of the Qurʾān) if you obstinately proceed with your own opinion (*raʾy*) and intellect (*ʿaql*). How can you understand this when you do not understand the language of states (*lisān al-aḥwāl*)? Instead, you only believe in propositional speech (*maqāl*)! You will not understand the meaning of His words, *There is nothing which does not proclaim His praise* (17:44) nor His words, *They [the heavens and the earth] said, "We have come*

> *willingly"* (41:11) so long as you think that the earth has a language (*lisān*) and a life. You will not understand the words of the speaker who said, "The wall said to the peg, "Why are you making a hole in me?" He said, "Ask the one who is hammering me and does not drop me! Behind me is the stone which hammers me." You are not aware that these words are true and more correct than propositional speech, so how will you understand the secrets that are behind this?[15]

The example of the talking inanimate objects, the wall and the peg, is one that al-Zamakhsharī also uses in his commentary, written some twenty years after al-Ghazālī's death, in his interpretation of verse 41:11.[16] Either al-Zamakhsharī borrowed from al-Ghazālī, which seems unlikely, or they both adopted the example from a previous commentator or theologian. Al-Zamakhsharī understands the words spoken by the heavens and the earth, "*We have come willingly*," as a figurative expression (*majāz*) which is either the creation of a similitude (*tamthīl*) or an imaginative representation (*takhyīl*) whose only purpose is to depict the effect of God's power over decreed things, having nothing to do with the real acts of speech and answering. He uses the example of the talking wall and peg both to illustrate the figurative use of speech and to confirm the meaning of the verse.

Whereas al-Zamakhsharī uses the concept of figurative language to solve the problem of the anthropomorphism of the verse, al-Ghazālī's point seems to be different. Although he might have agreed with al-Zamakhsharī's interpretation as it explains a verse which otherwise seems literally absurd, al-Ghazālī is saying something more than that; he is asserting that metaphorical and symbolic ways of speaking are superior modes of expression for facilitating deeper comprehension of the Qur'ān. Ibn 'Arabī develops this idea further in his writings by comparing the rational and imaginative faculties in man.

Ibn 'Arabī and the method of allusion (*ishāra*)

Unlike al-Ghazālī, Ibn 'Arabī rejects rational interpretation (*ta'wīl 'aqlī*) outright. Although there are aspects of the revelation which reason declares impossible, this only proves the imperfection of man's rational faculties, not the necessity of interpretation.[17] Man has two faculties by which he obtains knowledge of God. The faculty of reason (*'aql*) in man works by means of reflection (*fikr*), using the language of abstraction. It is capable of knowing God's incomparability, how He is utterly different from His creation. The imaginative faculty (*khayāl*) in man, on the other hand, works through sensory perceptions, using the language of images. It is capable of perceiving God's similarity in His self-disclosures (*tajallī*) in His creation. Perfect knowledge combines both of these faculties. Use of only the rational faculty turns God into an abstraction and use of only the imaginative faculty leads to polytheism and anthropomorphism.[18]

The Qur'ān uses both abstractions and images to communicate its message, but the latter predominate because revelation entails a descent of meanings into the imaginal realm and sense perception and is an act of connection, not separation. The rational faculty is unable to understand the images of the Qur'ān and therefore seeks to interpret it so as to make it conform to the dictates of reason, but this leads to a distortion of its meaning. Prophets and friends of God, on the other hand, accept the whole of the Qur'ān because they understand the language of images by means of unveiling (*kashf*).[19] To use al-Ghazālī's example described previously, the prophets and friends of God will understand what the verse *They said, "We have come willingly"* (41:11) means because they have experienced it through the seeing, hearing, and tasting of the imaginative faculty.

Only the prophets and friends of God understand the principles of "striking similitudes" (*ḍarb al-amthāl*). They can strike similitudes themselves because God has taught them how to do this, and they recognize the similitudes that God has struck for Himself because they have witnessed the connection between the similitude and the meaning it represents.[20] However, "striking similitudes" (*ḍarb al-amthāl*) is not the term Ibn ʿArabī uses to describe Ṣūfī interpretation of the Qur'ān, nor does he use the term *ta'wīl*, which he applies almost exclusively to the kind of rational interpretation (*ta'wīl ʿaqlī*) of which he is so critical.[21] Instead, the term Ibn ʿArabī prefers is "allusion" (*ishāra*). He explains that Ṣūfīs have chosen this word over "commentary" (*tafsīr*) in order to defend themselves from the ignorance of exotericists. The word *ishāra*, which literally means "to point," is used just once in the Qur'ān (19:29), in a verse referenced by Ibn ʿArabī as part of his explanation for the Ṣūfīs' adoption of the term. Just as Maryam (the Virgin Mary) "pointed" to the infant ʿĪsā (Jesus) so that he spoke in her defense against the accusations of her people, so do Ṣūfīs "point" or "make allusion" to what they know so that they will not be attacked by uncomprehending exotericists.[22]

Some of the examples of Ibn ʿArabī's own Qur'ānic interpretation in his *Futūḥāt al-makkiyya* resemble Abū Naṣr al-Sarrāj's method of allusion (*ṭarīq al-ishāra*)[23] and al-Ghazālī's "striking of similitudes" (*ḍarb al-mithāl*), albeit with the addition of his own technical vocabulary. Chittick translates one such example from the *Futūḥāt* on verses 52:1–8 of the Qur'ān:

> *By the mount* – the body, because of the natural inclination within it, since it is not independent through itself in its *wujūd* [existence].
>
> *And a book inscribed* from a divine dictation and a right hand writing with a pen of potency.
>
> *On a parchment*, that is your own entity – by way of allusion, not exegesis.
>
> *Unrolled*, manifest, not rolled up, so it is not curtained.
>
> *By the inhabited house*, that is, the heart that embraces the Real, so He is its inhabitant.
>
> *And the uplifted roof* – the sensory and suprasensory faculties in the head.
>
> *And the burning sea*, that is nature kindled with the ruling fire that necessitates movement.

> *Surely thy Lord's chastisement is about to fall.* In other words, something from which the animal self, the command spirit, and the high intellect take refuge but which derives from the self's nurturing Master, who makes its affair wholesome, is about to fall and come down upon it. For the self possesses the low waystations absolutely in respect to its possibility and relatively in respect to its nature.
>
> *There is none to avert it*, because there is only what I have mentioned. What we have is receiving His coming down and climbing up to His approach. Between these two properties become manifest the *barzakhs* [isthmuses], which possess towering splendor and firmly-rooted knowledge.[24]

In this interpretation, the five signs invoked to attest to the reality of the Day of Judgment are taken to refer to the spiritual makeup of man. Events which will occur at the end of time are taken to refer to events which happen in the here and now. What makes Ibn 'Arabī's correspondence between these two realities unique is the way in which he connects them. The first verse of this *sūra* is *By the mount (wa'l-ṭūr)*; as Chittick explains,

> The word *ṭūr* or "mount" derives from a root that means to approach something and to hover around it. The Shaykh takes the etymological sense as an allusion to the bodily nature's inclinations, which draw it toward things that it desires.[25]

It is this close attention to the etymological and grammatical possibilities of the text which distinguishes Ibn 'Arabī's approach to Qur'ānic interpretation, an approach based on the assumption that all the possible meanings which the Arabic language allows for any given word or group of words in the Qur'ān are valid. To reject any one of these meanings is to limit God's knowledge, to imply that He was unaware of the various ways in which His Book could be interpreted.[26]

One example which shows the difference between this kind of hyperliteralism and a more purely symbolic or allegorical approach is Ibn 'Arabī's interpretation of the verse, "*laysa ka-mithlihi shay'un*" (42:11), which can be translated as, *there is nothing similar to him*. The *ka* means "like" and *mithl* means "similar." Ibn 'Arabī accepts the common explanation that the *ka* here merely serves to reinforce the meaning of *mithl*. He also endorses an interpretation in which *ka* retains its meaning, making it possible to translate the verse as *there is nothing like His similar*, and to understand it as a reference to the Perfect Man.[27] Although the common interpretation of this verse is that it asserts God's incomparability, Ibn 'Arabī's acceptance of all possible interpretations allows him to find in it confirmation for God's incomparability and His similarity. Ibn 'Arabī understood this interpretative approach as an extreme fidelity to the possibilities of the Qur'ānic text. His critics denounced it as a distortion of its meaning (*taḥrīf ma'ānī 'l-Qur'ān*).[28]

Al-Nīsābūrī and al-Kāshānī and the method of esoteric interpretation (*ta'wīl*)

The terms *tafsīr* and *ta'wīl* have a complicated history.[29] In the first few centuries of Islam, they were used interchangeably to refer to any commentary on the Qur'ān. Over time, however, the word *tafsīr* began to be applied only to those works that relied heavily on the transmitted interpretative traditions from the first few generations of Muslims, while *ta'wīl* became a term used to describe other types of interpretations. In the fourteenth century both al-Nīsābūrī and al-Kāshānī used the word *ta'wīl* to describe their interpretative activity.

Al-Nīsābūrī divides his commentary *Gharā'ib al-Qur'ān* into three sections comprised of variant readings (*qirā'āt* and *wuqūf*), exoteric commentary (*tafsīr*), and esoteric commentary (*ta'wīl*). His understanding of how the last two relate to one another is set forth in his introduction:

> Know that the requirement of religion is that the Muslim should not interpret (*yu'awwilu*) anything in the Qur'ān or the *ḥadīth* according to meanings which would invalidate the essentials which the Prophet and the pious first generations (*al-salaf al-ṣāliḥ*) commented (*fassara*) on, like the Garden, the Fire, the Path, the Balance, the palaces, the rivers, the trees, etc. Instead, he must affirm these essentials just as they have been set forth.
>
> Then, if he understands from them other realities (*ḥaqā'iq*), symbols (*rumūz*), and subtleties (*laṭā'if*) which have been unveiled to him, there is no harm. For surely God has not created anything in the world of form (*'ālam al-ṣūra*) that does not have an equal (*naẓīr*) in the world of meaning (*'ālam al-ma'na*). And nothing is created in the world of meaning, which is the Hereafter, which does not have a reality (*ḥaqīqa*) in the world of Truth (*'ālam al-ḥaqq*), which is the unseen of the unseen (*ghayb al-ghayb*). And nothing is created in the two worlds that does not have patterns (*namādhij*) in the world of mankind (*'ālam al-insān*). But God knows best.[30]

The essentials (*a'yān*) that Nīsābūrī mentions here are elements of the Afterlife that Islamic philosophers interpreted allegorically, an act of interpretation for which they were strongly criticized. Al-Nīsābūrī emphatically states that these elements must be accepted as literal truth. His method of interpretation resembles that described by al-Ghazālī in his *Mishkāt al-anwār*, in which correspondences are uncovered between the physical and spiritual worlds.

Writing in the same period, al-Kāshānī uses the terms *tafsīr* and *ta'wīl* in much the same way as al-Nīsābūrī does, although al-Kāshānī writes only *ta'wīl*. In addition to the term *ta'wīl*, al-Kāshānī refers to "*taṭbīq*," a word that means "to make correspondences."[31] In the introduction to his commentary, al-Kāshānī writes that the process of *ta'wīl* is unending, while that of *tafsīr* is limited.

Al-Kāshānī believes that, while it is prohibited to alter the external sense of the Qur'ān, this prohibition does not extend to understanding its additional meanings.

> It is said that the one who interprets (*fassara*) by his own opinion (*ra'y*) has become an infidel (*kafara*). As for esoteric interpretation (*ta'wīl*), it never ceases because it varies according to the states of the listener and his circumstances in the stages of his traveling and his different phases. Whenever he rises from a station, a door of new understanding is opened to him, and he beholds (*iṭṭala'a*)[32] by means of it the subtlety of a ready meaning.[33]

Here, al-Kāshānī's view is not without precedent. Abū Naṣr al-Sarrāj had also pointed out this difference between exoteric and esoteric commentary:

> [The Ṣūfīs] differ in their deductions just as the exotericists (*ahl al-ẓāhir*) do. However, the differences of opinion between the exotericists lead to error while this is not so in the science of the inward (*'ilm al-bāṭin*) because the differences [represent] virtues, advantages, noble characteristics, states, morals, stations and degrees. It is said that the differences of opinion among the scholars (*'ulamā'*) in the science of exotericism (*'ilm al-ẓāhir*) is a mercy from God because the one who is right refutes the one who is wrong, thereby making the error of his opponent in religion clear to people so that they turn away from him. If this were not the case, people would leave their religion.
>
> But the differences of opinion between the people of realities is also a mercy from God because each one of them speaks from where he is at the moment (*waqtuhu*) in response to his state, making allusions from his ecstasy (*wajd*). There is a benefit in their words for everyone from amongst those who observe acts of obedience and the lords of the hearts, the aspirants and those who are realized, according to their different capacities, characteristics and degrees... [Abū Naṣr al-Sarrāj demonstrates his point here with different interpretations of what the "true *faqīr*" means from ten different Ṣūfīs...] They have all differed in their replies just as they have differed in where they were at the moment (*awqāt*) and their states, but all are sound (*ḥasan*). Each reply belongs to the group of people suitable for it, and each is a benefit, blessing, increase and mercy for them.[34]

Rūzbihān comments on this as well, speaking of the Ṣūfīs in the past:

> They spoke according to their stations (*maqāmāt*) in the presence of His Omnipotence (*jabarūt*) and according to the extent of their travelling in the open spaces of His Kingdom (*malakūt*). They spoke by means of convincing allusions (*ishārāt*) and suitable expressions (*'ibārāt*) from pure hearts, grounded intellects (*'uqūl rāsikha*), passionate spirits, and

> sanctified innermost secrets. The differences between their perceptions of the allusions of the Qur'ān is like their differences in degrees of what they have seen, the unveilings, states, approaches, visions of unseen things, and that which shines upon their innermost secrets from the lights of preeternal and everlastingly eternal things. What they attained is in what they said. They told of the depth of the sea of the Qur'ān because it is the qualities of the Merciful and all of its realities cannot be perceived by contingent beings.[35]

Al-Simnānī and commentary on the seven inner senses (*tafsīr al-buṭūn al-sab'a*)

In the introduction to his Qur'ānic commentary, al-Simnānī explains that the "student of commentary on the seven inner senses" will have to learn special technical terms (*iṣṭilāḥāt*). The "seven inner senses" is a reference to a *ḥadīth* which states, "The Qur'ān has an exoteric sense (*ẓahr*) and an inner sense (*baṭn*), and its inner sense has an inner sense up to seven inner senses (*buṭūn*)."[36] The "special technical terms" (*iṣṭilaḥāt*) refer to spiritual faculties of man called "subtle substances" (*laṭā'if*), each of which corresponds to a prophet mentioned in the Qur'ān.[37]

It is a system of correspondences based on Qur'ān 41:53: *We will show them Our signs in the horizons (āfāq) and in their souls (anfus) until it becomes manifest to them that this is the truth* (41:53).[38] Knowledge and deeper understanding of the Qur'ān, as well as the ability to benefit from it, requires the discovery of the connection between the horizons (*āfāq*) and souls (*anfus*), between the prophets and the subtle substances (*laṭā'if*) of man. Man has the potential to develop spiritually from a speaking animal to the bearer of the trust of God. At each level of his development, he becomes the possessor of a new subtle substance (*laṭīfa*) as shown in Table 4.1.

The reader of the Qur'ān should recognize these correspondences so as to be able to practically apply the lessons of the stories of the prophets to one's own struggle. Al-Simnānī explains this process with examples from each of the seven levels, as in this passage on the bodily subtle substance (*laṭīfa qālabiyya*) and the prophet Ādam:

> Whenever you hear a part of the Book addressing Adam, listen to it with your subtle bodily subtle substance (*laṭīfa qālabiyya*). Apply your bodily subtle substance practically in what has been commanded and prohibited for it, and take heed in the similitudes struck for it (*bi-mā ḍuriba mathal^{an} lahu*). Know with certainty that the inner sense (*baṭn*) of this Book is connected to you in [the realm of] souls (*anfus*) just as its external sense is connected to Adam in [the realm of] horizons (*āfāq*), to enable you to benefit from the Speech of the Truth and so that you may be one of those who read [the Qur'ān] fresh and anew.[39]

Table 4.1 Al-Simnānī's theory of subtle substances (*laṭā'if*)

Seven subtle substances (laṭā'if)	*Prossessor of the subtle substance*	*Corresponding prophet*
subtle bodily substance (*al-laṭīfa al-qālabiyya*)	man (*insān*)	Ādam
subtle soul substance (*al-laṭīfa al-nafsiyya*)	civilized man (*al-insān al-madanī*)	Nūḥ (Noah)
subtle heart substance (*al-laṭīfa al-qalbiyya*)	submitter (*muslim*)	Ibrāhīm (Abraham)
subtle innermost substance (*al-laṭīfa al-sirriyya*)	believer (*mu'min*)	Mūsā (Moses)
subtle spirit substance (*al-laṭīfa al-rūḥiyya*)	friend (*walī*)	Dāwūd (David)
subtle mystery substance (*al-laṭīfa al-khafiyya*)	prophet (*nabī*)	'Īsā (Jesus)
subtle reality substance (*al-laṭīfa al-ḥaqqiyya* or *al-laṭīfa al-anā'iyya*)	seal (*khātim*)	Muḥammad

On this initial level, the struggle is to respond to the Qur'ānic commands and prohibitions pertaining to the body. On the next level, the level of the subtle soul substance (*laṭīfa al-nafsiyya*) and the prophet Nūḥ, the struggle is to contain one's passion and anger which will otherwise be like an overwhelming flood, and so on. When one reads about the communities of each of these prophets, they should recognize its believers, unbelievers, and hypocrites as corresponding to the forces within each of their subtle substances (*laṭā'if*) which may act in harmonious or harmful ways.[40]

The discovery of these subtle substances and their correspondences with the stories of the prophets is an experiential one. Al-Simnānī explains that no one will believe what he has said until they have witnessed it for themselves. But once this scheme has been understood, the reader will know with certainty that the Qur'ān has seven inner senses. Al-Simnānī gives an example of how these can be discovered in a single verse of the Qur'ān 4:43. He addresses only the first part of it:

> *O you who believe, do not come to prayers while intoxicated until you are able to know what you are saying; nor in a state of ritual impurity, unless you are traveling, until you have done the major ablution.*

The external meaning of this verse is clear, admonishing the believer in a state of drunkenness or impurity to delay saying his prayers until he is sober and ritually pure. In al-Simnānī's commentary on the inner senses of the verse, the states of drunkenness and impurity refer to increasingly subtle forms of forgetfulness and attachment. In the first inner sense of this verse, drunkenness and impurity is the result of preoccupation with the affairs of the world. The ablution for it is the "water" of the traditional remembrance (*al-dhikr al-rasmī*). In the second inner sense of the verse, the state of drunkenness and impurity is brought about by passion (*hawā*) and its ablution is accomplished with the "water" of the instructional remembrance (*al-dhikr al-taʿlīmī*). In each of the inner senses that follow, the believer risks intoxication and impurity resulting from the ever-higher states he achieves. The ablution at each level is the "water" of the appropriate remembrance (*dhikr*). Without a state of sobriety and purity, there can be no prayer or intimate conversation with God.[41]

5

ATTACKING AND DEFENDING ṢŪFĪ QUR'ĀNIC INTERPRETATION

The problem of distinguishing sound exegesis from exegesis by mere personal opinion (*tafsīr bi'l-ra'y*)

Although there are indications that in the earliest period of Islam some Muslims objected to any kind of commentary on the Qur'ān, the necessity of interpretation was overwhelmingly accepted by the tenth century. Disagreements continued, however, over what constitutes legitimate commentary and exegetes had to justify their endeavors in light of a *hadīth* on interpretation transmitted from Ibn 'Abbās:

> The Prophet said, "Whoever speaks of the Qur'ān from his personal opinion (*ra'y*), let him take his seat in the Fire."[1]

A similar tradition quotes the first caliph Abū Bakr al-Ṣiddīq as saying,

> What earth would carry me, what heaven shelter me, if I were to speak of the Qur'ān from my personal opinion (*ra'y*) or of what I do not know?[2]

The question became how to distinguish sound and acceptable interpretation from the prohibited interpretation by personal opinion (*tafsīr bi'l-ra'y*). In the introduction to his *Jāmi' al-bayān*, al-Ṭabarī writes that the Qur'ān is comprised of three parts: the part whose interpretation is known only to God; the part whose interpretation is known only to the Prophet and, through his explanation or other indication, to his community; and the part known only to those who possess knowledge of the Arabic language.[3] The first part of the Qur'ān should not be interpreted by anyone and the second part can only be understood by means of an explanation of the Prophet; otherwise, it is interpretation by personal opinion (*tafsīr bi'l-ra'y*).[4] The best interpreters of the Qur'ān will be those who are clearest in proving their interpretations based on the most authentic traditions of the Prophet and their knowledge of Arabic language. Furthermore, they will not disagree with what has been said by the Companions and Followers of the Prophet, and the men of knowledge in the community.[5] After al-Ṭabarī there were religious scholars who believed that any commentary that did not base itself entirely on the early interpretative tradition (*tafsīr bi'l-ma'thūr*) was an interpretation by personal opinion (*tafsīr bi'l-ra'y*), and therefore prohibited. Al-Ghazālī was one of the first to contest this view.

Al-Ghazālī on *tafsīr bi'l-ra'y*

Al-Ghazālī addressed the problem of defining what constitutes *tafsīr bi'l-ra'y* as part of his defense of Ṣūfī Qur'ānic interpretation in his *Iḥyā' 'ulūm al-dīn*.

> What is intended by [the prohibition on commentary of the Qur'ān] must either be a restriction to what has been transmitted (*naql*) or heard [from authorities] (*masmū'*), abandoning any deduction (*istinbāṭ*) and independent understanding (*istiqlāl bi'l-fahm*), or what is intended is something else. It is completely wrong to think that what is intended is that one should not speak about the Qur'ān except according to what one has heard, for several reasons.[6]

Al-Ghazālī presents four arguments for not confining commentary to the transmitted tradition. First, the traditions traceable to the Prophet explain only part of the Qur'ān. Most of the transmitted exegetical tradition comes from Companions such as Ibn 'Abbās and Ibn Mas'ūd and represents their own opinions, not what they heard from the Prophet himself. Therefore, these interpretations can be called *tafsīr bi'l-ra'y*. Second, the Companions and early exegetes had disagreements over the interpretation of Qur'ānic verses. Third, there is a distinction between interpretation and revelation. This is demonstrated in the Prophet's prayer for Ibn 'Abbās, "O God, instruct him in religion and teach him interpretation (*ta'wīl*)." Al-Ghazālī asks, "If interpretation was what has been heard [from authorities] (*masmū'*) like what has been revealed (*tanzīl*), what would be the purpose of granting him that?"[7] Fourth, the Qur'ān confirms the possibility of deduction (*istinbāṭ*) independent of transmitted knowledge in Qur'ān 4:83, "*Truly, those among them who are able to deduce (the matter) (yastanbiṭūnahu) know it*."[8]

Having discussed what the *ḥadīth* on *tafsīr bi'l ra'y* does *not* mean, al-Ghazālī continues with what he believes is the correct interpretation of the ban on *tafsīr bi'l-ra'y*.

> The prohibition is for one of two reasons: The first is where someone has an opinion (*ra'y*) regarding something to which he is inclined by his nature (*ṭab'*) and inclination (*hawā*), so he interprets (*yata'awwalu*) the Qur'ān in accordance with his opinion and inclination so that he can argue for the authenticity of his own objective (*gharaḍ*). If he did not have that opinion and inclination, that meaning would not have appeared to him from the Qur'ān.
>
> Sometimes this is done knowingly like the one who argues for the authenticity of his innovation (*bida'*) by means of some verses of the

> Qur'ān, knowing that that is not what is meant by the verse, but he seeks to deceive his opponent by it.
>
> Other times it may be done unknowingly but, since the verse has a potentiality for more than one meaning, his understanding of it inclines to the sense which agrees with his objective, that view having been preferred because of his opinion and inclination. He has commented by means of his opinion, i.e., his opinion has led him to that commentary. If he did not have that opinion, then he would not have preferred that sense.
>
> Other times he may have a sound objective, and so he seeks some indication (*dalīl*) for that from the Qur'ān and then proves it with something he knows was not intended for that . . . this is like someone who calls for struggle with the hard heart and says, God says, "*Go to Pharoah. Truly, he has transgressed*," (20:24) and he points to his own heart and indicates that that is what was intended by Pharoah. This kind [of interpretation] is what some preachers do with sound intentions of beautifying their talk and attracting the listener, but it is prohibited. The *bāṭiniyya* have utilized this with corrupt intentions to deceive people and invite them to their false school of thought. In accordance with their opinion (*ra'y*) and school of thought, they bring the Qur'ān down to matters which they most certainly know are not what was intended by it.
>
> These categories are the first of the two reasons for the prohibition of *tafsīr bi'l-ra'y*. What is meant [in the *ḥadīth*] by personal opinion (*ra'y*) is the false personal opinion that agrees with inclination (*hawā*) without sound personal effort (*al-ijtihād al-ṣaḥīḥ*). Personal opinion (*ra'y*) includes the true and the false. That which agrees with inclination (*hawā*) can be designated by the term "*ra'y*."[9]

Al-Ghazālī is making a distinction between two types of personal opinion (*ra'y*): sound personal effort (*al-ijtihād al-ṣaḥīḥ*), which is praiseworthy, and opinion biased by inclination (*hawā*), which is not. The latter is blameworthy whether the interpreter is aware of his distortion of the meaning of the Qur'ān, and whether his intention is sound, as in the case of the preacher, or unsound, as in the case of the *bāṭiniyya*. His example of the sound-intentioned but nonetheless blameworthy interpreter who suggests that what is meant by Pharoah is the hard heart is a strange one, given that this is exactly the kind of interpretation practiced by some Ṣūfīs. Al-Ghazālī himself justifies it in his other works with his theory of correspondences, a theory we will return to shortly. Al-Ghazālī continues with the second reason for the ban on *tafsīr bi'l-ra'y*.

> The second is where someone hastens to comment on the Qur'ān on the basis of the external sense of the Arabic without seeking help from listening [to authorities] (*samā'*) and transmission (*naql*) regarding the strange words (*gharā'ib*) of the Qur'ān, its obscure and alternate expressions, its abridgment, elision, ellipsis, and word order. One who does not

> master the exoteric aspect of commentary and hastens to deduce meaning purely on [his own] understanding of the Arabic language will have made many errors and will have joined the group of those who interpret the Qur'ān by personal opinion (*ra'y*).
>
> Transmission (*naql*) and hearing [from authorities] (*samā'*) in the external aspect of commentary (*tafsīr*) are necessary for him first, so that by means of it, he will be wary of situations of error. After that, understanding (*fahm*) and deduction (*istinbāṭ*) will be expanded. The strange words (*gharā'ib*) that can be understood only through hearing [from authorities] (*samā'*) are many. We will point out some of them so that one can seek information about words like them and know that it is not permissible to neglect the memorization of exoteric commentary first; there is no hope of reaching the inner sense (*bāṭin*) before mastering the exoteric sense (*ẓāhir*). One who claims to understand the secrets of the Qur'ān without mastering exoteric exegesis is like one who claims to have reached the inside of the house before crossing through the door, or the one who claims to understand what Turks mean in their speech without his having understood their language. Truly, exoteric commentary is the same as learning the language that is necessary for understanding, and there are many areas that can only be learned by hearing from [authorities] (*samā'*) and there is no hope in reaching the inner sense (*bāṭin*) before mastering the external sense (*ẓāhir*).[10]

Al-Ghazālī is stating his belief that understanding the information transmitted from the Companions and Followers of the Prophet is necessary, but only as a first step in interpretation, and he appears to be limiting the usefulness of their commentary primarily to linguistic explanations. Because of the conflicting interpretations found among early exegetes, al-Ghazālī rejects an unquestioning acceptance of their interpretations in areas other than issues of language. Although al-Ghazālī's purpose here is to defend Ṣūfī exegesis in particular, his argument works as well for any exegete wishing to go beyond the interpretations of the first generations of Muslims. His argument was, in fact, adopted by one of the most well-known Qur'ānic commentators, Abū 'Abd Allāh Muḥammad al-Qurṭubī (d. 1272),[11] who quotes al-Ghazālī without due attribution to him almost word for word in the introduction to his commentary, *Al-Jāmi' li-aḥkām al-Qur'ān*.[12]

Ibn al-Jawzī and Ibn Taymiyya on the importance of transmitted information

Al-Ghazālī firmly believed that the interpretation of the Qur'ān should not be restricted to the transmitted tradition. He rather bluntly says that,

> the one who claims that the Qur'ān has no other meaning that what exoteric exegesis has provided should know that he has acknowledged his

> own limitations and therefore is right with regards to himself, but is wrong in an opinion that brings everyone else down to his level.[13]

A critical response to this view can be found in the *Kitāb talbīs Iblīs* (The Book of the Devil's Deception) written by Ibn al-Jawzī (d. 1200). Ibn al-Jawzī attempts in this book to identify and correct the errors he sees among his fellow Muslims, devoting approximately half of the book to the errors of Ṣūfīs even though he appears to have been a member of a Ṣūfī order himself.[14]

According to Ibn al-Jawzī, the starting point for all the delusions of the Ṣūfīs is their turning away from seeking transmitted knowledge.[15] The devil deceives them in this matter in several ways. First, he shows them how much work is involved in seeking knowledge while making ease and comfort seem attractive. Some Ṣūfīs have said that preoccupation with transmitted knowledge is idleness but this is only because they have seen the commitment it requires.

Second, he causes them to be content with just a little knowledge, so that they believe that those who seek extensive knowledge of *ḥadīth* do so only for prestige and their own pleasure. Ibn al-Jawzī concedes this desire for prestige, but compares it to the desire for marriage, a desire that is necessary for the greater goal of procreation.

Third, he causes some of them to believe that the objective is practice (*'amal*) without understanding that devotion to knowledge is the most perfect practice.

Last, the Devil deceives the Ṣūfīs into believing that knowledge is acquired from inner processes (*bawāṭin*) and inspiration (*ilhām*), without intermediary (*bi-lā wāsiṭa*). Ibn al-Jawzī does not deny the possibility of inspiration but insists that it is not knowledge in and of itself, but is rather the *fruit* of knowledge and piety. He insists that there can be no knowledge without the intermediary of transmitted knowledge; otherwise, there would be no way of knowing whether the inspiration received is sound or merely a Satanic suggestion. Those who belittle transmitted knowledge attack the religious law (*sharī'a*), a charge tantamount to infidelity. He notes that this is the case with Abū Yazīd al-Bisṭamī when he criticized religious scholars, saying, "Poor people! They get their knowledge from the dead, but we get our knowledge from the Living One who never dies."[16]

According to Ibn al-Jawzī, there is never a point where one moves beyond the need for transmitted knowledge. He disapprovingly relates a story regarding the Ṣūfī Aḥmad ibn Abū'l-Hawārī:

> Aḥmad ibn Abū'l-Hawārī threw his books into the sea and said, "Yes, you *were* proof (*dalīl*), but devotion to proof after attainment (*wuṣūl*) is absurd." Aḥmad ibn Abū'l-Hawārī had searched out *ḥadīth* for thirty years. When he attained all he could from them, he carried his books to the sea, submerged them and said, "O knowledge, I have not done this to you out of disdain, nor out of disdain for what is your due. Rather, I used to seek you out in order to be guided by you to my Lord. Now that I have been guided by you, I have no further need of you."[17]

Ibn al-Jawzī understands that Ṣūfīs justify their position concerning transmitted knowledge by dividing knowledge into the exoteric (*ʿilm al-ẓāhir*) and esoteric (*ʿilm al-bāṭin*), but it is a distinction he rejects.

> Many of the Ṣūfīs make a distinction between the law (*sharīʿa*) and the truth (*ḥaqīqa*) but this is an ignorant thing to say because all of the law is different kinds of truths (*ḥaqāʾiq*).[18]

Despite this criticism, Ibn al-Jawzī notes that there have been many Ṣūfīs who do insist upon the necessity and primacy of the law.

Ibn Taymiyya was an admirer of Ibn al-Jawzī, and he demonstrates a similar belief in the primacy of transmitted knowledge. He insists that knowledge can never be received directly without the intermediary of the *ḥadīth* and Traditions, and he attacks any belief to the contrary as a corrupt influence from philosophy.

> What is stated by different groups of the *bāṭiniyya* – the Shiʿī *bāṭiniyya* such as the writers of the "Epistles of the Brotherhood of Purity" and the Ṣūfī *bāṭiniyya* such as Ibn Sabʿīn and Ibn ʿArabī and others, and as also found in the writings of Abū Ḥāmid [al-Ghazālī] and others – that it is possible for men who practice spiritual exercises, purification of the heart, and development of the soul by means of praiseworthy characteristics, to come to know the realities that have been related from the Prophets concerning belief in God, angels, the Book, the prophets and the Last Day, and information about the jinn and devils, without the intermediary of communication from the prophets, is based upon this false premise, which is that when they purify themselves this will descend upon their hearts either through the "Active Intellect" or by some other means.[19]

He criticizes Abū Ḥāmid al-Ghazālī in particular for stating this belief frequently in his works and for suggesting that those who practice spiritual disciplines may hear the speech of God just as Mūsā did. According to Ibn Taymiyya this contradicts the correct beliefs held by the founders of the four Schools of Law, *ḥadīth* scholars and the "real" Ṣūfīs (*ṣūfiyya muḥaqqiqūn*) who follow the Messenger.[20] However, Ibn Taymiyya does not deny that there is a connection between knowledge and practice but rather insists that this knowledge will never be received other than by means of the prophets.

> Some theologians have criticized what is true in [al-Ghazālī's writings], claiming that the practice of spiritual disciplines and purification of the heart has no effect whatsoever in obtaining knowledge. They are also wrong in this denial since the truth is that piety and purification of the heart are among the strongest means to acquiring knowledge. However, the Book and the Sunna must be resorted to for knowledge and practice. It is not possible for anyone after the Prophet to know by himself without

> the intermediary of the Prophet these things from the Unseen. No one can do without that which has come from the messengers in understanding the Unseen. The speech of the Messenger is clear in and of itself. There is no unveiling to anyone nor is any analogy of it equal to it. An "unveiling" or "analogy" of someone is sanctioned only when it is consistent with [the speech of the Messenger]; otherwise it contradicts it. However what is called an "unveiling" (*kashf*) or an analogy (*qiyās*) does contradict the Messenger and is therefore a false analogy and false imagination (*khayāl*). This is what was meant when it was said, "I seek refuge in God from philosophical analogy and Ṣūfī imagination."[21]

Ibn Taymiyya affirms a limited role for inspiration in areas where there are inadequate *shar'ī* indications. In his *Sharḥ kalimāt li-'Abd al-Qādir*, he writes

> If the *sālik* [the person seeking knowledge] has creatively employed his efforts to the external *shar'ī* indications and sees no clear probability concerning the preferable action, he may feel inspired – along with his goodness of intention and reverent fear of God – to choose one of two actions as superior (to the other). This kind of inspiration is an indication concerning the truth. It may be even a stronger indication than weak analogies, weak *ḥadīths*, weak literal arguments (*ẓawāhir*) and weak *istiṣḥābs* which are employed by many of those who delve into the principles, differences, and systematizing of *fiqh*.[22]

Ibn Taymiyya's acceptance of a limited place for inspiration, however, does not extend to what Ṣūfīs call the knowledge of states (*aḥwāl*). A basic error of the Ṣūfīs, according to both Ibn al-Jawzī and Ibn Taymiyya, is their acceptance of the state they call ecstasy (*wajd*). We have already seen how the Ṣūfīs found a model for Qur'ānic recitation in Ja'far al-Ṣādiq, who is said to have repeated a verse continually in prayer until he heard it from the Speaker Himself and fainted. Ibn al-Jawzī does not refer to this particular story in his *Talbīs Iblīs*, but he states that there are many examples in books on asceticism of men fainting, crying, and even dying upon hearing the Qur'ān recited.[23] Although acknowledging that there may have been some sincere believers amongst them, he nonetheless rejects what he sees as a loss of control without precedence among the Companions of the Prophet. According to Ibn al-Jawzī, the Companions had the purest of hearts but their strong emotion (*wajd*) did not go beyond weeping and humility (*khushū'*).[24]

Ibn Taymiyya also makes it clear that those who faint or even die upon hearing a recitation of the Qur'ān are not to be emulated. In his *Al-Ṣūfiya wa'l-fuqarā'* he describes three ranks of those who listen to or recite the Qur'ān, knowingly or unknowingly contesting the levels found in the Ṣūfī versions:

> Instead, there are three ranks [to those hearing the *Qur'ān*]. One of them is the state of those unjust to themselves, those who are hard-hearted, not

> yielding to the audition [of the *Qur'ān*] nor to the remembrance [of God], and they are comparable to the Jews...
>
> The [second rank] is the state of the pious believer who is too weak to bear what suddenly afflicts his heart. So he is the one who is struck down, death-struck or swooning, and that is due only to the power of the sudden seizure *(al-wārid)* and the weakness of the heart to bear it...
>
> But those who retain their reason, in spite of the fact that they acquired from faith that which others acquired, or similar to it or more perfect, they [the former] are more excellent than they [the latter] are. This is the state of the Companions – may God be satisfied with them – and the state of our Prophet – God bless him and give him peace. For he was made to travel by night into the heaven, and God revealed to him what He revealed. Yet, he awoke as he had spent the night; his state did not change. Thus, his state is more excellent than that of Moses – God bless him and give him peace – who fell swooning (Q. 7:143) when his Lord manifested Himself to the mountain. Moses' state is a splendid, exalted, and excellent state, but the state of Muḥammad – God bless him and give him peace – is more splendid, exalted, and excellent.[25]

Ibn Taymiyya's views on the subject of losing consciousness are more complex than Ibn al-Jawzī's. Whereas Ibn al-Jawzī leans towards a complete condemnation of losing consciousness, Ibn Taymiyya carefully and clearly distinguishes the insincere who seek unconsciousness, even through alcohol and drugs, from the sincere who succumb because they have not yet realized the more perfect state of sobriety. It is a discussion similar to that found in many Ṣūfī texts.[26] Ibn al-Jawzī, however, rejects the entire notion of knowledge by means of states and stations, calling al-Qushayrī's description of them a worthless and confused mess (*al-takhlīṭ alladhī laysa bi-shay'*).

> ʿAbd al-Karīm b. Hawāzin al-Qushayrī wrote a book, *Al-Risāla*, for [the Ṣūfīs] in which he makes extraordinary remarks on annihilation (*fanā'*) and subsistence (*baqā'*), contraction (*qabḍ*) and expansion (*basṭ*), the moment (*waqt*) and the state (*ḥāl*), ecstasy (*wajd*) and existence/finding (*wujūd*), gathering (*jamʿ*) and separation (*tafriqa*), sobriety (*ṣaḥw*) and intoxication (*sukr*), tasting (*dhawq*) and drinking (*shurb*), obliteration (*maḥw*) and affirmation (*ithbāt*), self-disclosure (*tajallī*), presence of the heart before God's signs (*muḥādara)* and unveiling (*mukāshafa*), flashes (*lawā'iḥ*), rising stars (*ṭawāliʿ*) and glimmers (*lawāmiʿ*), originating (*takwīn*) and consolidating (*tamkīn*), the religious law (*sharīʿa*) and the truths (*ḥaqā'iq)* and so on – all that from a delirium without any basis, and his *tafsīr* is even more incredible.[27]

For both Ibn al-Jawzī and Ibn Taymiyya, valid Qur'ānic exegesis will not deviate in any way from the interpretations of the early Companions and Followers of the

Prophet. Ibn al-Jawzī specifically criticizes many of the books we have been mentioned so far and will be discussing in Part II. He mentions Abū Naṣr al-Sarrāj's *Kitāb al-luma'*, wherein are mentioned "repugnant beliefs" and "despicable statements." Abū Ṭālib al-Makkī's *Qūt al-qulūb* contains "false *aḥādīth*" and "corrupt beliefs." 'Abd al-Raḥmān al-Sulamī's *Ḥaqā'iq al-tafsīr* contains astonishing examples of Ṣūfī exegesis "which occur to them without the support of any of the fundamentals of knowledge." Al-Ghazālī's *Iḥyā' 'ulūm al-dīn* is full of false traditions which al-Ghazālī does not know are false.[28]

According to Ibn al-Jawzī, the problems in Ṣūfī interpretation occur as a result of linguistic error or distortion, deviation from the transmitted *tafsīr* tradition, abandonment of the obvious and clear meaning of a verse, and incorrect belief. He gives examples of these errors, taken primarily from al-Sulamī's *Ḥaqā'iq al-tafsīr*, and then ends with these dismissive words:

> The entire book is like this. I had intended to show quite a bit of it here but I see that time will be wasted in recording something which borders between infidelity (*kufr*), error (*khaṭa*) and drivel (*hadhayan*). It is like what we have related from the *bāṭiniyya*. These are examples for anyone who wants to know what the book is like; if anyone wants to know more, let him look at this book.[29]

Ibn Taymiyya on sound interpretation of the Qur'ān

Ibn Taymiyya's *Muqaddima fī uṣūl al-tafsīr*[30] can be seen as a point-by-point rebuttal of al-Ghazālī's arguments for not confining Qur'ānic commentary to the transmitted tradition. Al-Ghazālī, as we have seen, asserted that the Prophet explained only part of the Qur'ān, and that most of the transmitted exegetical tradition comes from the Companions of the Prophet and represents their own opinions, not what they heard from the Prophet himself. According to al-Ghazālī, this material is contradictory and should not be considered as authoritative as the revealed text. Instead, al-Ghazālī views the interpretative tradition from the first generations of Muslims (*salaf*) as a model for the independent exercise of judgment (*ijtihād*), not as conclusive proof (*ḥujja*) that demands acceptance.[31]

Ibn Taymiyya's approach, on the other hand, is to create a hierarchy of sources that are to be consulted in descending order until the explanation of a Qur'ānic verse is clear: the Qur'ān, the Sunnah of the Prophet, the statements of the Companions of the Prophet (*ṣaḥāba*), and the statements of the Followers of the Companions of the Prophet (*tābi'ūn*).[32] Ibn Taymiyya supports his methodology and rebuts the points made by al-Ghazālī by making two assertions. The first is that the Prophet completely explained the meaning of the entire Qur'ān to his Companions.[33] The second is that the Companions and the Followers have greater authority in interpreting the Qur'ān than any generation of Muslims after them, to the point where their consensus is conclusive proof (*ḥujja*).[34] Ibn Taymiyya differs from other Sunnī Muslim commentators, not so much in his degree of reverence for the Prophet and the pious predecessors (*salaf*), but in his confidence in the comprehensiveness, accuracy, and unity of the material transmitted from them.[35] He does not accept the assertion that the Companions or the Prophet and the early exegetes disagreed over interpretation of Qur'ānic verses. Instead, he gives examples proving that their differences amount to variation rather than contradiction.

According to Ibn Taymiyya, errors in interpretation are the result of error in one of two areas. He states that knowledge is either the result of authentic transmission (*naql muṣaddaq*) or verifiable deduction (*istidlāl muḥaqqaq*) and that, therefore, commentators make errors either through their imperfect knowledge of *aḥādīth* or by faulty thinking. Mostly these errors are the result of either preconceived ideas that are read into the Qur'an, or attention paid only to the words and not to the context of the revelation. Like al-Ghazālī, Ibn Taymiyya divides those who make these errors into those who know full well that they are distorting the message of the Qur'ān and those whose intention is good. According to Ibn Taymiyya, the second type includes many Ṣūfīs, preachers, jurists, and others who have the correct meanings but the wrong Qur'ānic verses to support those meanings. Ibn Taymiyya tells us that this is the case for much of what the Ṣūfī Abū 'Abd al-Raḥman al-Sulamī (d. 1021) includes in his commentary, *Ḥaqā'iq al-tafsīr*.[36] Ibn Taymiyya is not opposed to Ṣūfī exegesis per se, but rather considers it as falling into the category of *tafsīr bi'l-ra'y* if it does not agree with the interpretations of the earliest exegetes.

Al-Ghazālī's defense of *ta'wīl*

The fact that al-Ghazālī was criticized well before Ibn Taymiyya for defending Qur'ānic exegesis that goes beyond the transmitted interpretative tradition can be seen in his work *Fayṣal al-tafriqa*.[37] It is a book that calls for careful discrimination in evaluating the beliefs of other Muslims before charging them with disbelief (*takfīr*). It was apparently written to console an unnamed colleague upset by attacks on al-Ghazālī himself. Al-Ghazālī states that the problem of excessive *takfīr* stems from a lack of differentiation between those who deny the message of the Prophet and those who have different interpretations of that message. Al-Ghazālī agrees that those who deny the message of the Prophet are guilty of disbelief (*kufr*), a legal category in Islamic societies with serious consequences. But those who accept that message, differing only in their interpretations of it, are guilty only of innovation (*bida'*) or error (*khaṭa'*) if they are wrong in their interpretations, both lesser charges than disbelief.

Al-Ghazālī begins his argument with the statement that interpretation is essential for those verses of the Qur'ān and *aḥādīth* whose meaning, if taken literally, would be absurd. According to him, this interpretation is incumbent on every Muslim, however literal-minded, if they are not to prove themselves completely stupid and ignorant.[38] However, since al-Ghazālī agrees that some interpretations *do* constitute disbelief, he provides a system for evaluating interpretative activity.

The system is based on a conception of existence (*wujūd*) as comprised of five degrees (*marātib*), each of which has a different relationship to interpretation.[39] The first degree is essential (*dhatī*) or absolutely real existence (*al-wujūd al-muṭlaq al-ḥaqīqī*), which is made up of the heavens and the earth, the animals and the plants that exist whether or not we perceive them. Al-Ghazālī asserts that there is no need for interpretation (*ta'wīl*) of this degree of existence because it entails what is manifest (*al-ẓāhir*). Significantly, al-Ghazalī includes in this category the Throne, the Footstool and the Seven Heavens mentioned in the Qur'ān and the Traditions of the Prophet, elements of the Unseen world which he insists are solid, real things, and therefore not subject to interpretation.

The second degree of existence is sensible (*ḥissī*), that which we see but which has no existence outside of our perceptions. Included in it are the dreams and hallucinations of ordinary people and the visions of prophets and saints. An example of a *ḥadīth* which corresponds to this level of existence is the one in which the Prophet says, "The Garden was shown to me in the breadth of this wall." The person who has proof (*burhān*) that physical bodies do not intermingle and that the small cannot contain the large, knows that this means that the likeness of the Garden appeared (*tamaththala*) to the senses (*al-ḥiss*), so that it was as if the Prophet was witnessing it.

The third degree of existence is the imaginary (*khayālī*), referring to things that we create in our imaginations that are absent from our senses, for example, the likeness of an elephant that exists in our brain but not outside of it. The *ḥadīth* used to illustrate this degree of existence is one which begins with the Prophet saying, "It was as if I were looking at Yūnus (Jonah)..." Al-Ghazālī interprets this to mean that the Prophet was not really seeing (*lam yakūn ḥaqīqa 'l-naẓar*), but it was *like* seeing (*ka 'l-naẓar*). However, he seems unsure of his own example, saying that it would not be farfetched to say he was really seeing it, as described in the sensible degree of existence.

The fourth degree of existence is mental (*'aqlī*) existence, based on the difference between a thing's meaning (*ma'nā*) and its form (*ṣūra*). The hand is the form (*ṣūra*) for the meaning (*ma'nā*) "the ability to strike." When the Qur'ān or *ḥadīth* speak of God's hand, the person who has proof (*burhān*) of the absurdity of God's having a sensible or imaginable hand attests to God's having the power to strike, give, and withhold, which is the meaning or reality of "hand."

The fifth degree of existence is analogical (*shabahī*) and refers to something which does not exist in any of the prior degrees of existence, and can only be understood by its resemblance (*ishbāh* or *munāsaba*) to the attributes or qualities of something else. The examples al-Ghazālī gives are the qualities such as anger, longing, joy, and patience, when they are attributed to God. The person who has proof (*burhān*) knows that God cannot possess qualities that imply imperfection, so he understands anger, for example, as the will to punish.

It is the last two degrees of existence that produce the most radical interpretations through the use of metaphor (*majāz*) and figurative speech (*isti'āra*). Al-Ghazālī insists that this kind of metaphorical interpretation is unavoidable, supporting his claim by stating that even Aḥmad ibn Ḥanbal, the man most opposed to this form of interpretation, found himself unable to avoid it completely.[40] Having established the necessity of metaphorical interpretation, al-Ghazālī sets forth a rule of interpretation (*qanūn al-taʾwīl*) so as to define the parameters of its permissibility. In any given text of the Qurʾān or *ḥadīth*, the interpreter must accept the literal sense (*ẓāhir*) based on its essential existence (*al-wujūd al-dhātī*) unless he has proof (*burhān*) of its absurdity. If it is absurd, he looks to the next degree of existence for its meaning, unless this too is absurd. The metaphorical interpretation required by the mental and analogical degrees will only be permissible if the interpreter has proof of the absurdity of interpretation based on all the other levels.

Al-Ghazālī concludes that disagreements over interpretation are based on the matter of proof, with the Ḥanbalī declaring there is nothing inconceivable about God's being described by the direction "above," and the Ashʿarī declaring there is nothing inconceivable about the ocular vision of God. To avoid internal strife in the Muslim community, al-Ghazalī has two different recommendations, one for the common man untroubled by doubts in his faith, and one for intellectuals whose faith needs more proof. For the common man, he recommends the unquestioning acceptance of the literal meanings of the Qur'ān, *ḥadīth*, and the interpretations of the Companions of the Prophet. Speculative thinkers whose beliefs are more troubled may cautiously use this method of going beyond the literal sense in order to strengthen their faith. They should not, however, charge others with disbelief, unless there is denial of one of the roots of the faith (belief in God, in His Messenger, and in the Last Day), or one of its branches when based on the soundest Traditions.[41]

One of the examples al-Ghazālī gives to illustrate those who deny the fundamental tenets of Islam, and therefore deny the message as a whole, are the philosophers who deny God's knowledge of particulars or the physical reality of the Garden and the Fire in the Afterlife. He charges them with having abandoned the literal meaning of the Qurʾān and the soundest *ḥadīth* on these matters without any valid proof of the inconceivability of these concepts. What is particularly damning to them is their belief that the physical Afterlife is merely a fiction devised for those unable to grasp the intellectual Afterlife. This belief implies that the Prophet engaged in a kind of lie, however well meaning. This, according to al-Ghazālī, is what places them at the first degree of atheism (*zandaqa*).[42]

As for those who interpret matters that do not pertain to Islam's most basic beliefs, al-Ghazālī advises against accusations of disbelief, although one may still make accusations of innovation and error. Al-Ghazālī uses a Ṣūfī interpretation as an example. He states that a certain Ṣūfī found it inconceivable that the Prophet Ibrāhīm (Abraham) could have believed that a star, the moon, or the sun could be God (Qur'ān 6:76–9). Instead, al-Ghazālī explains, the Ṣūfi took this as an indication that the celestial bodies mentioned represent something non-physical, which he then understood to mean the angelic luminous substances (*jawāhir malakiyya nūrāniyya*). Al-Ghazālī is critical, saying that this rejection of the literal sense is not based on proofs (*barāhīn*) but on conjectural indications (*dalālāt ẓanniyya*). Nonetheless, he insists that the Ṣūfī should not be charged with disbelief as this matter is not one of the fundamental beliefs of Islam.[43] The interpretation referred to here is, in fact, al-Ghazālī's own, or at least one he quotes at length in other works. Versions of it can be found in both his *Iḥyā' 'ulūm al-dīn*[44] and *Mishkāt al-anwār*.[45]

Al-Ghazālī does not even identify himself as a Ṣūfī here, but rather says, "This is their kind of interpretation." He then refers to two other Ṣūfī interpretations, one of which is also discussed in his *Mishkāt al-anwār*.[46]

> They have interpreted (*ta'awwalū*) "the staff" and "the shoes" in God's words, "*Take off your shoes*" (20:12) and "*Throw down what is in your right hand*" (20:69). Perhaps conjecture (*ẓann*) in matters such as these that do not relate to the fundamentals of belief is analogous to proof (*burhān*) regarding the fundamentals, so there should be no accusations of disbelief or innovation. To be sure, if the opening of this door were to lead to confusing the hearts of the common people, then the author should be particularly charged with innovation in everything whose mention has not been related on the authority of the first generations (*salaf*).[47]

Al-Ghazālī advocates tolerance for this kind of Ṣūfī interpretation so long as it does not confuse people and so long as the Ṣūfī does not claim to be released from the obligations of religious law. Al-Ghazālī recommends that such a Ṣūfī be killed because, even if he were still a believer, his actions would open a door to licentiousness (*ibāḥa*) that cannot be closed, thereby causing great harm to religion.[48]

Problems with al-Ghazālī's defense of *ta'wīl*

Al-Ghazālī's uses the word *ta'wīl* in his *Fayṣal al-tafriqa* to refer to the interpretation of verses in the Qur'ān whose literal meaning can be definitively shown to be absurd. *Ta'wīl* used in this way is a concept that can be traced back to the theologian al-Ash'arī who strove to find a defensible exegetical stance between pure literalism and the type of metaphorical interpretation practiced by the Mu'tazila.[49] Ḥanbalī scholars felt that God should be described only as He described Himself, or as the Prophet described Him. They therefore felt that the anthropomorphic verses of the Qur'ān should not be interpreted as the Mu'tazila interpreted them, but rather should be understood *bi-lā kayfa*, without asking "how" or "why". The classic definition of the *bi-lā kayfa* doctrine goes back to a tradition from Mālik b. Anas,[50] quoted here from *Taḥrīm al-naẓar fī kutub ahl al-kalām* (Censure of Speculative Theology), written by the Ḥanbalī scholar Muwaffaq al-Dīn ibn Qudāma (d. 1146):

> Has he not heard the story of Mālik b. Anas when he was asked with regard to the Koranic verse, "The Merciful on the throne sits firm,"[51]

> "how 'sits firm'?"? Mālik inclined his head and was silent until the sweat of fever covered his brow; then he looked up and said: "The attribute *istawā*[52] is unknown, the modality of it is not rational; but belief in it is obligatory, and inquiring about it is a heretical innovation."[53]

Al-Ash'arī also relied on the *bi-lā kayfa* doctrine, but opened the door to some degree of interpretation if there was any proof (*ḥujja*) that the literal sense should be abandoned. The way that the later Ash'arite theologian Fakhr al-Dīn al-Rāzī understood this was to divide the verses of the Qur'ān into three parts. The first are the clear verses (*muḥkamāt*) whose apparent sense (*ẓāhir*) can be confirmed by rational indicators (*al-dalā'il al-'aqliyya*). The second type of verses are those whose apparent sense (*ẓāhir*) has been shown to be impossible by definitive indicators (*al-dalā'il al-qāṭi'a*). The third type of verses are ambiguous in meaning (*mutashābih*) and indicators like these cannot be found to either affirm or deny [one meaning or another].[54] The sound exegete, according to al-Rāzi, will know how to discover the truth concerning the first two types of verses, and will know to entrust the meaning of the third type to God.

When al-Ghazālī brings up examples of Ṣūfī interpretation in his *Fayṣal al-tafriqa*, he expands the definition of verses open to *ta'wīl* beyond the anthropomorphic verses that are usually the subject matter of this debate, verses whose literal meaning was generally accepted by Muslims as being absurd. In discussing the story of the Prophet Ibrāhīm and the celestial bodies, al-Ghazālī acknowledges that the rejection of the literal sense of this story is not based on proofs (*barāhīn*) but on conjectural indications (*dalālāt ẓanniya*). What al-Ghazālī is most likely referring to here are theological arguments objecting to the idea that the Prophet Ibrāhīm could have mistaken the celestial bodies for God. However, when al-Ghazālī proceeds from his comments on the story of Ibrāhīm to Ṣūfī interpretations of Mūsā's "staff" and "the two shoes," he is now addressing another kind of verse altogether, verses whose literal sense is not at all in question. Clearly, Mūsā's staff and shoes can be accepted as existing literally and therefore do not have to be interpreted metaphorically. Al-Ghazālī, however, seems unaware that he has violated his own hermeneutic principle. The weakness of al-Ghazālī's defense of Ṣūfī interpretation in his *Fayṣal al-tafriqa* is that his argument only works for the interpretation of Qur'ānic verses whose literal meaning is problematic, verses that constitute only a small portion of Ṣūfī exegesis.

Al-Ghazālī's final defense of Ṣūfī interpretation

Whether al-Ghazālī recognized the problem with his argument, his later writings address it nonetheless in two ways.[55] The first concerns defining who is qualified to interpret the ambiguous verses of the Qur'ān. In his *Fayṣal al-tafriqa*, al-Ghazālī had recommended that the common people (*'awāmm*) accept the ambiguous parts of the Qur'ān, such as the anthropomorphic verses, without interpretation. The rule of interpretation he suggests in this book is only for those people whose faith has become troubled. However, by the end of his life, as we have already seen, al-Ghazālī had expanded the definition of the common people in his *Iljām al-'awāmm* to include Qur'ānic exegetes, jurists, *ḥadīth* scholars and theologians, all of whom he believed should not go beyond the literal sense of Qur'ānic verses. Instead of confining *ta'wīl* to those whose faith has become troubled, al-Ghazālī now confined the right to interpret ambiguous verses to "those firmly rooted in knowledge" *(al-rāsikhūn fī'l-'ilm)*, defined by al-Ghazālī as individuals of high spiritual attainment. Al-Ghazālī shifts from using rational criteria for defining acceptable *ta'wīl* to criteria based on the interpreter's spiritual practice and divine grace.[56]

The second area in which a change can be seen in al-Ghazālī's exegetical thinking is in how he distinguishes Ṣūfī interpretations from *bāṭinī* interpretations. In his early writing on the subject in the *Iḥyā' 'ulūm al-dīn*, al-Ghazālī, he mentions the allegorization of the Qur'ānic figure Pharoah as an example of blameworthy interpretation in his discussion of *tafsīr bi'l-ra'y*:

> This is like one who calls for struggle with the hard heart and says, God says, "*Go to Pharoah. Truly, he has transgressed.*" (20:24), and he points to his own heart and indicates that that is what was intended by Pharoah. This is what some preachers do with sound intentions of beautifying their talk and attracting the listener, but it is prohibited. The *bāṭiniyya* have utilized this with corrupt intentions to deceive people and invite them to their false school of thought.[57]

The problem here is that equating Pharoah with the hard heart is exactly the kind of symbolic or allegorical commentary that Ṣūfīs do.[58] If one follows the rule of interpretation which al-Ghazālī proposes in his *Fayṣal al-tafriqa*, any interpretation that goes beyond the literal sense of a Qur'ānic verse is unacceptable unless the literal sense can be shown to be absurd. Al-Ghazālī revises his defense of Ṣūfī interpretations in the *Mishkāt al-anwār*,[59] now relying upon the Ibn Mas'ūd *ḥadīth* to insist that all the different levels of meaning in the Qur'ān must be accepted as valid. Unacceptable interpretation would be like saying that Mūsā did not have any shoes, or that he did not hear the words, "*Take off your shoes.*" Equally unacceptable is the denial of other levels of meaning.

> God forbid! Surely the annulment of the literal meanings (*ẓawāhir*) is the view of the *bāṭinyya* who have looked one-eyed towards one of the worlds, not knowing the parallelism (*muwāzana*) between the two worlds, nor understanding this aspect. Likewise, the annulment of secrets (*asrār*) is the teaching of the *ḥashawiyya*.[60] Whoever looks only to the external sense (*ẓāhir*) is a *ḥashawī*, and whoever looks only to the inner sense (*bāṭin*) is a *bāṭini*, and whoever joins the two is perfect (*kāmil*). Because of that [the Prophet] said, "The Qur'ān has an exoteric sense (*ẓāhir*) and an inner sense (*bāṭin*), a limit (*ḥadd*) and a point of

> ascent (*muṭṭala'*). It may be that this is transmitted from 'Alī and stops with him (*mawqūf 'alayhi*).[61]
>
> Rather, I say that Mūsā understood from the command to take off his shoes the removal of the two engendered worlds, so he followed (*imtathala*)[62] the command externally by taking off his shoes and inwardly by the removal of both worlds. This is "taking heed" (*i'tibār*), i.e., the crossing over (*'ubūr*) from one thing to another, from the external sense (*ẓāhir*) to the secret (*sirr*).[63]

Although it is questionable whether the Ismā'īlīs would have denied the reality of Mūsā's shoes, al-Ghazālī argument here is, nonetheless, his most effective defense of Ṣūfī interpretation. In adopting it, however, he abandons the condition contained within the Ash'arī defense which allows for *ta'wīl* only when the apparent sense of a verse can be shown to be absurd.

The success of al-Ghazālī's argument can be seen in the fact that al-Simnānī adopts it, with a few modifications, in the introduction to his *tafsīr*:

> Know with certainty that anyone who rejects commentary on the exoteric sense (*ẓāhir*) of the Qur'ān regarding the human world of horizons (*al-'ālam al-āfāq al-nāsūtī*) is a stubborn *bāṭinī* apostate. Anyone who rejects commentary on the inner sense (*baṭn*) of the Qur'ān regarding the kingly world of souls (*al-'ālam al-anfus al-malakūtī*) after having affirmed its external sense is a stupid and anthropomorphic idiot. But the one who combines the external and the inner sense is a happy Sunnī *muslim*. The one who knows the limit (*ḥadd*) of the Qur'ān in the World of Dominion (*'ālam al-jabarūt*) is a rightly guided gnostic believer (*mu'min*). The one who ascends to the lookout point (*muṭṭala'*) of the Qur'ān in the World of Divinity (*'ālam al-lāhūt*) is a perfectly virtuous man (*muḥsin kāmil*), witness for communities, looking out (*muṭṭali'*) over unseen things, praiseworthy and noble.[64]

Al-Simnānī adds an interesting interpretation of the *ḥadīth* on *tafsīr bi'l ra'y*, suggesting that the definition of unacceptable interpretation changes according to the level of meaning of the Qur'ān.

> The one who interprets the external sense (*ẓahr*) of the Qur'ān by his own opinion (*ra'y*), without hearing from a commentator whose authority derives from the Companions, has become a disbeliever because of his ignorance of most of its precepts (*aḥkām*), causes of revelation (*asbāb al-nuzūl*), and parables (*amthāl*).
>
> The one who interprets the inner sense of the Qur'ān by his own opinion (*ra'y*), without secret, spiritual, hidden or real inspiration (*ilhām sirrī aw rūḥī aw khafī aw ḥaqqī*), has becomes a disbeliever in all the allusions (*ishārāt*) coming from the presence of Lordship through the particulars

of the powers (*al-daqā'iq al-quwā*) and the kingly subtleties (*al-laṭā'if al-malakūtiyya*).

The one who interprets the limit (*ḥadd*) of the Qur'an by his own opinion (*ra'y*), without the permission emanating from the Ka'ba of Divinity, has become a disbeliever in the gnosis of the tenuities of the qualities pertaining to the Dominion (*ma'ārif raqā'iq al-ṣifāt al-jabarūtiyya*).

The one who interprets the lookout point of the Qur'ān by his own opinion (*ra'y*), before His permission to enter into the exalted presence and before obtaining great purity and comprehension of the core of the real subtle substance (*al-laṭīfa al-ḥaqqiya*) which nurtures the subtle "I" substance (*al-laṭīfa al-anā'iyya*), has become a disbeliever in the realities of the Qur'ān.[65]

Al-Simnānī's definitions of the different types of prohibited *tafsīr bi'l ra'y* can be compared to the restrictions which al-Ghazālī applies as to who may interpret the Qur'ān in non-literal ways. Determining the legitimacy of interpretations that go beyond the literal sense of the Qur'ānic text becomes far more difficult here because there are no external formulas to follow. There is a possibility of error at every level, and al-Simnānī therefore makes suggestions on how to combat them. Just as a healthy and sound ear is a requirement for hearing the external sense of the Qur'ān and learning its exoteric commentary, a healthy and sound "ear" of the heart is a requirement for hearing the inner sense of the Qur'ān and learning its esoteric commentary. Each higher level of comprehension requires a correspondingly healthy and sound "ear." Just as there are remedies for ailments of the physical ear, there are remedies for these inner ailments, consisting of the abandonment of attachments and various forms of remembrance (*dhikr*), for which al-Simnānī suggests several examples.[66]

The defense of Ṣūfī exegesis that al-Ghazālī ends up with is the one that most Ṣūfīs seem to have quietly adopted. As detailed in the *ḥadith* transmitted from Ibn Mas'ūd, the Qur'ān has many levels of meaning, and therefore it would be wrong to limit its meaning to only those meanings transmitted in the interpretative tradition. The literal or exoteric aspect of its message must be accepted wholeheartedly along with these other levels of meaning. The interpretations of other levels of meaning correspond to the different states experienced by individual Ṣūfīs, and are the result of their spiritual practices and divine grace. Their validity cannot be verified by external means, and communicating them will not necessarily be of larger benefit to the community of Muslims.

Part II

COMMENTARY

6

ṢŪFĪ COMMENTATORS ON THE QUR'ĀN

In a religion as firmly based on a book as Islam, almost any writing which emerges can conceivably be classified as commentary on the Qur'ān, leaving us with the difficult task of deciding which works should be included in the genre of exegesis. The task of identifying the formal characteristics of *tafsīr* has been tackled with great skill by Calder.[1] He suggests that, first and foremost, a work of *tafsīr* must follow a "canon and segmentation, lemma and comment" format that sequentially addresses the complete, or nearly complete, text of the Qur'ān."[2] Second, the *tafsīr* must allow for polyvalent readings through the citation of named authorities, a polyvalence that may, however, be limited by the selection of material included and the statement of preferred interpretations. Last, a *tafsīr* must measure the Qur'ānic text by use of outside disciplines, both linguistic (instrumental) and theological (ideological).[3] Given these defined characteristics, Calder does not include Ṣūfī works within the genre of *tafsīr*, although he accepts the use of Ṣūfī ideas as an ideological structure against which to measure the Qur'ān.[4]

As we have already seen, the Ṣūfīs themselves often reserved the term "*tafsīr*" for the types of commentaries following the characteristics that Calder describes, and used different terms like "allusion" (*ishāra*) and "interpretation" (*ta'wīl*), or more rarely, "understanding" (*fahm*), or "striking similitudes" (*ḍarb al-mithāl*), for their commentaries. What holds these writings together as a genre, however, is the fact that they follow the lemma and comment format of *tafsīr*, and address the Qur'ān in a sequential, even if in a more selective manner.[5] Works such as Jalāluddīn Rūmī's *Mathnawī* and Ibn 'Arabī's *Fuṣūṣ al-ḥikam* are examples of Ṣūfī works that present a large amount of Ṣūfī interpretations of the Qur'ān, but are not generally considered as part of the commentary genre because they do not follow this format.

Ṣūfī commentaries on the Qur'ān differ from the *tafsīr* genre described by Calder in another way, in the area of style. These works have been described as "allegorical"[6] and "symbolic,"[7] but these are terms that do not adequately convey their varied forms of discourse. As part of their interpretation of Qur'ānic verses, Ṣūfīs displayed literary characteristics that are not often found in work of *tafsīr*, creating their own metaphors, wordplay, narratives, and poetry as an integral part of their exegesis, and it is this use of language and style as much as specific Ṣūfī doctrines and beliefs that gives Ṣūfī commentary its distinctive character.

The commentaries chosen here to represent Ṣūfī exegesis consist of a variety of influential works, but is should be noted that many important Ṣūfī commentaries remain in manuscript form. Because the exegetical works included in this study will be excerpted as part of an analysis of selected Qur'ānic passages, the unique style of each of the commentaries may not be obvious. What follows, then, is a chronological introduction to each of the commentators, with biographical notes, and comments on the style and method of each.

Al-Tustarī

Abū Muḥammad Sahl b. ʻAbd Allāh al-Tustarī was born in the Persian province of Khūzistān and died in Basra in 896.[8] He became involved with Ṣūfism early in life under the influence of his uncle, a ḥadīth scholar and disciple of the Ṣūfī Maʻrūf al-Kharkhī (d. 815). His teachings are preserved in writings that reflect his own hand as well as the disciples who took oral instruction from him.

Al-Tustarī's *tafsīr* is the oldest continuous Ṣūfī commentary on the Qur'ān. Exegesis attributed to other early Ṣūfī figures exists in the compilation of al-Sulamī (d. 937 or 942), *Ḥaqā'iq al-tafsīr*, but al-Tustarī's commentary is the earliest work to survive independently. Although there is yet no critical edition of the commentary, which comprises a small volume, Böwering has made a thorough study of it on the basis of six extant manuscripts.[9] He describes it as a disjointed work, which "resembles a collection of jottings, noted down in loose sequence and linked to each other without any apparent principle of logical order."[10] These jottings appear to come from three different sources: al-Tustarī's exoteric and esoteric interpretations of Qur'ānic verses, his aphorisms and stories taken from other works no longer extant, and additions and glosses inserted into the text, either by disciples of al-Tustarī or later Ṣūfīs.[11]

Given the nature of the compilation of this work, its rather eclectic content is not surprising. According to Böwering,

> There are literal and metaphorical interpretations of the Qur'ānic phrases: illustrations from the Prophet's normative and customary behavior; examples from the legends of the prophets of old; traces of mystical views shared by earlier Ṣūfīs and anecdotes concerning their practical conduct; fragments of Tustarī's mystical themes, his religious thought, and ascetic practice; exhortations and guidelines for disciples and answers to their questions; and finally, episodes about Tustarī's life, glosses and explanatory insertions into the text.[12]

Al-Tustarī's *tafsīr* hints at the possibilities but leaves to others the task of a more conscious and comprehensive presentation of Ṣūfī exegesis.

Al-Sulamī

Abū 'Abd al-Raḥmān Muḥammad b. al-Ḥusayn al-Sulamī was born in the city of Nīsābūr (Nishapur in Persian).[13] Although he traveled extensively to study *ḥadīth* and perform the pilgrimage, most of his life was spent in his home city, where he died in 1021. Like the grandfather who educated him and the Ṣūfī teacher who initiated him, al-Sulamī was a Shāfi'ī scholar of *ḥadīth*. He was a prolific writer, with more than 100 books to his name, about 30 of which are extant. His *Ṭabaqāt al-Ṣūfiyya*, the oldest extant Ṣūfī hagiographical collection, and his two compilations of Ṣūfī exegesis, the *Ḥaqā'iq al-tafsīr* and the *Ziyādāt ḥaqā'iq al-tafsīr* are invaluable because they preserve oral teachings and written works from Ṣūfīs of the eighth to tenth centuries.

The *Ḥaqā'iq al-tafsīr* comprises two volumes in a recently published edition.[14] Portions of the work were previously published by Massignon and Nywia.[15] The *Ziyādāt ḥaqā'iq al-tafsīr* is an appendix to the *Ḥaqā'iq* recently discovered and published by Böwering in one volume.[16] According to Böwering, al-Sulamī gathered the material for his commentaries from both written and oral sources. The only written sources which al-Sulamī mentions explicitly are those attributed to Abū'l-'Abbās Aḥmad al-Adamī, known as Ibn 'Aṭā' (d. 921) and Ja'far al-Ṣādiq (d. 765).[17] The most frequently cited authorities in the *Ḥaqā'iq* are Ibn 'Aṭā', Abū Bakr al-Wāsiṭī, known as Ibn al-Farghānī (d. 932), Sahl al-Tustarī, Abū Sa'īd al-Kharrāz (d. 899), al-Junayd (d. 910) and Abū Bakr al-Shiblī.[18] In the *Ziyādāt*, the most frequently cited authorities are Sahl al-Tustarī, Ja'far al-Ṣādiq, and Ibn 'Aṭā'.[19] Both books include anonymous quotations as well.

In the introduction to his *tafsīr*, al-Sulamī states that he included two types of quotations in his compilation. The first he calls *āyāt*, by which he means interpretations of specific verses, and the second he calls *aqwāl*, which are Ṣūfī sayings related to key Qur'ānic terms. Noting the wealth of commentaries based upon the exoteric sciences and the relative lack of the same for Ṣūfī exegesis, al-Sulamī writes that he has deliberately confined himself to the latter. Böwering remarks that, in preserving the earliest Ṣūfīs' exegetical comments, al-Sulamī performed a function similar to that of al-Ṭabarī in his *Jāmi' al-bayān*, and in doing so established Ṣūfī commentary by allusion (*ishāra*) as a distinct genre within the *tafsīr* tradition.[20]

The style of al-Sulamī's commentaries reflects their structure as a compilation. Because there is no unifying voice behind the many citations that follow one another, linked only by the verse being interpreted, themes remain underdeveloped and terms unexplained. Without a larger context, many of these comments are somewhat cryptic. The focus is on key Qur'ānic words, rather than on larger segments of the verse and its context. Böwering understands the interpretations as encounters between key Qur'ānic words and mystical experience.

> These allusions are the result of the merger between Qur'ānic keynotes and the matrix of the Ṣūfī world of ideas. The keynotes, Qur'ānic words

> or phrases striking the Ṣūfī's mind, may be taken up in total isolation from the actual context or, less frequently, presuppose familiarity with a wider frame of Qur'ānic reference. It is significant to realize that these keynotes are not studied as a text, but aurally perceived by men experienced in listening attentively to Qur'ān recital and intent on hearing God, the actual speaker of the Qur'ānic word. Listening to the Qur'ānic word, the Ṣūfī is captured by a keynote, a fleeting touch of meaning communicated to him by the divine speaker. This keynote signals to the Ṣūfī the breakthrough to God, revealing himself in His divine speech and opening a way to Himself through and beyond His divine word.
>
> With these keynotes the listener associates a cluster of images emerging from the content of his personal experience. These images merge with the Qur'ānic keynotes and find their expression in the allusions that are jotted down in the commentary in a condensed, abbreviated form. These jottings thus reflect the gist of the listener's encounter with the divine word merging inextricably with the matrix of the Ṣūfī world of ideas. In this process the allusions achieve a synthesis that makes it impossible to discern where "exegesis" ends and "eisegesis" begins, and where the discovery of man's own existence disappears in the revelation of the divine word.[21]

This interaction between the Qur'ānic text and Ṣūfī experience in Ṣūfī commentary was first noted by Nwyia. One of the most distinctive examples of this is found in what Nwyia calls the "intériorisation des figures prophétiques." He writes,

> In their meditation on the Qur'ān, the figures of the prophets become prototypes of mystic experience or figures of religious consciousness. That which they read in the stories of the ancients *(akhbār al-awwālin)* are not "histories" but a lesson (*'ibrā*), a doctrine on the relationships between God and man. In this way Abraham becomes the figure of suffering but faithful consciousness or the prototype of friendship with God, Moses, the figure of spiritual experience as dialogue with God, etc.[22]

While many of these comments can be obscure because of their use of esoteric symbolism or technical Ṣūfī terminology that is left unexplained, other comments cited in the *Ḥaqā'iq al-tafsīr* could be characterized as homiletic, especially when compared to the reticence in this area of other types of commentaries that confine themselves to the interpretative tradition.

The *Ḥaqā'iq al-tafsīr* was recognized almost immediately as representing a very different approach to understanding the Qur'ān, an approach deemed unacceptable by some. Al-Sulamī's near contemporary, the Qur'ānic scholar al-Wāḥidī (d. 1076), said, "If al-Sulamī thinks that this is a *tafsīr*, he is an infidel."[23] In his *Talbīs iblīs*, Ibn al-Jawzī wrote that 'Abd al-Raḥmān al-Sulamī's *Ḥaqā'iq al-tafsīr* contains astonishing examples of Ṣūfī exegesis "which occur to them without the supports of any of the fundamentals of knowledge,"[24] and he quotes numerous examples from it in order to point out the errors of Ṣūfī exegesis. Critical judgments of the *Ḥaqā'iq al-tafsīr* were also made by such later scholars such as Ibn Taymiyya, Shams al-Dīn al-Dhahabī (d. 1348), and Abū'l Faḍl 'Abd al-Raḥmān al-Suyūṭī (d. 1505).[25]

Al-Qushayrī

Abū'l-Qāsim 'Abd al-Karīm b. Hawāzin al-Qushayrī (d. 1074) was an Arab from Northeastern Iran who studied with al-Sulamī after his primary spiritual teacher and father-in-law, Abū 'Alī al-Daqqāq, died.[26] Upon meeting his first teacher, al-Qushayrī abandoned his life as a wealthy landowner, and, at the urging of his teacher, adopted the life of a scholar of *ḥadīth* and Ash'arī theology. This quiet life was interrupted when the Saljūqs began to persecute al-Qushayrī and other prominent and vocal Shāfi'ī-Ash'arīs. Al-Qushayrī was imprisoned for a short time before escaping to live in exile, returning to Nīsābūr only when the political situation became more amenable to Ash'arīs.

Although al-Qushayrī wrote theological works and an exoteric Qur'ānic commentary, his fame rests upon his Ṣūfī works. The most famous of these is *Al-risāla fī 'ilm al-taṣawwuf*, considered by Ṣūfīs to be the classic formulation of their doctrine. His expressed purpose in writing the book was to reconfirm the orthodoxy of Ṣūfism against those Ṣūfīs who no longer observed the religious law (*sharī'a*). Al-Qushayrī was a cautious writer, avoiding the type of excessive statements attributed to al-Ḥallāj and other Ṣūfīs; consequently, his Ṣūfī commentary, the *Laṭā'if al-ishārāt*, has never been attacked in the manner of the commentaries of al-Sulamī and al-Kāshānī.

The *Laṭā'if al-ishārāt* consists of al-Qushayrī's own comments on Qur'ānic verses as well as anonymous Ṣūfī sayings. According to Basyūnī, the editor of a critical six-volume edition,[27] al-Qushayrī's goal in writing this *tafsīr* was to help his fellow Ṣūfīs and, as such, is a better example of his school of thought than the *Risāla*.[28] Although many of the elements found in al-Sulamī's *Ḥaqā'iq al-tafsīr* are present here, al-Qushayrī avoids the extensive use of Ṣūfī terminology and far-reaching wordplay and allegory, instead adopting a consistently homiletical style. Al-Qushayrī searches Qur'ānic verses for something to inspire the reader whether those verses are parts of narratives or religious legislation. The qualities of the prophets become lessons for the aspiring mystic. A verse on the distribution of booty prompts al-Qushayrī to comment on the booty to be enjoyed when one succeeds in capturing the soul from the enemies of passion and Satan.[29] Foreshadowing al-Ghazālī's *Iḥyā' 'ulūm al-dīn*, al-Qushayrī continually stresses the importance of the inner aspect of acts of worship, the need to go beyond mere bodily compliance to discover layers of meaning in these acts.[30]

As Basyūnī points out, al-Qushayrī's method is more literary than intellectual, a fact which he attributes to the Ṣūfī emphasis on "tasting" (*dhawq*) and an appreciation for the inimitability (*'ijāz*) of the Qur'ān. This method is apparent in the attention al-Qushayrī pays to individual words and phrases, drawing upon the roots of the language, etymology, inflections and rhetoric.[31] In addition to showing his appreciation for the literary subtleties of the Qur'ānic text, al-Qushayrī responds himself to the text in a literary manner by the use of elegant prose, metaphors, and poetry.[32]

Abū Ḥāmid al-Ghazālī

Abū Ḥāmid Muḥammad b. Muḥammad al-Ṭūsī al-Ghazālī was born in Ṭūs near present day Mashhad in Iran.[33] His studies brought him to Nīsābūr as a young man where he studied with the prominent Shāfi'ī jurist and Ash'arī theologian Imām al-Ḥaramayn al-Juwaynī (d. 1085), a colleague of al-Qushayrī. Al-Ghazālī resided in the court of the Saljūq vizier Niẓām al-Mulk until he was appointed as rector and professor at the Niẓāmīya *madrasa* in Baghdad. Four years later he resigned from this prestigious position as the result of a personal crisis that he later described in his intellectual autobiography, *Al-Munqidh min al-Ḍalāl*, which also details al-Ghazālī's disenchantment with theology, philosophy and Ismā'īlism, and his consequent adoption of Ṣūfism. Al-Ghazālī spent the next ten years in practicing and studying Ṣūfism in Damascus, Mecca and Medina before returning to his hometown. He taught once again in Nīsābūr before he died in Ṭūs in 1111.

Al-Ghazālī is said to have written over 400 works, of which about 70 are extant manuscripts. His writings cover a broad range of the intellectual sciences of the classical Islamic world. Among his early works is an exposition of Islamic philosophers entitled *Maqāṣid al-falāsifa*, which was followed by a criticism of the same in the *Tahāfut al-falāsifa*. Among his juridical works is *Al-Mustaṣfā min 'ilm al-uṣūl al-fiqh*, a work which is still used as a textbook on the sources of Islamic law today. The *Fayṣal al-tafriqa bayn al-Islām wa'l-zandaqa* deals with the specific issue of taxing others with disbelief. The *Iljām al-'awāmm 'an 'ilm al-kalām*, written at the very end of al-Ghazālī's life, expresses his reservations about the study of theology. Among al-Ghazālī's Ṣūfī works is the *Iḥyā' 'ulūm al-dīn*, a four-volume book that attempts, as its title announces, "the revivification of the religious sciences." Borrowing extensively from Abū Ṭālib al-Makkī's *Qūt al-qulūb*, al-Ghazālī reorganized and amplified this material into a systematic work written in a clear and lucid style, addressing the topics of knowledge, worship, and behavior from a pietistic and mystical standpoint. His shorter works include *Al-Risāla al-laduniyya*, a treatise dealing with the distinctive epistemology of Ṣūfism, the *Jawāhir al-Qur'ān* containing various theories regarding the Qur'ān and its interpretation, and the *Mishkāt al-anwār*, a short hermeneutical and exegetical work concerning the Light Verse of the Qur'ān and the Veils *ḥadīth*. Al-Ghazālī is said to have written a forty-volume commentary on the Qur'ān as well, but an extant copy has yet to be found.[34]

Al-Ghazālī's commentary on the Light Verse in the *Mishkāt al-anwār* is, unique among the Ṣūfīs studied here in the extent to which it combines theory and exegesis.[35] If al-Ghazālī abandoned philosophy and theology as a means for attaining truth, he nonetheless continued to employ their analytical and logical tools in his writing. We need not go so far as Ibn Taymiyya in saying, "Ghazālī went into the belly of the philosophers (*falāsifa*) and when he wished to come out he was unable to do so,"[36] but it could be said that al-Ghazālī's contribution to Ṣūfī exegesis is more intellectual than poetic and literary, as it is with al-Qushayrī and al-Maybudī. However, he writes in a very accessible and non-obscure manner, and therefore functions quite effectively as an apologist for Ṣūfī theory. The style of the commentary is consistently allegorical, although, as we have seen, al-Ghazālī had distinctive ideas regarding the use of metaphors in the Qur'ān.

Rashīd al-Dīn al-Maybudī

We know very little of the life of Rashīd al-Dīn Abū'l-Faḍl Aḥmad al-Maybudī (fl. 1135), the author of the ten-volume commentary *Kashf al-asrār wa-'uddat al-abrār*.[37] From his name we know he was from Maybud, a small town near Yazd in central Iran. On the basis of the contents of his commentary, Rokni has concluded that al-Maybudī was a Shāfi'ī Sunnī *ḥadīth* scholar who showed his respect for the Shī'ī tradition by quoting 'Alī 185 times and other Shī'ī imams 68 times.[38]

Al-Maybudī explained the purpose of his writing the *Kashf al-asrār* in his introduction. He had read and been greatly impressed by the *tafsīr* of 'Abd Allāh al-Anṣarī al-Harawī (d. 1089) but was disappointed by its brevity, and so set out to expand it.[39] Although al-Anṣarī's commentary was purely mystical, al-Maybudī decided to add other dimensions of *tafsīr* as well. He divided the Qur'ān into reading sections (*majlishā*), and then divided each of these sections into three parts. The first part in each section is a literal Persian paraphrase of the Qur'ānic Arabic verses. The second part, the largest of the three parts, is exoteric *tafsīr* written in both Persian and Arabic which addresses philological, narrative, juridical, and theological issues as found in the transmitted *salafī* and post-*salafī* exegetical tradition. The third part, also written in both Persian and Arabic, contains what al-Maybudī calls "symbols" (*rumūz*), "allusions" (*ishārāt*) and "subtleties" (*laṭā'if*),[40] and it is this part that makes his *tafsīr* distinctive.

The *Kashf al-asrār* has sometimes been called the *tafsīr* of Khwājā 'Abd Allāh al-Anṣarī, but, in fact, al-Anṣarī is only one of the sources al-Maybudī used in the third part of his *tafsīr*. When al-Maybudī quotes al-Anṣarī, he sometimes refers to him by name and sometimes calls him "the spiritual guide of the way" (*pīr-i ṭarīqat*), or "the learned one of the way" (*'ālim-i ṭarīqat*). Al-Maybudī's other primary source for this part of his *tafsīr* is the *Laṭā'if al-ishārāt* of al-Qushayrī who is quoted or paraphrased anonymously in Arabic or in Persian translation. Other sources must have been used as well for the sayings and interpretations attributed to early Ṣūfīs which he includes. Böwering states that, at least in the case of those sayings attributed to Sahl al-Tustarī, the material appears to have been taken from Abū Naṣr al-Sarrāj's *Kitāb al-luma'*, Abū Ṭālib al-Makkī's *Qūt al-qulūb*, and the hagiographical work, *Ḥilyat al-awliyā' wa-ṭabaqāt al-aṣfiyā'* of Abū Nu'aym al-Iṣfahānī (d. 1038).[41]

Rokni has identified three different types of interpretation within this third part of al-Maybudī's *Kashf al-asrār*.[42] The first kind he calls *ta'wīl*, by which he means interpretation that uncovers Ṣūfī doctrines and beliefs in Qur'ānic verses. Rokni illustrates this with al-Maybudī's commentary on verses 2:67–71, in which Mūsā commands his people, on God's behalf, to sacrifice a heifer and they question him regarding what kind of cow this might be. The qualities of the cow to be sacrificed are taken as an allusion to the qualities needed for the mystical aspirant. Another kind of *ta'wīl*, according to Rokni, is the juxtaposition of Ṣūfī terminology with Qur'ānic verses. His example is the commentary on Qur'ān 3:31. Al-Maybudī compares the first part of this verse, *Say*, "*If you love God*," to the Ṣūfī concept of dispersion (*tafriqa*) and the second part, "*God will love you*," to the concept of union (*jam'*).

The second kind of interpretation that Rokni identifies in al-Maybudī's Ṣūfī exegesis is homiletic elucidation (*tawḍīḥ... bi-ravish-i majlis-i ghūyān va khuṭabā'*). Adopting the style of preachers, al-Maybudī uses rhymed prose, poetry, puns, stories, similes, and metaphors to exhort and inspire the believer. The subject matter might be the inward qualities and outward practices of the believer, the stations of the prophets, or God's glory. It is in this kind of interpretation that al-Maybudī's literary skills are most apparent, and as Rokni points out, the value of the *Kashf al-asrār* lies in its mystical and literary aspects, its Ṣūfī *ta'wīl*, and its homilies.

Rokni's third type of interpretation occurs less frequently. He calls it *tashqīq*, by which he means the way in which al-Maybudī breaks apart a Qur'ānic verse and then expands these various parts by means of related verses, *ḥadīth*, or poetry. As an example he cites al-Maybudī's commentary on Qur'ān 3:191, *those who remember God standing, sitting and on their sides*, in which al-Maybudī identifies three different types of people who remember God. The first type remembers God with the tongue while forgetting Him in the heart. This is the remembrance (*dhikr*) of the unjust. The second type remembers God with the tongue and a present heart. Yet he seeks reward, so this is the remembrance of those who adopt a middle way. The third type remembers God with a heart full of Him, while his tongue has become silent as one who knows God. This is the remembrance of those who have outdistanced all others (*ṣābiqūn*).[43]

Rūzbihān al-Baqlī

Abū Muḥammad Rūzbihān b. Abī Naṣr al-Baqlī began his life in the Persian town of Fasā (Pasā in Persian), where he was born, as he put it in his autobiography, "to ignorant folk who were a prey to drunkenness and error, gross and vulgar men like unto 'startled asses fleeing before a lion' (Koran 74:50–1)."[44] He claims to have experienced mystical states beginning in childhood, states which increased in intensity until he fled into the desert as a young man, and was overwhelmed daily by visions in which he perceived the heavens and the earth as pure light. Following this period, he lived with Ṣūfīs and began to balance his extraordinary experiences by studying the exoteric sciences of Islam as a Shāfi'ī and an Ash'arī. Most of his life was spent in Shīrāz, where he established a Ṣūfī lodge and a following, and died in 1209.

Rūzbihān wrote over forty works in Arabic and Persian dealing with both exoteric and Ṣūfī topics, many of which are no longer extant or exist only in fragmentary form. Among those which have been published in critical editions, at least in part, are the aforementioned autobiography, *Kashf al-asrār*,[45] the *'Abhar al-'āshiqīn*[46] which presents Rūzbihān's theories on love and beauty, the *Sharḥ-i shaṭḥiyāt*[47] containing the ecstatic sayings of al-Hallāj and other Ṣūfīs, and the *'Arā'is al-bayān fī ḥaqā'iq al-Qur'ān*, his Ṣūfī commentary on the Qur'ān.

The *'Arā'is al-bayān* has been published so far only in lithographic form, comprising two large volumes in the edition used for this study.[48] Alan Godlas is currently working on a critical edition and English translation of this work.[49] The commentary on each Qur'ānic verse begins with Rūzbihān's own exegesis, followed by quotations from al-Sulamī's *Ḥaqā'iq al-tafsīr* and *Ziyādāt ḥaqā'iq al-tafsīr*, and al-Qushayrī's *Laṭā'if al-ishārāt*. The style of Rūzbihān's comments is quite distinct from the Ṣūfīs he quotes. Jāmī (d. 1492) remarked on its difficulty, saying, "he has sayings that have poured forth from him in the state of overpowering and ecstasy, which not everyone can understand."[50] The Moghul prince Dārā Shikūh (d. 1659) was impressed enough with Rūzbihān's writings to have written an abridgement and update of his *Sharḥ-i shaṭḥiyāt*, and to have had Rūzbihān's Qur'ānic commentary translated into Persian, yet he found his style "fatiguing."[51] On the other hand, modern scholars have noted the literary merits of Rūzbihān's writings. Mu'īn writes,

> His speech is like a rose that flutters apart once grasped in the hand, or like an alchemical substance that turns into vapor when barely heated. His language is the language of perceptions; he praises the beautiful and beauty, and loves them both.[52]

Similarly, Schimmel writes,

> What so profoundly impresses the reader in Rūzbihān's writings, both in his commentary on the *Shaṭḥiyāt* and his *'Abhar al-'āshiqīn* – "*Le Jasmin des fidèles d'amour*," as Henri Corbin translates its title – is his style, which is at times as hard to translate as that of Aḥmad Ghazzālī and possesses a stronger and deeper instrumentation. It is no longer the scholastic language of the early exponents of Sufism, who tried to classify stages and stations, though Baqlī surely knew these theories and the technical terms. It is the language refined by the poets of Iran during the eleventh and twelfth centuries, filled with roses and nightingales, pliable and colorful.[53]

In his Qur'ānic commentary, however, Rūzbihān's role changes from creator of symbols and metaphors to interpreter of those he locates in the Qur'ān, and in these interpretations the influence of Ṣūfī theories and technical terms is more evident, and above all, mystical experience. Unlike the popular homiletical and didactic style of the commentaries of al-Qushayrī or al-Maybudī, Rūzbihān's is visionary and esoteric.

Al-Kāshānī

Other than the fact that 'Abd al-Razzāq Kamāl al-Dīn b. Abī'l-Ghanā'im al-Kāshānī (or Qāshānī, Kāshī or Kāsānī) came from the province of Kāshān in Iran and died in 1329, we know little of his life.[54] He studied logic and philosophy as a young man before turning to Ṣūfism, where his philosophical bent found new expression in the school of Ibn 'Arabī.[55] Al-Kāshānī became one of the most widely read of the early interpreters of Ibn 'Arabī, having studied with Mu'ayyid al-Dīn al-Jandī (d. 1291), himself a student of Ibn 'Arabī's stepson, Ṣadr al-Dīn al-Qūnawī (d. 1274). Al-Kāshānī wrote an influential commentary on Ibn 'Arabī's *Fuṣūṣ al-ḥikam*, a commentary on al-Anṣarī's *Al-Sā'irīn*, and a dictionary of technical terms, the *Iṣṭilāḥāt al-Ṣūfīyya*, which explains the terms found in his own and other Ṣūfīs' writings. His Qur'ānic commentary, the *Ta'wīlāt al-Qur'ān* has been published several times in two large volumes inaccurately attributed to Ibn 'Arabi.[56]

It has been shown that, in fact, al-Kāshānī had an attitude towards exegesis very different from Ibn 'Arabī. The school of Ibn 'Arabī, beginning with al-Qūnawī, focused on the more philosophical and abstract areas of Ibn 'Arabī's thought, reducing if not eliminating Ibn 'Arabī's strong emphasis on the role of imagination and Islamic practice.[57] Al-Kāshānī was no exception here. As Morris writes,

> Kāshānī's Koranic commentaries, like his other books, are all clearly distinguished by a thoroughgoing pedagogical concern and didactic procedure that is manifested in such interrelated characteristics as their rigorous systematization, the clarification and simplification of vocabulary (especially if compared with Ibn 'Arabī), and the conceptualization (often in an openly reductionistic manner) of what were originally multivalent symbols. These tendencies are not merely stylistic particularities; they also reflect a shift in the content and underlying intentions of Kāshānī's writing (when compared with Ibn 'Arabī) that brought him very close to the prevailing systems of Avicennan philosophy (especially in their interpretations of the phenomena and claims of Sufism) and related schools of kalam – to such a degree that their verbal formulations are sometimes virtually indistinguishable.[58]

Morris judges al-Kāshānī's commentary as an aberration from the usual norms of Ṣūfī exegesis, replacing personal spiritual realization with "the *application* to the Koran of a coherent metaphysical system."[59] Whereas Ibn 'Arabī emphasized the primacy of knowledge by unveiling (*kashf*) over reason (*'aql*), Morris suggests that al-Kāshānī alters or even reverses this perspective. The result is "a sort of allegorical reduction of the complex symbolism of the Koran and *ḥadīth* to a single (or at most twofold) plane of reference."[60]

What Morris is responding to here is al-Kāshānī's primary methodology, which is that of finding correspondences between Qur'ānic verses and spiritual psychology and the stages of an individual's spiritual path. According to Lory, this is the methodology al-Kāshānī calls *taṭbīq*.[61] Al-Kāshānī is not the first commentator to use this technique, but he is the first to use it so extensively and exclusively, and the first to apply it to entire passages of the Qur'ān. It is this method that invites the charge of allegorical reductionism, and yet, however one judges the results, this does not appear to have been al-Kāshānī's intention. We have already seen how he characterizes the Qur'ān in the introduction to his commentary as a sea containing endless treasures to be found and *ta'wīl* as a process of ever changing interpretation related to the ever changing states of the reader.[62]

Al-Nīsābūrī

Niẓām al-Dīn b. al-Ḥasan al-Khurāsānī al-Nīsābūrī (d. 1327), known as Niẓām the Lame, was born and lived in Nīsābūr.[63] He was a renowned scholar who wrote on subjects ranging from astronomy and mathematics to morphology and Qur'ānic recitation. His most important work was his Qur'ānic commentary, *Gharā'ib al-Qur'ān wa raghā'ib al-furqān*, printed in thirty parts in twelve volumes.[64] The *Gharā'ib al-Qur'ān*, like al-Maybudī's *Kashf al-asrār*, divides the Qur'ān into sections made up of both exoteric and Ṣūfī commentary. After quoting a group of Qur'ānic verses, al-Nīsābūrī gives different readings (*qirā'āt*) and recitation pauses and stops (*wuqūf*). This is followed by commentary (*tafsīr*) primarily derived from al-Rāzī's *Al-Tafsīr al-kabīr*, as well as al-Zamakhsharī's *Al-Kashshāf 'an ḥaqā'iq al-tanzīl* and other commentaries. These sources are quoted without attribution throughout most of the commentary, although al-Nīsābūrī acknowledges his debt to al-Rāzī and al-Zamakhsharī in the introduction and names a few additional sources in a postscript. He also states in his postscript that the final part of each section, entitled *ta'wīl*, was taken mostly from the *tafsīr* of the Ṣūfī Najm al-Dīn al-Rāzī Dāya (d. 1256).[65]

Dāya was a disciple of the founder of the Kubrawī order, Najm al-Dīn al-Kubrā, who is said to have begun a commentary on the Qur'ān that he was unable to complete before his death, a commentary that ends in *sūra* 51. A number of manuscripts credit Dāya with the work, and it is therefore unclear to what degree this commentary was co-authored or revised by him. The commentary of 'Alā al-Dawla al-Simnānī (d. 1336), also from the Kubrawī order, contains an introduction and commentary on the first *sūra* followed by commentary from *sūra* 52 to the end of the Qur'ān. It exists independently and as a work appended to the *tafsīr* of Kubrā and Dāya. This collective work of the Kubrawī order is sometimes called *Al-Ta'wīlāt al-najmiyya*. Dāya may have written a different, independent *tafsīr* as well.[66] Because these *tafsīr*s exist only in manuscripts it is difficult to ascertain at this point in time which *tafsīr* al-Nīsābūrī used for his *ta'wīl*, and the extent to which his material is indebted to it.

In some ways al-Nīsābūrī's *ta'wīl* resembles that of al-Kāshānī in that al-Nīsābūrī frequently establishes correspondences between elements of Qur'ānic verses and the spiritual psychology and states of man. In general however, al-Nīsābūrī is less philosophical and theoretical than al-Kāshānī and often demonstrates a more lyrical response to the Qur'ānic text. In the introduction to his commentary, al-Nīsābūrī provides a context to understand *ta'wīl* as part of the methodology of "extracting many issues from brief expressions" (*istinbāṭ al-masā'il al-kathīra min al-alfāẓ al-qalīla*). These issues pertain to either topics of wording or content. Included in the first are matters related to recitation (*qirā'a*), lexicology (*lugha*), etymology (*'ilm al-ishtiqāq*), morphology (*'ilm al-ḥarf*), grammar (*'ilm al-naḥw*), and rhetoric (*'ilm al-badī'*). Included in the second are matters related to meanings (*ma'ānī*), explanation (*bayān*), deduction (*istidlāl*), the fundamentals of religion (*uṣūl al-dīn*), the fundamentals of jurisprudence (*uṣūl al-fiqh*), jurisprudence (*fiqh*), and the science of mystical states (*'ilm al-aḥwāl*). It is the science of mystical states that forms the basis for *ta'wīl* interpretations.[67]

7

QUR'ĀNIC VERSES 18:60–82

The story of Mūsā and al-Khaḍir

And when Mūsā (Moses) said to his boy, "I will continue until I reach the junction of the two seas or spend years and years traveling. But when they reached the junction, they forgot their fish, which took its way through the sea as in a tunnel. When they had gone on, [Mūsā] said to his boy, "Give us our meal. Truly, fatigue has overwhelmed us on our journey." [The boy] said, "Did you see when we betook ourselves to the rock? I forgot the fish and what caused me to forget to mention it was none other than Satan. It took its way through the sea in an amazing way!" [Mūsā] said, "That is what we were seeking." So they retraced their steps.

They found one of Our servants to whom We had given mercy from Ourselves and to whom We had taught knowledge from Our very presence (min ladunnā). Musa said to him, "May I follow you so that you can teach me something of that which you have been taught – right judgement?" He said, "You will not be able to be patient with me. How can you be patient with what you do not fully understand?" [Mūsā] said, "You will find me patient, God willing, and I will not disobey you in anything." He said, "If you follow me, do not ask me anything until I myself mention it to you."

So they proceeded until they embarked on the ship and he made a hole in it. [Mūsā] said, "Did you put a hole in it in order to drown its people? You have done a terrible thing!" He said, "Didn't I say to you that you would not be able to be patient with me?" [Mūsā] said, "Do not call me to account for what I forgot and do not be hard on me for what I did." They proceeded until they met a young man and he killed him. [Mūsā] said "Have you killed an innocent soul who has killed no one? You have indeed done an awful thing!" He said, "Didn't I say to you that you would not be able to be patient with me?" [Mūsā] said, "If I ask you anything after this, do not keep me in your company. You have had enough excuses from me." Then they proceeded until they came upon a people of a village. They asked them for food but they refused them hospitality. They found a wall in it that was almost falling down, so he fixed it. [Mūsā] said, "If you had wished, you could have been paid for it."

> *He said, "This is the parting between you and me. I will tell you the interpretation (ta'wīl) of that which you were unable to bear patiently.*
> *As for the ship, it belonged to some poor people who worked in the sea. I wanted to make it unusable because a king was behind them seizing every boat by force. As for the young man, his parents were believers and we feared that he would be hard on them on account of his insolence and ingratitude. We wanted that their Lord would give to them in exchange one better than he in purity and closeness of affection. As for the wall, it belonged to two young men who were orphans in the town. Underneath it was a buried treasure that was theirs. Their father had been a righteous man so your Lord wanted them to mature and reach their full strength and take out their treasure as a mercy from your Lord. I did not do it for myself. That is the interpretation (ta'wīl) of that which you were unable to bear patiently.*

Many stories are related in the Qur'ān in this elliptical manner, suggesting that the first Muslims hearing these verses were already familiar with these tales, or that they received further narrative detail or explanation from the Prophet himself. In this case there is an evidence for the latter in a *ḥadīth* transmitted on the authority of the Jewish convert Ubayy b. Kaʿb (d. 642), a *ḥadīth* which identifies the servant of God mentioned in these verses as al-Khaḍir (or al-Khiḍr), "the green man." Early Western scholars attempted to identify external sources for the Qur'ānic story and found common features in the Gilgamesh epic, the Alexander romance, and the Jewish legend of Elijah and Rabbi Joshua ben Levi.[1] While Wensinck claimed that the Qur'ānic story is derived from Jewish legend,[2] Wheeler has demonstrated more recently that it is, in fact, the Jewish legend that can be traced to Arabic sources.[3] He states that the common narrative elements isolated by Wensinck and earlier scholars conflate the Qur'ānic version with material from later Qur'ānic commentaries. For example, the theme of the water of eternal life, common to the Gilgamesh epic and the Alexander romance, is mentioned explicitly in the story of Mūsā and Khaḥir only in the commentaries and not in the Qur'ān itself. Wheeler views the appropriation of themes from earlier sources as part of a purposeful interpretative strategy for uncovering meaning rather than as an attempt to "get the story straight." It should be pointed out, however, that while Wheeler attributes these narrative elements to Qur'ānic commentators, the classical commentators themselves attribute details such as the water of eternal life and the salted fish that comes to life to the Prophet himself through the *ḥadīth* attributed to Ubayy b. Kaʿb, giving them a near canonical status.

The *ḥadīth* related from Ubayy b. Kaʿb contextualizes the Qur'ānic narrative by explaining the reason for Mūsā's journey. Mūsā is looking for a man whom he has been told has more knowledge than he does.

> Mūsā stood up amongst the people of Israel in order to preach. Someone asked, "Which person is the most knowledgeable?" Mūsā said, "I am."

> God rebuked him since he did not attribute his knowledge to Him. [God] said, "Nay, I have a servant at the junction of the two seas." Mūsā said, "O Lord, what is the way to him?" It was said, "You will take a fish and place it in a basket . . ."[4]

Al-Ṭabarī quotes an embellishment of this dialogue transmitted from Ibn 'Abbās:

> Mūsā asked his Lord, "Lord, which of your servants is most beloved to you? He said, "The one who remembers Me and does not forget Me." Mūsā said, "And which of your servants is most judicious?" He said, "The one who judges by the truth and does not follow his own inclination (*hawā*). Mūsā said, "O Lord, which of your servants is the most knowledgeable?" He said, "The one to whose knowledge the knowledge of the people aspire, that perhaps they might receive a word that would lead them to guidance or save them from ruin." Mūsā said, "Lord, is there such a one on earth?" He said, "Yes." Mūsā said, "Lord, who is he?" He said, "Al-Khadir." Mūsā said, "Where shall I look for him?" He said, "Upon the shore by the rock where the fish will slip away."[5]

Although al-Khaḍir is presented as being more knowledgeable than Mūsā, al-Khaḍir emphasizes the complementary nature of their knowledge, saying, "O Mūsā, I have knowledge from God that He has taught me that you do not know, and you have knowledge from His knowledge that He has taught you that I do not know."[6] Al-Ṭabarī quotes an interpretation from Ibn 'Abbās on the nature of their respective knowledge stating that al-Khaḍir practised the knowledge of the Unseen (*'ilm al-ghayb*) while Mūsā only understood external standards of justice[7] and he characterizes al-Khaḍir's knowledge as inward (*bāṭin*) and Mūsā's as external (*ẓāhir*).[8] Al-Khaḍir, however, points out the relative insignificance of the knowledge they both possess as he and Mūsā proceed on their journey; when the two of them board a boat they see a small bird pecking at the water, causing al-Khaḍir to remark that their combined knowledge takes from God's knowledge an amount equal to what the bird has taken from the sea.[9]

As mentioned earlier, the *ḥadīth* of Ubayy b. Ka'b contains details common to other stories of late antiquity that do not occur in the Qur'ānic verses. These details are explicit in only one of the versions of the *ḥadīth*.

> Mūsā set out with his boy and a salted fish. It had been said to him, "When this fish comes to life in a certain place, your companion will be there and you will have found what you are looking for." So Mūsā set out with his boy and the fish that they carried. He traveled until the journey wore him out and he reached the rock and the water, the water of life (*mā' al-ḥayāt*). Anyone who drank from it became immortal and nothing that was dead could approach it without coming to life. When they had stopped and the water touched the fish, it came to life *and took its way through the sea, as in a tunnel.*[10]

In the Alexandrian romance, Alexander's cook Andreas follows the fish, jumping into the spring of life after him, thereby attaining an immortality that he does not know what to do with. A similar narrative appears in an account attributed to Ibn 'Abbās, but it is unclear upon whose authority he speaks.

> Ibn 'Abbās was asked, "Why don't we hear any mention of a *ḥadīth* concerning Mūsā's boy even though he was with him?" Regarding this, Ibn 'Abbās said, "The boy drank from the water and became immortal. The wise man took him, found him a suitable boat, and sent him out into the sea. It will rock in the waves with him until the Day of Resurrection and that is because it was not for him to drink from it but he did."[11]

As for al-Khaḍir's immortality, it is not mentioned in al-Ṭabarī's *tafsīr*, but can be found in his *Ta'rīkh al-rusul wa'l-mulūk* where he mentions reports that al-Khaḍir drank from the water of life and became immortal and that he meets the Prophet Ilyās (Elijah) every year in Mecca during the pilgrimage season.[12] Al-Qurṭubī spends three and half pages discussing the matter of al-Khaḍir's immortality in his *tafsīr*. He writes that most people believe that al-Khaḍir died on the basis of a *ḥadīth* that states that not a soul living at the time of the Prophet would be alive 100 years after his death. Al-Qurṭubī, however, sides with those who interpret this as a general statement for which there are exceptions, including al-Khaḍir, 'Īsā (Jesus), Ilyās, and the Dajjāl (Antichrist). Although the *ḥadīth* states that "no on will remain on the earth *(arḍ)*," al-Qurṭubī argues that *arḍ* here refers only to the Arab world. He finds additional support for al-Khaḍir's immortality in traditions that mention the yearly pilgrimage of al-Khaḍir and Ilyās to Mecca, and a treatise attributed to al-Qushayrī that contains many reports from pious men and women who have seen and met al-Khaḍir. Additionally, 'Alī is said to have received a private prayer (*du'ā'*) directly from al-Khaḍir. A *ḥadīth* in the *Ṣaḥīḥ* of Muslim tells of the Dajjāl's meeting with the best of men at the end of time, and al-Qurṭubī cites those who identify this man as al-Khaḍir and who say that the Dajjāl will finally end al-Khaḍir's long life. As always, though, he admits that "God knows best."[13]

Although al-Khaḍir's immortality is often mentioned in other Ṣūfī works, especially in his role as a spiritual initiator,[14] this idea is not mentioned in the Ṣūfī commentaries studied here. Instead, the focus on al-Khaḍir concerns the knowledge which he is said to have possessed, knowledge received directly from God (*'ilm ladunī*).

'Ilm ladunī

In non-Ṣūfī commentaries, exegetes attempt to clarify ambiguous or difficult words and phrases and to explain variant readings of the text. When Ṣūfīs address a word or phrase, as they do in the story of Mūsā and al-Khaḍir with the phrase *'ilm ladunī*, their writings often raise more questions than they resolve. Ernst has suggested that these definitions are best understood as teaching tools. In discussing a passage from al-Qushayrī's *al-Risāla* that lists various definitions for the term Sufism, Ernst writes

> [the definitions] accomplish a powerful rhetorical transaction; the person who listens to or reads these definitions is forced to imagine the spiritual or ethical quality that is invoked by the definition, even when it is paradoxical.[15]

The definitions in Ṣūfī commentaries for *ʿilm ladunī* serve this function, being didactic rather than descriptive or explanatory. In commenting on the knowledge that God taught al-Khaḍir *from Our very presence* (*ladunnā*), al-Ṭabarī, as we have seen, compares the inner and outer aspects of the knowledge possessed by al-Khaḍir and Mūsā. Ṣūfīs commentators provide much more extended definitions and meditations on this type of knowledge.

Al-Tustarī defines al-Khaḍir's special knowledge as inspiration (*ilhām*), understood as a kind of revelation (*waḥy*) that is not restricted to prophets:

> Inspiration (*ilhām*) acts as a substitute for revelation (*waḥy*), just as He said, *and your Lord revealed* (*awḥā*) to the bees (16:68)[16] and *We revealed to the mother of Mūsā* (28:7).[17] Both of these were inspiration (*ilhām*).[18]

After al-Tustarī, numerous tenth-century Ṣūfīs are quoted in the commentaries of al-Sulamī and Rūzbihān al-Baqlī with different definitions of *ʿilm ladunī*. According to Ibn ʿAtā, *ʿilm ladunī* is not book learning, but knowledge from the Unseen:

> [It is] knowledge by unveilings (*kushūf*), not by the dictation of letters. Rather, the place to encounter it is in witnessing (*mushāhada*) the spirits (*arwāḥ*).[19]

For al-Qāsim (d. 953–4),[20] *ʿilm ladunī* is bestowed rather than acquired knowledge.

> The knowledge of deduction (*istinbāṭ*) comes with exertion (*kulfa*) and intermediaries but *ʿilm ladunī* comes without these.[21]

Not only is this knowledge not from this world, it distracts one from anything other than its source in the Unseen, bringing about a total absorption in God.

> Al-Shiblī said, "[*and to whom We had taught*] *knowledge* that made him preoccupied with Us from anything other than Us." It is said, "it directs him to Us and cuts him off from created things or anything concerning them."[22]

This early material is confirmed and expanded upon in the eleventh-century commentary of al-Qushayrī. He adds that this is knowledge reserved for God's elite, but as a benefit for all believers. Al-Qushayrī's definitions also illustrate the inherent tension between Ṣūfī beliefs and traditional theology, since *'ilm ladunī* takes precedence over the proofs of rational thought.

> It is said that knowledge from the very presence (*min ladun*) of God is something that is obtained by means of inspiration (*ilhām*) without being burdened by seeking (*taṭallub*).
>
> One can say that it is that which God (*al-ḥaqq*) teaches the elite (*khawāṣṣ*) among His servants.
>
> One can also say that it is something that God (*al-ḥaqq*) teaches His friends (*awliyā'*) according to what is appropriate in it for His servants.
>
> It is said that it is something whose benefit does not belong to its possessor, but rather that which is in it from the truth of God belongs to His servants.
>
> One can also say that it is something that its possessor cannot find a way to deny. Evidence (*dalīl*) of soundness would be what one finds definitively, but if you were to ask him about his proof (*burhān*) he will not be able to produce any evidence (*dalīl*), for the most powerful kinds of knowledge are those which are farthest from evidence (*dalīl*).[23]

Although several of these definitions seek to define *'ilm ladunī* in relation to other types of knowledge, none do so systematically. This task was taken up by al-Rāzī in his commentary on the verse, beginning with a rebuttal to those who believed that *'ilm ladunī* could only be bestowed on a prophet. For the exegetes who believe al-Khaḍir was a prophet, the fact that God describes him as one *to whom We taught knowledge from Our very presence* (*ladunnā*)

> requires that God taught him without the intermediary of the instruction of a teacher and the spiritual guidance (*irshād*) of a spiritual guide (*murshid*). Any person whom God teaches without the intermediary of a human being must be a prophet who knows things by means of revelation (*waḥy*).[24]

We have already seen that this issue is a contentious one, with those like Ibn al-Jawzī and Ibn Taymiyya insisting that only prophets can receive knowledge directly from God. Al-Rāzī disagrees, claiming that there are many types of knowledge that come to man directly without an intermediary.

> This deduction (*istidlāl*) is weak because different types of necessary knowledge (*al-'ulūm al-ḍarūriyya*) are obtained initially from God, but that does not indicate prophecy.[25]

The term "necessary or self-evident knowledge" (*'ilm ḍarūrī*) refers to sensory (*ḥissī*) knowledge from both internal and external sensory perceptions; intuitive (*badīhī*) knowledge of self-evident truths such as the fact of one's existence and the fact that one half of two is one; and information established by multiple reports (*mutawātir*). It is usually contrasted with acquired knowledge (*'ilm muktasab* or *kasbī*), which consists of rational (*'aqlī*) and religious (*shar'ī*) knowledge.[26] Although al-Rāzī compares *'ilm ladunī* to *'ilm ḍarurī* for the sake of his argument here, he classifies *'ilm ladunī* among the types of knowledge that are acquired (*'ulūm kasbiyya*). Al-Rāzi mentions that al-Ghazālī has a treatise concerning God-given types of knowledge (*'ulūm al-laduniyya*), and al-Rāzī proceeds to "verify what has been said regarding this matter."[27] He begins by saying that we become aware of things either by conceptualization (*taṣawwur*) or assent (*taṣdīq*). Each of these types of perception, in turn, are either considerative (*naẓarī*) or acquired (*kasbī*).[28]

> Considerative types of knowledge (*al-'ulūm al-naẓariyya*) are obtained in the soul (*nafs*) and intellect (*'aql*) without acquisition (*kasb*) or study (*ṭalab*), like our conceptualization (*taṣawwur*) of pain and pleasure, and existence and nonexistence; and our assent (*taṣdīq*) that negation and affirmation cannot coexist nor be mutually eliminated, and that one is half of two.
>
> Acquired types of knowledge (*al-'ulūm al-kasbiyya*) are those that cannot be initially obtained in the substance of the soul (*jawhar al-nafs*) but rather their acquisition must be arrived at by means of some path. This path has two parts. One of them is where man combines these considerative and intuitive types of knowledge (*al-'ulūm al-badīhiyya al-naẓariyya*) until he reaches knowledge of unknown things. This way is called consideration (*naẓar*), reflection (*tafakkur*), pondering (*tadabbur*), contemplation (*ta'ammul*), deliberation (*tarawwin*), and deduction (*istidlāl*). This mode of obtaining different types of knowledge is the path that can only be completed by effort and study.
>
> The second mode [of obtaining types of knowledge] is when man strives by means of spiritual disciplines (*riyāḍāt*) and efforts (*mujāhadāt*) in which the sensual and imaginative faculties (*al-quwwat al-ḥissiya wa'l-khayāliyya*) become weak. When they become weak the power of the rational faculty (*al-quwwat al-'aqliyya*) becomes strong and the divine lights shine in the substance of the intellect (*jawhar al-'aql*). Gnostic sciences (*ma'ārif*) are obtained and different types of knowledge (*'ulūm*) are perfected without the intermediary of effort or study in reflecting and contemplation. These are what are called the God-given types of knowledge (*al-'ulūm al-laduniyya*).[29]

If the treatise written by al-Ghazālī that al-Rāzī refers to is, in fact, *Al-Risālat al-laduniyya* that has come down to us,[30] al-Rāzī has stripped al-Ghazālī's description of *'ilm ladunī* of its Neoplatonic terminology.

In al-Ghazālī's work, the acquisition of knowledge is said to be achieved either by human (*insānī*) or divine (*rabbānī*) teaching.[31] When it is the latter, it may be either an internal or an external process. The internal process is the process of reflection (*tafakkur*). Reflection (*tafakkur*) differs from knowledge gained by human teaching because reflection is what one gains from the Universal Soul (*al-nafs al-kullī*), while learning from another human being is confined to what one gains from a particular individual. When the divine (*rabbānī*) teaching involves an external process, this will either be revelation (*waḥy*) or inspiration (*ilhām*). When it is revelation, the teacher is the Universal Intellect (*al-ʿaql al-kullī*)[32] and knowledge is inscribed within the sanctified soul (*al-nafs al-qudsiyya*) without learning or reflection. According to al-Ghazālī, revelation (*waḥy*) is reserved for prophets alone.

Revelation (*waḥy*) is engendered from the emanation (*ifāḍa*) of the Universal mind (*al-ʿaql al-kullī*), while inspiration (*ilhām*) is engendered from the illumination (*ishrāq*) of the Universal Soul (*al-nafs al-kullī*).[33] Inspiration is the awakening of the individual human soul by the Universal Soul according to the degree of its purity and receptivity (*qabūl*), and the strength of its preparedness (*istiʿdād*). The knowledge received from this process, which occurs in both prophets and saints, is called God-given knowledge (*ʿilm ladunī*), and is the type of knowledge that al-Khaḍir received.

What is common to the theories presented by al-Rāzī and al-Ghazālī here is the way in which they seek to confirm the possibility of individuals who are not prophets acquiring God-given types of knowledge (*al-ʿulūm al-laduniyya*); this validation is accomplished by incorporating *ʿilm ladunī* into existing philosophical and theological epistemological frameworks. Using the verse on al-Khaḍir's knowledge as a proof-text, al-Rāzī and al-Ghazālī provide a theoretical framework for the Ṣūfī's belief in knowledge through inspiration (*ilhām*). It is an expositional and apologetic approach that differs from Ṣūfī commentaries that take this form of knowledge as a given. Although all of the Ṣūfī commentators studied here understood *ʿilm ladunī* as a kind of knowledge that might be received by the rare individual, none of them addressed the issue of whether these individuals, like al-Khaḍir, are entitled or even obliged to follow a different set of rules than the common believer. But apparently there were those who did propose such an argument, and al-Qurṭubī attacks them in his *tafsīr* not only for believing that they could receive knowledge by any means other than the prophets, but especially for claiming that this special knowledge frees them from the need to follow the religious law.[34]

> Our shaykh, Imām Abū'l-ʿAbbās said that the esotericist heretics (*zanādiqa al-bāṭiniyya*) are of the opinion that traveling a path requires these religious precepts but they say, "These general religious precepts are only imposed upon the stupid and the common. As for the friends of god (*awliyāʾ*) and elect (*ahl al-khuṣūṣ*), they don't need these texts; the only thing meant for them is what happens in their hearts and they are ruled by whatever seizes them in their thoughts." They say, "That is because of the purity of their hearts from all kinds of turbidity

> and the freedom of their hearts from all others, so that the divine kinds of knowledge (*al-'ulūm al-ilāhiyya*) and lordly realities (*ḥaqā'iq al-rabbāniyya*) are disclosed to them and they understand the secrets of created things. They know the principles of individual things and by means of them they are able to dispense with universal religious principles just as happened with al-Khaḍir. Because of what was disclosed to him from different types of knowledge, he was able to dispense with the understanding Mūsā had of these things." Included in what they have transmitted is, "Seek the legal opinion of your heart even if the Muftis give a legal opinion for you."
>
> Regarding that, our shaykh said that this is the talk of heresy (*zandaqa*) and infidelity (*kufr*), the proponent of which should be killed without being given a chance to seek repentance, because it is a denial of what is known from the religious laws. Truly God has imposed his practice (*sunna*) and implemented his wisdom through his precepts which can only be known by means of His messengers who mediate between Him and His creation. They convey His message and word from Him explaining His religious laws and precepts. They have been chosen for that just as He said, *God chooses messengers from angels and from men. Truly, He is Hearing, Seeing* (22:75). He also said, *God well knows where to place His message* (6:124), and *Mankind was a single community and God sent prophets to give glad tidings and warn* (2:213) in addition to other verses.
>
> In sum, definitive knowledge (*al-'ilm al-qaṭ'ī*), necessary certainty (*al-yaqīn al-ḍarūrī*) and the consensus (*ijmā'*) of the pious predecessors and descendants all agree on the fact that there is no way that anyone can have knowledge of the precepts of God referring to His command and prohibition except by way of the messengers. And the one who says, "Here is another way by which to know His command and prohibition without the messengers," so that he dispenses with them, is an infidel (*kāfir*) who should be killed. His repentance should not be sought and there is no need for questions and answers from him. It is a belief in the perpetuation of prophets after our Prophet whom God has made the seal of His prophets and messengers. There is no prophet or messenger after him.[35]

Al-Qurṭubi would seem to be denying the possibility of what al-Rāzī and al-Ghazālī defended, *'ilm ladunī* received by those who are not prophets, at least with regards to knowledge of God's commands and prohibitions. But al-Qurṭubī does not deny the possibility of there being friends of God (*awliyā'*) to whom charismatic acts (*karāmāt*) occur. Although he agrees with other exegetes who say that al-Khaḍir was a prophet, al-Qurṭubī nonetheless uses him as a starting point for discussing charismatic acts (*karāmāt*) occurring in individuals who are not prophets, and the question of whether it is permissible for a friend of God (*walī*) to know that he is a friend of God.[36] In the latter discussion, al-Qurṭubī quotes

Ṣūfī hagiographical material approvingly,[37] demonstrating that his criticism of some Ṣūfīs should not be taken as a general condemnation of Ṣūfism.

The journeys of Mūsā

The fact that al-Rāzī describes *ʿilm ladunī* as acquired knowledge that requires spiritual disciplines (*riyāḍāt*) and efforts (*mujāhadāt*) on the part of those seeking it does not contradict the Ṣūfis who say that it comes without exertion or seeking. Their comments refer to the actual bestowal of the knowledge from God, whereas al-Rāzī's comments refer to the preparation needed to receive this knowledge. According to the Ṣūfīs, the difficulties that Mūsā underwent in his journey to and with al-Khaḍir, were part of the process of learning proper behavior (*ta'dīb*). Their comments in this area demonstrate another distinctive characteristic of Ṣūfī exegesis, one that seeks to uncover the edifying potential of the characters and events described in the Qur'ān in a manner similar to that of preachers. They place Mūsā's journey with al-Khaḍir in the context of the other journeys in his life, and compare this to the different states (*aḥwāl*) and stations (*maqāmāt*) through which a spiritual seeker continually moves. The fact that al-Khaḍir possessed *ʿilm ladunī*, while Mūsā did not, at least not at that point in his life, relates to their different stations.

> Fāris[38] said: *Mūsā* said, "*God willing*" about himself in "*You will find me patient, God willing*," but al-Khaḍir did not do the same when he said, "*You will not be able to be patient with me*," because the knowledge of Mūsā at that time was the knowledge of what religious law has prescribed and deduction (*istidlāl*), but the knowledge of al-Khaḍir was God-given knowledge (*ʿilm ladunī*) from one unseen to another. Mūsā was in the station (*maqām*) of learning proper behavior (*ta'dīb*) while al-Khaḍir was in the station (*maqām*) of unveiling (*kashf*) and witnessing (*mushāhada*).[39]

Mūsā's task in this journey, however, was not to learn about states, but rather to learn about proper behavior, and this could not be achieved by asking questions. In response to al-Khaḍir's request to Mūsā, *If you follow me, do not ask me anything until I myself mention it to you*, al-Ḥuṣrī[40] is said to have said,

> There was no way to learn the knowledge of al-Khaḍir from a place of questioning. Mūsā came to him to learn proper behavior (*taʿdīb*), not for instruction regarding any particular state (*ḥāl*).[41]

While the purpose of the journey with al-Khaḍir was to learn proper behavior, al-Qushayrī points out that this was not the case in the journey of Mūsā to Mount Sinai, nor when he set out into the desert fleeing from Pharoah.

> In this journey Mūsā was the one who carried a burden (*mutaḥammil*). It was a journey to learn proper behavior (*ta'dīb*) and to endure difficulty

> because he had gone to ask for greater knowledge, and the state (*ḥāl*) of seeking knowledge is the state (*ḥāl*) of learning proper behavior (*ta'dīb*) and a time for bearing difficulty. Because of this he was overwhelmed by hunger and said, "*Truly fatigue has overwhelmed us on our journey*." When he fasted at the time of waiting to hear the Word of God he was patient for thirty days and neither hunger nor difficulty overcame him, because his journey was to God and so he was the one who was carried (*maḥmūl*).[42] One can say that this was a journey for learning proper behavior (*ta'dīb*) and he had been sent back to endure the difficulty. This is not as it was when he watered [the animals] for the daughters of Shu'ayb, for the toil and hunger that afflicted him [in the search for al-Khaḍir] was greater. In that time he was the one who was carried (*maḥmūl*) while this time he was the carrier of the burden (*mutaḥammil*).[43]

Al-Qushayrī's analysis here of the different journeys of Mūsā is not original. In *'Arā'is al-majālis fī qiṣaṣ al-anbiyā'*, a book on the stories of the prophets, Aḥmad Abū Isḥāq al-Tha'labī (d. 1036) states that wise men (*ḥukamā'*) have said that Mūsā had a total of five journeys. The first of these was the journey of escape (*harab*) after killing a man in Egypt (Qur'ān 26:21). The second was the journey to Ṭūr where Mūsā saw a fire and heard a voice (Qur'ān 27:8 and 28:30). The third was the journey of seeking (*ṭalab*) when he left Egypt with his people (Qur'ān 20:77). The fourth was the journey of war (*ḥarb*) when he exhorted his people to enter the Holy Land (Qur'ān 5:27). The fifth was the journey of hardship (*naṣab*) and this was his journey to find al-Khaḍir.[44]

While the stories found in the genre of *qiṣaṣ al-anbiyā'* were viewed with some suspicion, their engaging details and style led some commentators to loosen their standards of authenticity so as to include excerpts from them.[45] Al-Qurṭubī was one such commentator whose critical comments on *isrā'īliyyat* material did not keep him from including some of the more amusing anecdotes from al-Tha'labī's *tafsīr*.[46] However, the homiletic and literary style considered acceptable and even praiseworthy in preaching was not generally accepted within the genre of *tafsīr*, except when it could be shown to be transmitted from traditions whose authenticity was unquestioned. In contrast, Ṣūfī exegesis incorporates *isrā'īliyyāt* material and original homiletic and literary material into a style most fully developed in the commentary of Rashīd al-Dīn al-Maybudī. As we have already mentioned, al-Maybudī incorporates a good deal of al-Qushayrī's work in his own *tafsīr*, without attribution, but displays his originality in the way he weaves al-Qushayrī's comments into a decidedly literary format. In al-Maybudī's version of the journeys of Mūsā, there are four journeys and four rhyming words used to describe them: *harab*, *talab*, *ṭarab*, and *ta'ab*.

> Mūsā had four journeys. The first was the journey of escape (*harab*) just as God told in the story of Mūsā, "*So I fled from you when I feared you*" (26:21). The second was the journey of the search (*ṭalab*) at night for

fire: *When he came to it, a voice cried from the right shore of the wādi* (28:30). The third was the journey of rapture (*ṭarab*) *when Mūsā came to Our appointed time* (7:143). The fourth was the journey of toil (*ta'ab*): *Truly fatigue has overwhelmed us on our journey* (18:60).

As for the journey of flight (*harab*), it was the affair in the desert when he had fled from the enemy and had turned his face towards Madyan. He had killed the Copt, just as the Lord said, *Mūsā struck him and killed him* (28:15). How remarkable was the salvation and victory in God's solicitude in forgiving him that killing! Mūsā said, "The hand of him who has struck reaps the harvest," but He said to Mūsā, "There was no sin in that. The sin belonged to the devil and that act was from him." *He said, "This is the work of Satan"* (28:15). Thus the believing servant is excused by His grace and receives His pardon. He said, *Satan made them slip in some of what they earned but indeed God has forgiven them* (3:155). God overlooked their sin because that was the whispering of Satan and the work of the devil.

After this there was the journey of searching (*ṭalab*), the night when Mūsā went in search of fire, a fire that was such that the entire world would be extinguished by it. The entire world falls in love with every place where the tale of the fire of Mūsā has gone. Mūsā went in search of fire and found light while the brave youth (*javānmard*) went in search of light and found fire. If Mūsā received the sweetness of hearing the word of God (*ḥaqq*) without intermediary, how amazing is it that the smell of that reaches His friends (*dustān*)? If the fire of Mūsā was manifested publicly, the fire of these brave youths is hidden. And if the fire of Mūsā was in the bush, the fire of these brave youths is in the soul (*jān*). He who has this fire knows that it is such. All of the fires of the body burn and the fire of the friendship of the soul cannot endure the soul-burning fire.

As for the journey of rapture (*ṭarab*), it has been mentioned previously in [the commentary on] His words *when Mūsā came to Our appointed time* (7:143).

The fourth journey of Mūsā was a journey of toil (*ta'ab*). It is an allusion (*ishāra*) to the journey of aspirants (*murīdān*) in the beginning of their desires (*irādāt*),[47] the journey of discipline (*riyāḍa*), bearing difficulty, and the polishing of three things: the soul (*nafs*), the disposition (*khūy*) and the heart (*dil*).

Polishing the soul (*nafs*) consists of three things: replacing complaining with giving thanks, forgetfulness with wakefulness, and extravagance with sobriety. Polishing the disposition (*khūy*) also consists of three things: replacing irritation with patience, niggardliness with generosity, and vengefulness with forgiveness. Polishing the heart (*dil*) also consists of three things: replacing the danger of security with fear, the misfortune of despair with the blessing of hope, and the tribulation of the distraction in the heart with thanksgiving of the heart.

> The substance of this polishing consists of three things: pursuing knowledge, [eating] permissible food, and persistence in litany (*wird*). The fruit of it consists of three things: an innermost heart (*sirr*) which has become adorned with knowledge of the Lord, a soul (*jān*) set ablaze by the sun of eternity, and God-given knowledge (*'ilm ladunī*) found without intermediary.[48]

As part of his effort to extract lessons from the story of Mūsā and al-Khaḍir for the individual believer, al-Maybudī uses the characters, details and events of the story as symbolic indicators of the stages of the soul in its progress towards attaining knowledge of higher realities. The boat which al-Khaḍir ruins represents the poverty that one must embrace in order to escape the notice of Satan who is attracted to prosperity and the outward display of one's religion.[49] The boy he kills is an allusion (*ishāra*) to the desires and opinions that shoot up in the field of spiritual discipline (*riyāḍa*), and struggle (*mujāhada*) that must be cut off because this "offspring" will become a disbeliever as it grows.[50] Finally, the wall which al-Khaḍir rebuilds is an allusion (*ishāra*) to the soul at peace (*nafs muṭma'inna*)[51] that must not be destroyed. The purpose of spiritual effort is to purify the soul, not annihilate it, for the Prophet said, "Your soul has a right over you."

> The treasures of the secrets of eternity have been placed underneath it. If the wall of the soul becomes ruined, the treasure of the lordly secrets will fall upon the desert and any feeble idiot will covet it. The secret of these words is that the treasure of reality has been placed in the human qualities and the natural manners of dervishes have been built upon this partition. This is the very thing that brave youth (*javānmard*) has said:
>
> Religion for dervishes is searching (*ṭalab*)
> for it is the custom of kings to
> bury treasures in deserted places.[52]

In contrast to al-Maybudī's very readable and didactic style, Rūzbihān's commentary on the story of Mūsā and al-Khaḍir is mostly a commentary on the commentary of his predecessors, written in a difficult style made all the more obscure by unexplained terminology and concepts. The interpretation of Mūsā's journey to al-Khaḍir as a journey of toil, mentioned in al-Qushayrī, is used by al-Maybudī to address the practical aspects of the spiritual path that must be undertaken before mystical knowledge can be attained. Rūzbihān refers to al-Qushayrī's interpretation as well, and even quotes it in full, but his own interpretation is less practical than esoteric.

> When [Mūsā and his boy] mistook their way, they did not proceed with the heart (*qalb*) and fatigue affected them. That was God's way of teaching them that they had disregarded intuition (*ḥads*) and the heart (*qalb*).

> Perhaps he knew the order (*ḥukm*) of the Unseen, but the heart and intellect (*'aql*) did not so the soul (*nafs*) suffered on account of ignorance. If the heart (*qalb*) and the soul (*nafs*) had known just as the innermost heart (*sirr*) knew, the effects of fatigue would not have overcome them. The fatigue overcoming them was because of their being in the station (*maqām*) of struggle (*mujāhada*) and trial (*imtiḥān*).
>
> If Mūsā had been the one who was carried (*maḥmūl*)[53] there by the good fortune of witnessing (*mushāhada*), then he would have been as he was on Mount Sinai when he did not eat food for forty days, and yet weariness did not overcome him. This is the state (*ḥāl*) of the people of intimacy (*uns*) while the first is the state of the people of desire (*irāda*)... When he was seeking an intermediary he was veiled from the station (*maqām*) of witnessing (*mushāhada*), and he was tested with struggle (*mujāhada*) by means of which God taught him proper behavior (*addabahu*) until nothing of the different types of knowledge of realities entered into his mind, for God is jealous of the one whom He entrusts with reaching the secret of secrets, for the sake of which he draws him out to learn the knowledge of the Unseen.[54]

Just as al-Rāzī's *tafsīr* requires a background in theology and its terminology, Rūzbihān's *tafsīr* is best understood by those who have read other Ṣūfī commentaries and are familiar with their special vocabulary.

What distinguishes the commentaries of al-Kāshānī and al-Nīsābūrī from earlier Ṣūfī exegetes is their almost exclusive use of allegoresis as a method of interpretation. Al-Kāshānī explicitly refers to such in his initial comments on the narrative of Mūsā and al-Khaḍir. It is the kind of interpretation that al-Ghazālī called "striking similitudes" (*ḍarb al-mithāl*) in his *Mishkāt al-anwār*.

> *And when Mūsā said to his boy*. The external sense (*ẓāhir*) of it is in accordance with what has been mentioned in the stories and there is no way to deny the miracles. As for its inner sense (*bāṭin*), it can be said: "*when Mūsā*, the heart, *said to his boy*, the soul, at the time of the attachment to the body, "*I will not stop*," i.e., I will keep on travelling and journeying "*until I reach the junction of the two seas*," i.e. the intersection of the two worlds, the world of the spirit (*'ālam al-rūḥ*) and the world of body (*jism*). They are the sweet and the bitter[55] in human form and the station (*maqām*) of the heart (*qalb*).[56]

Whereas al-Maybudī used allegoresis sparingly in his commentary, in his interpretation of the three actions of al-Khaḍir, al-Kāshānī applies it consistently and extensively throughout his exegesis of the Qur'ānic narrative. Also distinctive is the way in which he combines terminology and concepts taken from the writings of Ibn Sīnā with that of the Ṣūfīs.[57] Mūsā's search for al-Khaḍir, according to al-Kāshānī, is a search for the holy intellect (*al-'aql al-qudsī*) necessary to achieve perfection.[58] Mūsā's saying, "*God willing, you will find me patient*," testifies to his own aptitude or preparedness (*isti'dād*) and perseverance in searching. The path to perfection requires devotion to spiritual exercises until the soul is disengaged (*mujarrad*) from the body. Only then can one become acquainted with deeper realities.

> *If you follow me* in travelling the path of perfection *do not ask me anything*, i.e., you must practice emulation (*iqtidā'*) and following the path by works (*a'māl*), spiritual disciplines (*riyāḍāt*), moral traits (*akhlāq*), and struggles (*mujāhadāt*). Do not seek realities (*ḥaqā'iq*) and meanings (*ma'ānī*) *until* the time comes and *I myself mention it to you*, i.e., I tell you that knowledge of unseen realities upon your disengagement (*tajarrud*) by means of transactions (*mu'āmalāt*) of the body and heart.[59]

The ship which al-Khaḍir scuttles represents the body (*badan*) in the sea of matter (*hayūlā*) travelling to God. The poor people who own it are the animal and vegetable faculties (*al-quwā'l-ḥayawāniyya wa'l-nabātiyya*).[60] The ten brothers mentioned in tradition represent the five external and five internal senses (*al-ḥawāss al-ẓāhira wa'l-bāṭina*). The boat of the body must be ruined by spiritual discipline (*riyāḍa*) so that the king of the commanding soul (*al-nafs al-ammāra*) will not seize it and use it for his passions and demands.[61]

The youth which al-Khaḍir kills also represents the commanding soul (*al-nafs ammāra*) whose qualities of anger and passion veil the heart. His parents, the spirit (*rūḥ*) and the corporeal nature (*al-ṭabī'a al-jismāniyya*), will be consoled with the birth of a new child, the soul at peace (*al-nafs al-muṭma'inna*).[62] The wall that is about to fall down represents the soul at peace as well.

> The wall that *was about to fall* is the soul at peace (*al-nafs al-muṭma'inna*). It is expressed as a wall because it came into being after the killing of the commanding soul (*al-nafs al-ammāra*) whose death was by means of spiritual discipline (*riyāḍa*). It became like an inanimate object without movement in its soul or desire (*irāda*). Because of the intensity of its weakness, it was almost destroyed, so its state is expressed as being about to fall. His fixing it is its being altered by moral perfections and beautiful virtues by the light of the faculty of rationality (*al-quwwat al-nuṭqiyya*) until the virtues take the place of its vices.[63]

The two orphans are the possessors of the theoretical and practical intellects (*al-'āqil al-naẓariyya wa'l-'amaliyya*) cut off from their father whom al-Kāshānī identifies as either the Holy Spirit (*rūḥ al-qudus*) or the heart (*qalb*).[64] The treasure is knowledge that can only be obtained in the station (*maqām*) of the heart (*qalb*) because it is here where all of the particulars and universals are combined in actuality when perfection is achieved.[65]

Although there are similarities between the interpretations of al-Kāshānī and al-Nīsābūrī, the latter is far more careful to emphasize the role of the Ṣūfī shaykh in the process of attaining perfection.

> *And when Mūsā said to his boy*. In this is the fact that the traveller must have a companion on the path. There is also the condition that one of them must be a commander and the other the one who is commanded. The companion must know his resolve and intention so that he understands the [nature of] his companionship and does not become fed up with the hardships of the journey before he succeeds in his goal. His intention should be to seek a shaykh to emulate, for seeking a shaykh, in truth, is seeking God (*al-ḥaqq*).
>
> *The junction of the two seas* is the junction of the sanctity (*walāya*) of the saint and the sanctity of the aspirant (*murīd*). There is the real spring of life. When a drop of it fell upon the fish, the heart (*qalb*) of the aspirant, it came to life *and took its way* in the sea of sanctity (*walāya*) *as in a tunnel*.
>
> *When they had gone on*. There is an allusion (*ishāra*) in this to the fact that if the aspirant becomes weary in the course of his travels, his heart will succumb to exhaustion and he will allow himself to be seduced into relinquishing the companionship of the shaykh, thinking that his goal can be obtained by other means. What an idea! This is false and worthless thinking if the divine solicitude does not reach him and return the sincerity of desire (*irāda*) to him.[66]

The knowledge which al-Khaḍir possesses is knowledge of the inner nature of things (*bawāṭin al-ashyā'*) and their realities (*ḥaqā'iq*), a knowledge which cannot be taught but can only be obtained by the purification (*taṣfiya*) of the soul and the disengagement (*tajrīd*) of the heart from corporeal attachments. This process is illustrated by the allegorical interpretation of al-Khaḍir's actions.

The scuttling of the ship represents the destruction of one's outward reputation and one's pride in devotional acts, for only devotional acts performed in a spirit of brokenness and humility are safe from Satan. The youth killed by al-Khaḍir is the commanding soul (*al-nafs al-ammāra*) killed with the knife of spiritual discipline (*riyāḍa*) and the sword of struggle (*mujāhada*). His parents are the heart (*qalb*) and spirit (*rūḥ*) who will receive a better child in his stead, the soul at peace (*al-nafs al-muṭma'inna*). The wall is the attachment (*ta'alluq*) that acts as a barrier between the rational soul (*al-nafs al-nāṭiqa*) and the world of disengaged things (*'ālam al-mujarradāt*). Al-Khaḍir's fixing the wall is the strengthening of the body and kindliness shown to the different faculties (*quwā*) and senses (*ḥawāss*), just as it is said, "Your soul is your mount, so be kind to it." The two orphans are the soul at peace and the inspired soul (*al-nafs al-muṭma'inna wa'l-mulhama*) and the treasure waiting for them is the obtainment of theoretical and practical perfections (*al-kamālāt al-naẓariyya wa'l-'amaliyya*). Their father is the discerning intellect (*al-'aql al-fāriqa*) who wanted to protect this treasure until they matured under the instruction of the shaykh and his kindly and indulgent guidance.[67]

Although the content of al-Nīsābūrī's interpretation remains more faithful to the terminology and concepts of Ṣūfīsm rather than philosophy, the style is very much like al-Kāshānī's, a kind of allegoresis that involves finding one-to-one equivalences between each element of the Qur'ānic text and a Ṣūfī or philosophical concept. The common objective of all these commentaries, despite their different styles and methods with regards to the story of Mūsā and al-Khaḍir, is what al-Ghazālī calls applying the Qur'ānic text to oneself (*takhṣīṣ*) and what al-Simnānī calls recognizing the correspondences between the prophets and the subtle substances (*laṭā'if*) of man.

"I wanted," "we wanted," and "your Lord wanted"

When al-Khaḍir finally explains his mysterious actions to the frustrated Mūsā before their parting, there is a shift in pronouns in his words from "*I wanted*" to "*we wanted*" to "*your Lord wanted*." This narrative oddity was understood by Ṣūfīs as a reference to the ambiguous nature of human volition.

> Ibn 'Aṭā said: When al-Khaḍir said, "*I wanted*," it was revealed to him in the innermost heart (*sirr*), "Who are you that volition (*irāda*) should belong to you?" Then, in the second situation he said, "*We wanted*," and it was revealed to him in the innermost heart, "Who are you and Mūsā that volition (*irāda*) should belong to you?" They he came back and said, "*Your Lord wanted*."[68]

Al-Ḥallāj explains these as different stations.

> The first station (*maqām*) is the total mastery (*istīlā'*) of God (*al-ḥaqq*). The second station is conversation with the servant. The third station is a return to the inner understanding (*bāṭin*) of [God's] supremacy in the outer world (*al-ẓāhir*)... because to get closer to something by means of egos (*nufūs*) is to get farther away while to approach [the supremacy] by means of [the supremacy] itself is to draw near.[69]

What al-Ḥallāj seems to be describing here is a change in awareness as the mystic draws nearer to God. Initially, al-Khaḍir said, "*I wanted*," because he perceived the distance between himself and the all-powerful Creator and therefore judged himself as a separate entity acting on his own volition. When he said, "*We wanted*," he judged the intimate conversation between himself and his Lord as indicating a kind of partnership in action, but this was also an illusion which kept him from true nearness.[70] Finally, when he said, "*Your Lord wanted*," he returned to the awareness of God's Omnipotence, achieving true intimacy by recognizing the secret of His pervasive agency and allowing his own ego to be eclipsed.[71]

As we have already seen, Rūzbihān often builds his meditations on the ideas of his Ṣūfī predecessors, and his comments here are followed by the interpretations attributed to Ibn ʿAṭā and al-Ḥallāj.

> These expressions of volition (*irādāt*) are in different forms but in truth they are one because volition (*irāda*) is the volition of God since desires (*irādāt*) emanate (*ṣadarat*) in their various types from His volition. His words, "*I wanted*" tell of the source of gathering (*ʿayn al-jamʿ*) and unity (*ittiḥād*).[72] His words, "*We wanted*" tell of taking on the attributes (*ittiṣāf*) and becoming expanded (*inbiṣāt*). His words, "*Your Lord wanted*" tell of the separation of eternity (*qidam*) from the temporally originated (*muḥdath*), and the obliteration of temporality (*ḥadath*) and the annihilation of the one who declares God one (*muwaḥḥid*) in the unified (*muwaḥḥad*).

In its quality (*waṣf*), this volition (*irāda*) is the inward dimension (*bāṭin*) of will (*mashīʾa*) and the inward dimension of will is that which is the unseen of the attribute (*ṣifa*). That which is the unseen of the attribute is the secret (*sirr*) of the essence (*dhāt*) and the secret of the essence is that which is the unseen of all Unseen things. When al-Khaḍir moved from the quality (*waṣf*) of unity (*ittiḥād*), jealousy (*ghayra*) cut him off from pure unity to the source of gathering (*ʿayn al-jamʿ*), and cut him off from the gathering (*jamʿ*) to taking on the attributes (*ittiṣāf*), and from taking on the attributes to becoming expanded (*inbiṣāt*). Then it drowned him in the sea of divinity and annihilated him in its depths from any vision (*ruʿya*), knowledge (*ʿilm*), volition (*irāda*), act (*fiʿl*), and allusion (*ishāra*). By his act (*fiʿl*) God (*al-ḥaqq*) spoke in the first, second, and third case and nothing remained in the explanation except God.[73]

The switch in pronouns from "*I wanted*" to "*we wanted*" to "*your Lord wanted*" is something which is only minimally addressed in non-Ṣūfī commentaries. By carefully focusing on the exact wording, Ṣūfī interpretations demonstrate something like the phenomenon Chodkiewicz notes in Ibn ʿArabī's writings, which he calls "rigorous fidelity" to the Qurʾānic text.[74]

8

QUR'ĀNIC VERSES ON MARYAM

Maryam (Mary), the mother of 'Īsā (Jesus), occupies a significant position in the Qur'ān, being set forth as an example to believers (66:12) and, with her son, as a sign to the worlds (21:91 and 23:50). Extended references to Maryam occur in the Qur'ān 3:35–3:47, 19:16–29, and 66:12; other verses containing brief references to Maryam are 4:156, 4:171, 5:17, 5:75, and 5:116. In addition, Maryam's name is mentioned twenty-three times as part of 'Īsā's name, "the son of Maryam." Only three other persons are mentioned more frequently in the Qur'ān and she is the only woman mentioned by name.[1] Maryam has been referred to as the prototype of the mystic in Islam,[2] a characterization that certainly holds true for the Ṣūfī commentaries studied here. Even more so than the figures of Mūsā and al-Khaḍir, the figure of Maryam illustrates the way in which Ṣūfīs adopt a Qur'ānic figure as a prescriptive model for themselves. The fact that she is a woman only makes this all the more striking.

What interests Ṣūfīs is Maryam's unusual relationship with the world and the divine, especially as seen through her detachment from the world, her special relationship with prayer, and the virginal conception of her son. Her detachment from the world is tied to the special vow and prayer made by Maryam's mother for her unborn child and Maryam's resulting service in the temple as a child. As in the passages quoted on the concept of *'ilm ladunī* in the previous chapter, Ṣūfī commentary here is distinguished by its focus on an unusual Qur'ānic word, whose meaning is explored in a consciously didactic manner.

Muḥarrar

When a woman of 'Imran said, "O my Lord, I have vowed to you what is in my womb in consecration (muharrar^{an}). So accept it from me, for you are the Hearing, the Knowing." When she gave birth she said, "My Lord, I have given birth to a female!" God knows best what she gave birth to and the male is not like the female. "I have named her Maryam and I seek refuge for her and her offspring in You from the accursed Satan."

(Qur'ān 3:35–36)

Ibn Isḥāq (d. *c.*767), an early source for explanatory details on the narratives in the Qur'ān, is quoted in al-Ṭabarī as saying that the *woman of 'Imrān* mentioned here was a woman named Ḥannā who had been barren for many years. One day she was sitting beneath a tree and saw a mother bird feeding her young. She so longed for a child that she prayed to God and He answered her prayer. When she realized that she was pregnant, she vowed to give the child up to be a servant in the temple. Although this was an accepted practice of the Jewish people in her time, only boys could serve. In light of her vow, Ḥannā was dismayed when she gave birth to a girl, Maryam. Nonetheless, *Her Lord accepted her with a gracious acceptance* (3:37), and she grew up in the temple.[3]

The word *muḥarrar* in this passage is explained by al-Ṭabarī and others[4] as referring to this practice of giving up one's children for service in the temple. It is a passive participle of the verb *ḥarrar*, a verb which occurs five times in the Qur'ān, always with the meaning of setting free a slave, and it is this sense of emancipation that Ṣūfī commentators focused on. Ja'far al-Ṣādiq is said to have said that *muḥarrar* means:

> in emancipation from the bondage of the world (*dunyā*) and its people. *Muḥarrar*^an means, I have vowed to you what is in my womb as a sincere servant (*'abd*) to You, not in servitude to any created being.[5]

Al-Tustarī writes that it means:

> [the child's] being freed and emancipated from the bondage of the world (*dunyā*), the following of its personal inclination (*hawā*), and the desired objects of its self (*nafs*). She made [the child] a servant to the worshippers of the temple in exclusive dedication to God.[6]

Al-Qushayrī adds,

> God (*al-ḥaqq*), glory be to Him in His preeminent wisdom, has emancipated this one from the bondage of being preoccupied with all appearances (*wujūh*) and states (*aḥwāl*).[7]

The references here are brief definitions of a concept developed more fully in other Ṣūfī works. In his *Risāla, al-Qushayrī* explains the relationship of freedom (*ḥurriyya*) to servitude (*'ubūdiyya*), devoting one chapter to each. He writes, "Let it be known to you that the real meaning of freedom lies in the perfection of slavery (*'ubūdiyya*)."[8] The relationship of the human being toward God is always that of a slave subject to His commands and prohibitions; those who have achieved the difficult and rare station of freedom experience it in relation to the world, not God. Al-Qushayrī suggests the importance of such people for others in quoting Abū'l-'Abbās al-Sayyāri (d. 953–4):

> If a prayer could be performed at all properly without recitation of the Qur'ān, it would be with the recitation of this verse:
>
> "I wish something to happen that is completely impossible for [this time], namely, for my eyes to behold the face of a free man (*ḥurr*).[9]

To be a free man is to be subject only to God and no one and nothing else, and to serve others from this state of nobility for His sake. Maryam's freedom (*ḥurriya*) was in her servitude (*'ubūdiyya*). She was not subject to the tumult of the world, its people and its objects of desire and was freed from preoccupation with all transitory things. Al-Maybudī writes,

> The following is an example of freedom. They tell of that gem of his time, Bū Bakr Qaḥṭubī,[10] that he had a son who rejected all rules and regulations and kept company with foolish, corrupt and impure youths. One of the Pīrs of the Way passed by this boy sitting in one of his wanton and forbidden assemblies, holding hands with those lawless ones. People began criticizing him behind him back. That Pīr was sympathizing with Bū Bakr Qaḥṭubī, thinking of the consequences of all this, and that the prattle of people about his son would follow him to the end of his days. With these thoughts, he went to Qaḥṭubī and found him in such a state that he was beside himself and unaware of that tale and condition! Clearly, he knew neither relatives nor strangers. Clearly, he knew neither the world nor people. The Shaykh was astonished by this state and said, "I'd give my life for one who is unaffected by the soaring mountains!" He asked Qaḥṭubī about the state that so astonished him and he replied, "Indeed, we were freed from slavery to things from beginningless eternity (*azal*)."[11]

According to Ṣūfī commentaries, it is this quality of servanthood that warrants the special status granted to Maryam in Qur'ānic verse 3:42, *And when the angels said, "O Maryam, truly God has chosen you and purified you, chosen you above the women of the world."* In al-Ṭabarī, the verse prompts a discussion of the hierarchy of the four perfect women in the world, namely, Āsiya (the wife of Pharoah), Maryam, Khadīja (the wife of Muḥammad), and Fāṭima (the daughter of Muḥammad);[12] and the question of whether Maryam is preferred over all women for all time or just the time in which she was living.[13] Al-Qurṭubī states that some interpret this verse to mean that Maryam is a prophet, an opinion he agrees with, on the grounds that God spoke to her by the intermediaries of the angels.[14] Ṣūfī commentators, however, consider Maryam's state to be one that is more broadly attainable by saints and the elect who possess this same quality of servanthood. Commenting on Qur'ān 3:43, "*O Maryam, be obedient to your Lord, and prostrate and bow with those who bow*," Rūzbihān writes,

> "and bow with those who bow," that is to say, draw near with your humility with those who are humble among the saints, prophets, and the elect of the people of My love so as to attain the blessings of unification (*jam'*), because the companionship of the saints is firmly rooted in servanthood (*'ubūdiyya*) and purification from the bondage of human nature (*bashariyya*).[15]

In commentary on Qur'ān 66:12, Rūzbihān adds an element of consciousness to this quality: Maryam chooses servanthood with full knowledge of its value.

> And Maryam, the daughter of 'Imrān, who guarded her chastity, so We breathed into her Our Spirit and she testified to the words of her Lord and His books and was one of the devout (*qānitūn*).

Rūzbihān writes,

> She testified to the words of her Lord. When the lights of Holiness and the spirit of intimacy (*uns*) appeared, her soul almost inclined to intoxication in the (*divine*) solicitude, since she had experienced the solicitude before and had negated it in the stage of servanthood (*'ubūdiyya*) so as not to fall by intoxication from the station of sobriety. Don't you see how He said, *and His books and was one of the devout* (*qānitūn*), that is to say one of the righteous in her knowledge of her Lord and her knowledge of the worth of her soul subservient (*musakhkhar*) and powerless to its Lord.[16]

Maryam has knowledge that a human being's value lies in his or her utter subservience to God, a concept perhaps better understood if one looks at the ways in which the words "subservient" (*musakhkhar*) and "to make subservient" (*sakhkhara*) are used in the Qur'ān. *Do they not see the birds held subservient (musakhkhar) in mid-air? Nothing holds them up but God!* (16:79). The sun, moon, stars, and clouds have all been made subservient, by God's command, and all that is in the heavens and the earth, held in this divine thrall, has been made subservient to man.[17] The perfect man or woman remains in a state of constant servitude towards God and in doing so, becomes His representative before creation. Maryam is one of the obedient (*qānitūn*), a word that the Qur'ān applies to both believing men and women, and the cosmos.[18] It is because Maryam represents the soul in complete submission and receptivity towards the divine that she is sometimes referred to as the soul at peace (*al-nafs al-muṭma'inna*).[19]

Prayer

If the portrayal of Maryam were to be confined to her consecration to God from the world (*muḥarrar*), she would remain an ascetic but ideal attainable by only a few. But the Ṣūfī commentaries studied here look to other, more visceral elements in the Qur'ānic and extra-Qur'ānic narratives, creating evocative meditations on the meaning of prayer as an expression of human longing and pain, and hope for God's response. The story of Maryam's uncle, the prophet Zakariyyā, and his awakening to the possibilities of prayer occurs in Ṣūfī comments on Qur'ān 3:37–9.

> *Her Lord accepted her graciously and caused her to grow in a beautiful manner and He made Zakariyya her guardian. Whenever Zakariyya went into the* miḥrab *to (see) her, he found her with food. He said, "O Maryam, how does this come to you?" She said, "It is from God. Truly God provides to whom He pleases without measure." Zakariyya prayed there to his Lord, saying, "Lord, grant me from Yourself goodly offspring. Truly You are the hearer of prayer." So the angels called to him as he stood praying in the mihrab. "God gives you the good news of Yahya who shall confirm a word from God, noble, chaste, and a prophet from among the righteous."*

Al-Ṭabarī tells us that it was Zakariyyā who built Maryam a special chamber in the temple (*miḥrāb*) and took care of her needs. According to numerous traditions reported from the Companions and Followers of the Prophet, the food mentioned here refers to fruits miraculously sent to Maryam, winter fruits in the summer and summer fruits in the winter. When Zakariyyā saw this miraculous provision given to Maryam, he desired a similar miracle for himself, to have a son even though he was old and his wife was barren.[20]

Ṣūfī commentaries on these verses note the importance of Zakariyyā serving Maryam, quoting an inspiration said to have been sent to the prophet Dāwūd (David), "If you see someone seeking me, be a servant to him."[21] Rūzbihān says that *He made Zakariyyā her guardian* (3:37) because only a saint (*walī*) can serve a saint.[22] Zakariyyā's desire to serve Maryam is such that he is concerned when he finds her in the *miḥrāb* already provided with food, since he did not initially believe that this food was the result of a miracle. According to al-Qushayrī, "He was afraid that someone other than him would seize the opportunity of serving her and beat him to performing these duties,"[23] but it was one of the signs of the "gracious acceptance" that she was not entrusted to Zakariyyā entirely but received provision from God directly "so that the worlds might know that God does not burden others with the concerns of His saints."[24] Rūzbihān writes that Zakariyyā was initially afraid that Maryam's charismatic gifts (*karāmāt*) were the result of a ruse of Satan but was reassured that this was not the case after questioning her.[25]

Al-Kāshānī suggests that the food described here may also refer to special knowledge given to Maryam.

> He found her with (*'indahā*) food. It is possible that what is meant here is the spiritual food (*al-rizq al-rūḥānī*) from the gnostic sciences (*ma'ārif*), realities (*ḥaqā'iq*), sciences (*'ulūm*) and abundant wisdom bestowed upon her from God, since the specification of "withness" (*'indiyya*) indicates their being provisions divinely bestowed (*laduniyya*).[26]

Similarly, al-Nīsābūrī writes,

> He found her with food, that is to say from the openings of the unseen (*futūḥāt al-ghayb*) that God feeds the elect of His servants who spend the night with Him, not with themselves nor creation, just as the Prophet said, "I spend the night with (*'inda*) my Lord feeding me and giving me to drink."[27]

Al-Nīsābūrī also describes the foods as "teachings directly from God (*al-'ulūm al-laduniyya*) without an intermediary."[28] But whether it was food or knowledge being given to Maryam, Zakariyyā is portrayed as having had difficulty believing that her position was so high as to warrant charismatic gifts (*karāmāt*). Ja'far al-Sādiq is quoted as having said,

> Her Lord accepted her until the prophets were amazed, in spite of the grandeur of their own fates, at the exaltedness of her situation with God. Don't you see that Zakariyyā said to her, "*How does this come to You?*" *She said,* "*It is from God,*" that is to say, from the one who has accepted me.[29]

Although surprised and even jealous of Maryam's spiritual states and gifts, Zakariyyā is consoled by being able to observe Maryam in her states and by his continued service to her.

> Maryam said, "It is from God, not from any created being," and in that were two things to relieve Zakariyyā: one of them was in the witnessing of her station (*maqām*) and her charismatic gift (*karāma*) from God and the second was that no one had beaten him to serving her. When He says, *Whenever (kullamā) Zakariyyā went into the* miḥrāb *to [see] her*, the word *kullamā* means "repeatedly" and this is an allusion to the fact that Zakariyyā did not cease serving her even though he found her with provision, but rather every day and at every moment he was studying her state (*ḥāl*) because the charismatic gifts (*karāmāt*) of the saints do not necessarily remain absolutely. It is possible that God will make something appear in them indefinitely or He might not, so Zakariyyā did not

> rely on that nor neglect to study her state. Then he began to question her again by saying, "*O Maryam, how did this come to you?*" because of the possibility that that which exists today is not how it was yesterday, since this is not incumbent on God.[30]

It is this witnessing of Maryam's states and gifts that inspires Zakariyyā to pray himself.

> Zakariyya prayed there to his Lord, saying, "*Lord, grant me from Yourself goodly offspring. Truly You are the Hearer of prayer,*" (3:38) that is to say when he saw the charismatic gift (*karāma*) of God with her, he grew more certain and more hopeful, so he asked for a son in spite of his advanced age and the fact that his request was granted was contrary to ordinary reality (*naqḍ*^{an}*l-il-ʿāda*).[31]

Rūzbihān describes Zakariyyā's desire for a miracle as the jealousy (*ghayra*) of prophecy.

> Zakariyyā prayed there to his Lord. When Zakariyyā went to [see] Maryam, he found her with all kinds of fruits, knowledge given to her from the precious charismatic gifts (*karāmāt*) of God. The jealousy (*ghayra*) of prophecy was aroused in him and he dwelt there in retreat (*khalwa*) and asked God for a son and God gave him what he asked for.[32]

God answers Zakariyyā's prayer out of compassion for this jealousy[33] and because the request is a worthy one. Both al-Qushayrī and Rūzbihān write that Zakariyyā asked for a son to help him in obeying God and to be a successor to him in carrying out the message and guiding the community. Al-Qushayrī extends the meaning beyond Zakariyyā to include all such prayer.

> It was a request that deserved to be granted, for when a request is for the sake of God (*al-ḥaqq*) and not for the pleasure of the self (*nafs*), then He will not refuse it.[34]

Zakariyyā's jealousy and longing are seen as positive so long as the object of his desire is not one of mundane gratification. There is a tension here between this desire and supplication, and the acceptance of God's will. In commenting on Qur'ān 3:39, *So the angels called to him as he stood praying in the miḥrāb*, al-Qushayrī writes,

> In this is an allusion to the fact that one who needs something from kings should stay at the door incessantly until the request is granted. It is said that the wisdom of God is such that He only consents to the request of one who embraces His service and throws the one who rejects obedience into the humiliation of loneliness.[35]

The right to petition God is a boldness that is tempered by the reminder that *Truly God provides to whom He pleases without measure* (3:37) and *God does what He wills* (3:40). Al-Maybudī tells us that when Zakariyyā received news from the angels that his prayer for a son would be answered, he said, "By what merit of mine do I deserve this reply, if not by Your will and grace?"[36] Furthermore, if man desires this grace, he should know that even his desire is the result of God's act. In a beautiful passage describing how God creates man's desires, al-Nīsābūrī writes,

> There are secrets belonging to God in every single atom of all existing things and in every one of their movements (*ḥarakāt*) and God has secrets that only God knows. Look at what secrets God expresses through the bird's feeding its young [before Ḥannā] and what signs and miracles He reveals from this moment to the Day of Resurrection through Maryam and ʿĪsā. Just as God made the bird feeding its young the cause of movement (*taḥarraka*) of Hannah's heart (*qalb*) to seek a child, so did He make the state of Maryam and the food miraculously given to her the cause of the movement of Zakariyyā's heart.[37]

The theme of human longing and supplication is further developed in commentary that compares Maryam's contemplative prayer in the *miḥrāb* to the prayer she makes in the pain and distress of childbirth.

> *So she conceived him and withdrew with him to a remote place. Labor pains drove her to the trunk of a palmtree. She said, "O would that I had died before this, and had been completely forgotten." But the one that was below her called to her, "Do not grieve, your Lord has placed a brook below you. Shake the trunk of the palmtree towards you and fresh dates will fall down to you."*
>
> (Qur'ān 19:22–25)

When Maryam received the food in her *miḥrāb*, it was a miracle of pure grace occurring without any effort on her part. The dates she is provided with here are also considered to be a miracle, since the tree is said to have been dried up and without fruit until she shook its trunk.[38] Several Ṣūfī commentators point out that in this second miracle, Maryam is required to act. Al-Qushayrī writes,

> It is said that when she was isolated (*mujarrad*) and without attachment (*ʿalāqa*), Zakariyyā would find her with food without her having been instructed to exert herself. When the attachment to the child occurred, she was instructed to shake the dried palmtree and this was in her weakest state as the time of the birth of the child became closer, in order to know that attachment necessitates pain and hardship.[39]

Ja'far al-Ṣādiq writes: "*O would that I had died before*" seeing my heart (*qalb*) attached to something other than God.[40] Rūzbihān quotes Abū Bakr. b. Ṭāhir as saying,

> "*O would that I had died*" in the days of trusting in God alone before being reduced to the pain of petitioning as referred to in His words, "*Shake the trunk of the palmtree towards you.*"[41]

But al-Maybudī would have us know that this "pain of petitioning" is itself a blessing:

> Maryam rose up in her weakness and seized the dry tree. When her hand touched the dry tree, it turned green, moist and fresh, bearing fruit, and in its freshness bent towards her. A divine voice came saying, "We had the power so that even without your touching the tree it would have become green and bent towards you, but We wanted by your shaking it to bring forth two miracles; first was that in childbirth, weakness and illness, We gave you power to shake the tree, which was to verify the miracle for you. The other was that We wanted the blessing of your hand to reach the tree so that it would bear fruit. Then the people of the world would understand that whoever is sad and grieved for Us, their hand is a remedy for pains.[42]

The pleading quality of the prayers of Ḥannā, Zakariyyā and Maryam, and God's responsiveness to them appealingly demonstrates the significance and value of human suffering and supplication. Maryam's contemplative life ends with her pregnancy, the pain of childbirth, and being slandered, making her a model for Ṣūfīs in balancing the concerns of the world with worship and trust in God.

The virgin Maryam

We have already seen in Ṣūfī interpretations of the story of Mūsā and al-Khaḍir the type of allegoresis that finds one-to-one correspondences between philosophical concepts and Qur'ānic references. In the commentary of al-Kāshānī, which makes use of the approach more than any other, the results of this interpretative approach can seem reductionistic or rich, depending on the passage. Al-Kāshānī's comments on Maryam's chastity display him at his best. In two passages of the Qur'ān, Maryam is described as *she who guarded her chastity* (21:91, 66:12). The Arabic phrase used is *aḥṣanat farjahā*, which literally means *she guarded her private parts*. Commenting on verse 21:91, al-Kāshānī writes,

> And she who guarded, that is to say the chaste (*zakiyya*) and pure (*ṣafiyya*), prepared (*musta'idda*) and worshipping soul (*nafs*), which guarded the private parts of its preparedness (*isti'dād*), and the locus (*maḥall*) of the effects of the spirit (*rūḥ*) belonging to its inward dimension by protecting it from the fornicators of the physical forces within it.[43]

The idea of the preparedness (*isti'dād*) of the soul refers to the different capabilities of souls to receive light from the Divine manifestation, a receptivity that can be damaged.[44] Commenting on the Qur'ānic verse in which Ādam and Hawwā (Eve) say, "*Lord, we have wronged ourselves and if You do not forgive us we will surely be among the lost*" (7:23), al-Kāshānī writes that *the lost* are

> those who waste their original preparedness (*isti'dād*), which is the substance of felicity and subsistence, by employing it in the abode of annihilation. Thereby they would be deprived of reaching perfection through becoming disengaged because they kept on clinging to the imperfections of nature.[45]

Similarly, Najm al-Din Rāzī (d. 1256), a Ṣūfi of the Kubrawī order, uses the concept of preparedness in his *Mirṣād al-'ibād*:

> Wretched is the person who is deprived of his own perfection and looks upon himself with the eye of disdain! He employs preparedness (*isti'dād*) of the human level, which is the noblest of existent things, in acquiring the objects of animal appetite, while animals are the meanest of existent things! He fails to recognize his own worth![46]

Human beings are the most perfect form of creation because they have the potential for becoming the locus in which the Divine manifestation occurs most fully, but this is a potential that can be squandered if the soul clings to the pleasures of the temporary and corporeal world. Maryam protected herself from these "fornicators of the physical forces within [the soul]"[47] and thereby protected her potentiality for perfection. Commenting on Qur'ānic verse 66:12, al-Kāshānī writes,

> What is taken into account in worthiness for the charismatic gift (*karāma*) from God is good work and true belief, such as the chastity (*iḥṣān*) of Maryam, her believing the words of her Lord, and her obedience, which prepared her for the acceptance (*qabūl*) of the breath of the spirit of God to her... The soul adorned by the excellence of abstinence and the aforementioned chastity is a receptacle (*qābila*) for the effusion (*fayḍ*) of the holy spirit and the pregnancy of 'Īsā, the heart (*qalb*), illuminated by the light of the spirit, believing in the words of the Lord, the wise tenants, and the divinely revealed religions, obeying god absolutely with knowledge and deed, secretly and openly, participating in the unity in everything large and small, inwardly and outwardly, and God knows best.[48]

Because Maryam guarded the preparedness of her soul, her soul was able to become a receptacle (*qābila*) for the effusion of the holy spirit and the pregnancy of ʿĪsā, described most fully in Qur'ānic verses 19:16–22:

> *Mention Maryam in the book when she withdrew from her family to an eastern place and veiled herself from them. Then We sent to her Our Spirit and it appeared to her as a well-proportioned man. She said, "I seek refuge in the Merciful from you if you fear God. He said, "I am only a messenger from your Lord, to grant you a pure son." She said, "How can I have a son when no man has touched me nor have I been unchaste!" He said, "Thus said your Lord: It is easy for Me and (We give him to you) so that We may make him a sign to men and a mercy from Us. It is a matter decreed." So she conceived him and withdrew with him to a remote place.*

The complexity of Ṣūfī symbolic interpretation is amply illustrated in Rūzbihān's commentary on these verses. He begins by equating Maryam's essential nature with the very nature of holiness itself. Her withdrawal to the *eastern place*, the source of divine lights (*maʿdin al-anwār al-ulūhiyya*),[49] refers to her profound mystical experiences and intimacy with the unseen world.

> The real allusion here is that the essential substance (*jawhar*) of Maryam is itself the primordial substance of holiness (*qudus*). Raised by God (*al-ḥaqq*) in the light of intimacy, with every one of her breaths she was drawn by the quality of nearness (*qurb*) and intimacy (*uns*) to the source of divine lights. She became watchful at every moment for the appearance of the sun of omnipotence (*jabarūt*) from the place in the east of dominion (*malakūt*). She withdrew from created things by her high aspiration characterized by the light of the unseen. She turned towards the places of the east of the suns of the Essence and the Attributes, inhaling the breezes of union (*wiṣāl*) from the world of eternity without beginning (*azal*).[50]

"The places of the East" and the suns that can be witnessed rising there are symbols for the different levels of reality or worlds of the Unseen, with the first referring to the unseen intermediary world of jinn and angels (the *malakūt*) and the second to the divine world of God's names and attributes. In his commentary on 19:16, al-Kāshānī calls the *eastern place* the holy world (*al-ʿālam al-qudsī*) and the western place from which Maryam withdrew and to which she returns the world of nature (*al-ʿālam al-ṭabīʿa*) and the horizon of corporeality (*al-ufuq al-jismānī*), or the dwelling place of the soul (*nafs*). In describing what happens to Maryam in this *eastern place*, Rūzbihān uses two concepts to describe the meeting of the divine and human: divine self-disclosure (*tajallī*) and clothing (*libās*).

> When we have finished describing the holiness (*qudus*) of the divinity (*lāhūt*) from human nature (*nāsūt*) and that human nature is incapable of reaching the divinity, far removed is the Majesty of God (*ḥaqq*) from

> mixing with creation, and eternity is segregated from contingency, exalted is His beauty and the grandeur of His beginninglessness (*azal*) above likeness and resemblance), we can say regarding God (*ḥaqq*) sending His spirit to her that the Spirit is the visible manifestation (*tajallī*) of the holiness of the essence (*dhāt*) in the light of qualities (*ṣifāt*); and the light of qualities is in the clothing (*libās*) of the acts (*af'āl*) in accordance with the beautiful form made desirable to her, which draws every spirit to it through the attribute of yearning (*shawq*), and that was the spirit of the act (*fi'l*), the spirit of the quality (*ṣifa*) and the spirit of the essence (*dhāt*) in the clothing of His light according to the capacity of her intellect (*'aql*). Because of that, He said, and it appeared to her as a well-proportioned man. This is the usual way of the appearance of the God (*ḥaqq*) in the beginning of the passionate love (*'ishq*) of the lovers, so that their spirits and hearts may be attracted by it to the treasure of being granted knowledge of the qualities and the essence, turning away after separating the truth (*ḥaqīqa*) from creation (*khalīqa*). The Prophet, peace be upon him, said about that, "I see my Lord in the most beautiful form."[51]

Elsewhere in his Qur'ānic commentary, Rūzbihān quotes al-Tustarī as defining the divine self-disclosure (*tajallī*) as one of the ways in which God gives knowledge to His servants, the others being revelation (*waḥy*), and knowledge with (*al-'indī*) and from (*al-ladunī*) God, all of these being subsumed within the category of knowledge by unveiling (*mukāshafa*).[52] The verb *tajalla* occurs in Qur'ānic verse 7:143, in which Mūsā asks to see God. God replies, "*You will never see Me, but look at the mountain. If it remains in its place, then you will see Me." When His Lord manifested Himself (tajalla) to the mountain, He made it as dust and Mūsā fell down in a swoon.*

Like Mūsā, Maryam does not perceive God directly. The holiness (*qudus*) of the essence (*dhāt*) descends in the light of the qualities (*ṣifāt*), which are "clothed" in the acts (*af'āl*), the level of reality visible to her. The acts function as a mirror for the manifestation (*tajallī*) of the essence and the qualities. The divine self-disclosure (*tajallī*) is always clothed or made ambiguous (*iltibās*) in this manner and is therefore hidden from those who are unaware of the secret. As evidence for his statements, Rūzbihān quotes the *ḥadīth*, "I saw my Lord in the most beautiful form." A more complete version of this *ḥadīth*, called the *ḥadīth* of vision (*ḥadīth al-ru'yā*), reads,

> I saw my Lord in a form of the greatest beauty, as a youth with abundant hair, seated on the throne of grace: he was clad in a garment of gold; on his hair a golden mitre; on his feet golden sandals.[53]

It is a *ḥadīth* whose authenticity was mostly rejected outside of Ṣūfism and caused some problems within Ṣūfism itself from those who saw in it license for the practice of gazing at youths.[54] The *ḥadīth* plays a central role in the thought of Rūzbihān because he believed the form of human beauty is the most perfect locus for the divine self-disclosure (*tajallī*) and that love of the form can lead to love of God.[55] It is not only the form of the well-proportioned man that acts as a mirror in which the *tajallī* occurs, but also Maryam.

> A breath of the union of eternity (*azal*) came to her and the sun of witnessing of holiness rose upon her. When she witnessed the rising of the manifestation (*tajallī*) of the eternal (*azal*), its lights shown and its secrets reached her spirit (*rūḥ*) and her spirit was impregnated by the breath of the unseen (*ghayb*). She became pregnant with the great Word and the light of the highest Spirit. When her state became exalted by the reflection in her beauty of the manifestation of the eternal, she veiled herself from created beings and became intimate with the bridegroom of reality (*ḥaqīqa*).[56]

If Rūzbihān seems to be suggesting a union of the human and divine here, elsewhere in his writings he qualifies this. Commenting on verses of al-Ḥallāj that would seem to describe union with the divine, Rūzbihān writes that this is a fancy (*wahm*) born of human weakness as it contemplates God, and he notes that "the intoxicated speak in this way frequently, even though they know that the essence of divinity is unattainable by the created."[57] But if Rūzbihān is careful to stress God's distance from created things, nonetheless his description of the intimacy Maryam enjoys with the "bridegroom of reality" is a provocative one that includes desire, yearning, and passion; the erotic imagery would be even more apparent if Rūzbihān's writing style was not so dense and his terminology so technical.

9

QUR'ĀN 24:35 (THE LIGHT VERSE)

> *God is the light of the heavens and the earth. The similitude of His/his light is as a niche in which is a lamp and the lamp is in a glass, and the glass is like a glittering star lit from a blessed olive tree neither of the east nor the west, whose oil would well-nigh shine even if no fire touched it. Light upon light. God guides whom He wills to His light and strikes similitudes for mankind, and God has knowledge of all things.*

The Light Verse has often been closely associated with Ṣūfī thought, primarily because of al-Ghazālī's well-known and influential commentary on it. Goldziher somewhat questionably stated that the verse is one of the few in the Qur'ān amenable to mystical thought.[1] It has been selected for discussion here because of the questions it raises concerning literal and metaphorical language, and how one can speak of God and His attributes.

God is the light of the heavens and the earth

The majority of non-Ṣūfī classical commentators considered the expression *God is the light of the heavens and the earth* to be a metaphor or idiom which must be understood in such as way as to avoid equating God with the phenomenon of light. In his *Jāmiʿ al-bayān*, al-Ṭabarī states that the Ibn ʿAbbās' interpretation, "God is the guide (*hādī*) of the people of the heavens and the earth," is the best of the interpretations from the Companions and Followers because it is the logical continuation of the preceding verse, *We have sent down to you signs making things clear, as a similitude of those who passed away before you, and as an admonition for those who are Godfearing* (24:34).[2] Another interpretation al-Ṭabarī cites suggests that the phrase means that God "governs (*yudabbiru*) the affair (*amr*) with regards to [the heavens and the earth], their stars, sun and moon," an expression taken from Qur'ānic verses 10:3, 13:2, and 32:5.[3] Other commentators quote additional interpretations traced back to the Companions and Followers, which make God the agent of illumination rather than light itself; that is, God is the illuminator (*munawwir*) or ornamentor (*muzayyin*) of the heavens and the earth.[4]

Only one interpretation cited in al-Ṭabarī retains the original wording of the phrase by suggesting a synonym for "light" (*nūr*), i.e., "light" (*ḍiyā'*).[5]

Al-Zamakhsharī's commentary is one of the first to reject the literal reading of the phrase and to insist upon its being interpreted. Like other Mu'tazila, al-Zamakhsharī was intent upon protecting the unity of God by denying that there could be a plurality of eternals, that is, a power, a knowledge, or a light that have existed independently with Him for all eternity. Their preferred manner of expressing the relationship between God and His attributes was to say that God is powerful, knowing, etc., by His very essence. In other words, the attributes are not distinct from His essence, but neither are they equivalent to it. One can say, "God is powerful," but not "God is Power," because this would be likening God to a created thing. Therefore, Qur'ānic phrases such as *God is the light of the heavens and the earth* must be interpreted because God is not like anything created, in this case light. Al-Zamakhsharī suggests that the phrase *God is the light* is like our saying, "Zayd is generous and munificent" (*Zayd^{un} karam^{un} wa jūd^{un}*) and then saying, "He revives men with his generosity and munificence" (*yun'ashu al-nās bi-karamihi wa jūdihi*). The first sentence does not mean that Zayd is generosity and munificence per se, but rather that Zayd possesses these attributes. Similarly, the meaning of the phrase *God is the light of the heavens and the earth*, according to al-Zamakhsharī, is that

> He is the possessor of the light of the heavens and the owner of the light of the heavens. The light of the heavens and the earth is the truth (*al-ḥaqq*), which can be compared to light in its manifestation and clarification, just as He says, *God is the friend of those who believe; He brings them forth from the shadows to the light* (2:257), i.e., from the false to the true (*al-ḥaqq*).[6]

The Mu'tazilī doctrine concerning the attributes of God was one of the most significant differences setting them apart from their Ash'arī counterparts who labeled them "deniers" (*mu'aṭṭila*) for supposedly denying the existence of the attributes of God, leaving God as an abstract symbol of unity.[7] In his commentary on this verse, however, the Ash'arī theologian al-Rāzī has more in common with al-Zamakhsharī than differences. Like al-Zamakhsharī, al-Rāzī insists that the phrase *God is the light* must be interpreted. As we saw in the discussion of Qur'ān 3:7, al-Rāzī believes that the abandonment of the probable meaning of any expression in the Qur'ān requires a clear-cut indicator (*dalīl munfaṣil*) that demonstrates the absurdity of the apparent sense (*ẓāhir*).[8] Al-Rāzī applies the methodology to this verse, setting forth argument after argument for proving the absurdity of calling God "light." He begins by explaining various definitions of the word "light" (in its physical sense), and then demonstrates the absurdity of applying any of these definitions to God.

Further evidence to support his rational arguments is drawn from three Qur'ānic verses, one of which is the Light Verse itself. Al-Rāzī finds a contradiction between the phrase *God is the light of the heavens and the earth* and the phrases *the similitude of His/his light* and *God guides whom He wills to His light*, since the first phrase appears to equate light with God's essence while the other phrases imply that light is attributed (*muḍāf*) to God. One of the ways in which al-Rāzī attempts to resolve this seeming contradiction is by referring to common usage of the Arabic language. He quotes the same sentences found in al-Zamakhsharī, although he does not mention al-Zamakhsharī by name.[9] Like al-Zamakhsharī, al-Rāzī understands the verse as meaning that God is not "light" per se but rather the possessor and creator of light, since Qur'ān 42:11 states *There is nothing like Him*. According to al-Rāzī, if God were a light, this verse would be false because all lights resemble one another. Nothing resembles Him and therefore He cannot be called light. Another verse al-Rāzī quotes to support his view is Qur'ān 6:1, *He made the shadows and the light*. This verse proves that the quiddity (*māhiyya*) of light was created by God, making it impossible that the divine being could be a light.[10]

Based on this rational and Qur'ānic evidence, al-Rāzī insists that the phrase *God is the light of the heavens and the earth* must be interpreted (*la budda min al-ta'wīl*). His preferred interpretation is the one attributed to Ibn 'Abbās and "the majority," which states that the verse means, "God is the Guide of the heavens and the earth." Al-Rāzī mentions several Qur'ānic verses that support this interpretation.[11] He considers it the best interpretation because the last part of the Light Verse, *God guides whom He wills to His light*, "indicates that what is meant is the light of guidance to knowledge and action." Al-Rāzī briefly mentions other traditional interpretations such as God as governor (*mudabbir*), arranger (*nāzim*), and illuminator (*munawwir*).[12]

This discussion of traditional interpretations is followed by an extensive summary and expansion of the first part of al-Ghazālī's *Mishkāt al-anwār*, a commentary on the Light Verse that will be discussed in greater depth in what follows. For now however, we can state that al-Ghazālī's basic premise is that light is a word used for many different types of phenomena. The relationship between these different kinds of phenomena is a hierarchical one, and lights that are higher are more worthy of the term "light" than lights that are lower. The light of the physical eye is inferior to that of the intellect (*'aql*), a fact that al-Ghazālī proves by listing seven imperfections of physical sight when compared to rational insight; al-Rāzī expands this list to a total of twenty imperfections. Even higher than the light of rational insight is the light of God. According to al-Ghazālī, the perfection of His light is such that He alone is worthy of the term "light." God is light in reality (*ḥaqīqa*) while all other light is metaphorical (*majāz*) in relationship to His light; in truth there is no light but He.[13]

At first glance this view would seem to be antithetical to that of al-Rāzī, who began his own exegesis by arguing that God cannot be called light. Nonetheless, al-Rāzī concludes after his long summary of al-Ghazālī's work that no contradiction exists between al-Ghazālī's interpretation and the traditional interpretation of light as "Guide," al-Rāzī's preferred interpretation.[14] Al-Rāzī's acceptance of al-Ghazālī's interpretation makes more sense when seen in the context of other discussions of God's attributes. A precedent for al-Ghazālī's statement that God is light in reality (*ḥaqīqa*) while all other light is metaphor (*majāz*) can be found in the work of the Mu'tazilī theologian al-Nāshi' al-Akbar (d. 906), who attempted to solve the problem of anthropomorphic descriptions of God in the Qur'ān by the theory that the attributes of God, when applied to God are "true" (*ḥaqīqa*) but when applied to men are "metaphor" (*majāz*). The more common way to solve anthropomorphic problems was to say the opposite, that attributes are *majāz* with regards to God but *ḥaqīqa* with regards to mankind. But, as Heinrichs has pointed out, either theory works well to solve the problem of anthropomorphism. The first theory, however, raises an additional issue, which is whether Nāshi' al-Akbar understands the distinction between the real (*ḥaqīqa*) and metaphor (*majāz*) to be on an ontological or a linguistic level.[15] Nāshi' al-Akbar's view is ambiguous, but al-Ghazālī's is not. He clearly asserts that God's light, like His existence, is the only real Light and Existence. Al-Rāzī's position is less clear; while he repeats al-Ghazālī's emphatic phrase, "There is no light but He," he omits key passages explaining what al-Ghazālī means by this. Al-Rāzī's main concern is the theological problem of eliminating any possibility of equating God with the physical phenomenon that we call light.

Ibn Taymiyya wrote a commentary on the Light Verse that is structured as a rebuttal to an unnamed adversary. Many of the arguments quoted from this adversary are arguments found in al-Rāzī's *Tafsīr al-kabīr* and the section on God's name "light" (*nūr*) in his *Sharḥ asmā' Allāh ta'ālā wa'l-ṣifāt*.[16] The wording is similar enough to suspect that Ibn Taymiyya's opponent is, in fact, al-Rāzī, but the fact that some of the arguments quoted are not found in either of the two works of al-Rāzī, at least not in the passages studied here, makes it difficult to definitively identify him as such. Ibn Taymiyya's commentary is highly polemical; he accuses his opponent of distorting the Qur'ān (*taḥrīf*), apostasy (*ilḥād*) with regards to God's signs and names, lying (*kidhb*), iniquity (*ẓulm*), and enmity towards the rights of God.[17] Ibn Taymiyya attempts to highlight, point by point, what he deems to be the contradictions in his opponent's arguments and their pervertedness (*fasād*). For our purposes the most important material pertains to Ibn Taymiyya's response to the claim that the phrase *God is the light of the heavens and the earth* must be interpreted. Ibn Taymiyya not only rejects the necessity of interpreting this phrase, he insists that the majority of Muslims do not interpret it, this being the view of the first generations (*salaf*), the Attributionists (*ṣifātiyya*)[18] among the theologians, jurists, Ṣūfīs, and others. The interpretation of God's attribute "light," according to Ibn Taymiyya goes back to the *jahmiyya*[19] and the Mu'tazila.

Ibn Taymiyya's opponent claims that the phrase *God is the light of the heavens and the earth* must be interpreted because "light is a mode of being (*kayfiyya*) existing in corporeality, which is the opposite of darkness, and far be it from God (*al-ḥaqq*) to have an opposite"[20] Ibn Taymiyya understands the term "light" as possessing different meanings appropriate to different contexts. He disagrees with the definition of light as a mode of being existing in corporeality, stating that created light can be either an essence (*'ayn*) or an accident (*'araḍ*). An example of the first is fire while the second would be the reflective light of the fire on a wall. Only the second can be said to be a "mode of being existing by means of a body." In other words, sometimes the word light refers to a substance (*jawhar*) and sometimes to a quality (*ṣifa*). Similarly, the names of God sometimes refer to His essence and sometimes to His attributes. As an example of this, Ibn Taymiyya quotes a *ḥadīth*, "You are the real (*ḥaqq*), Your speech is the real (*ḥaqq*), the Garden is real (*ḥaqq*), the prophets are real (*ḥaqq*) and Muḥammad is real (*ḥaqq*)."[21]

Similarly, Ibn Taymiyya understands the phrase *God is the light of the heavens and the earth* as meaning that light is part of God's essence as well as being one of His attributes; that is to say God is both light and possesses light. Therefore, there is no contradiction between the first phrase, *God is the light of the heavens and the earth* and the second phrase *the similitude of His/his light*, and it would be wrong to interpret the first phrase to mean "God is the possessor of light," as do al-Zamakhsharī and al-Rāzī. Ibn Taymiyya finds further proof for accepting the exact Qur'ānic wording as it is in the *ḥadith*, "O God, praise be to You, light of the heavens and the earth and what is in them," and the Prophet's reply to the question of how he saw his Lord, "I see a light."[22]

Ibn Taymiyya's insistence that God is light, however, does not mean that he rejects the metaphorical interpretations of the first generations (*salaf*) regarding this light, comments that he does not call *ta'wīl* but rather *tafsīr*. According to Ibn Taymiyya, saying that "God is the guide of the heavens and the earth" does not negate the fact of God being Himself a light. Using many of the same examples that he uses in his book on Qur'ānic methodology, *Muqaddima fi uṣūl al-tafsīr*, Ibn Taymiyya explains that the custom of the first generations was to use different expressions and examples to explain the meaning of the Qur'ān. When they said, "God is the guide of the heavens and the earth," they were making a statement regarding one of the meanings of *God is the light of the heavens and the earth*, a statement that does not invalidate its other meanings. Likewise, when they said, "God is the illuminator (*munawwir*) of the heavens and the earth," they were not contradicting the fact of His being a light, because part of the definition of light is being something that illuminates something else.[23] Ibn Taymiyya, then, accepts both the interpretation that *God is the light of the heavens and the earth* as "God is the guide of the heavens and the earth" and the interpretation that insists upon the literal meaning. However, he does not explore the implications of accepting the literal meaning.[24]

Ṣūfī interpretations of *God is the light of the heavens and the earth*

It is the literal understanding of the phrase *God is light* that interests al-Ghazālī in his *Mishkāt al-anwār*, although the conclusions he draws regarding it are not ones that Ibn Taymiyyya would have accepted. He explains that the various interpretations of the Light Verse are due to the different definitions of light they presuppose. He judges the understanding of light found amongst the Ṣūfīs to be superior to that of other interpretations, but suggests that it is not an interpretation that should be widely broadcast. As we saw in the commentaries on Qur'ān 3:7, the Ṣūfīs asserted that the Qur'ān contains both public knowledge that should be disseminated and private knowledge that is made deliberately obscure except to those few intended to receive it. Al-Ghazālī refers to this principle in the introduction to his *Mishkāt al-anwār* and explains why, then, he is revealing some of this private information:

> What is more, not every mystery is to be unveiled and divulged, and not every reality (*ḥaqīqa*) is to be presented and disclosed. Indeed, "the breasts of the free (*aḥrār*) are the graves of the mysteries."[25] One of the gnostics has said, "To divulge the mystery of Lordship is unbelief (*kufr*)." Indeed, the Master of the First and the Last [the Prophet] said, "There is a kind of knowledge like the guise of the hidden; none knows it except the knowers of God. When they speak of it, none denies it except those who are arrogantly deluded by God." And when the people of arrogant delusion become many, it becomes necessary to preserve the coverings upon the face of the mysteries. But I see you as one whose breast has been opened up by God through light and whose innermost consciousness (*sirr*) has been kept free of the darknesses of delusion. Hence, in this discipline I will not be niggardly toward you in alluding (*ishāra*) to sparks and flashes or giving symbols of realities and subtleties, for the fear of holding back knowledge from those who are worthy of it is not less than that in disseminating it to those who are not worthy of it.
>
> He who bestows (*manaḥa*) knowledge on the ignorant wastes it,
> And he who withholds (*mana'a*) it from the worthy has done them wrong.[26]

With this said, al-Ghazālī proceeds to the first section of his treatise on the definition of different types of light, and his interpretation of the phrase *God is the light of the heavens and the earth.*

Al-Ghazālī asserts that the term "light" is understood in three different ways. The first usage (*waḍ'*) is that of ordinary people (*'āmmī*) and indicates manifestation (*ẓuhūr*) to visual perception. "Light" here is "an expression for what can be seen in itself and through which other things can be seen, like the sun." The Arabic language, however, also includes the possibility of using the word "light" to refer to the organ of perception involved, the eye, as in the phrase "the light of the eyesight of the bat is weak (*fī'l-khuffāsh inna nūr 'aynihi ḍa'īf*)."[27] Al-Ghazālī suggests that this second definition of the term "light" is more appropriate than the first definition because the eye perceives and through it perception takes place, whereas seen light is merely the place where perception takes place. An even more perfect organ of perception is the "eye" of the intellect (*'aql*) and so this too can be referred to as a "light." It is in this sense that "light" can be used to refer to the Prophet and, to a lesser degree, the other prophets and religious scholars.[28]

While this second definition of "light" occurs among the elect (*khawāṣṣ*), the elect of the elect (*khawāṣṣ al-khawāṣṣ*) have a third definition, which defines "light" as "the first light" (*al-nūr al-awwal*) and "the real light" (*al-nūr al-ḥaqq*) because it is the only light that does not borrow its luminosity from something else. The use of the term "light" for anything other than this real light is metaphor (*majāz*). God is light, there is no light but He, and He is the totality of lights and the universal light. God is hidden from us because He is pure light. In everything other than God light is mixed with darkness, allowing us to see, but God has no opposite, no darkness mixed with His light and He is therefore veiled from His creation by the very intensity of His manifestation. He is everywhere but cannot be seen.

Just as the real light (*al-nūr al-ḥaqq*) is God, the real existent (*al-mawjūd al-ḥaqq*) is God. And just as our light is "borrowed," so is our existence "borrowed (*isti'āra*)." Once one has recognized what is real and what is metaphor, one will understand that "there is nothing in existence except God," and *Everything is being annihilated except His face* (28:88). The state (*ḥāl*) of seeing this is attained either by cognitive gnosis (*'irfān 'ilmī*) or "tasting (*dhawq*)." In the latter case there is an intoxication that overcomes the intellect and gives rise to such statements as those made by al-Ḥallāj and Abū Yazīd al-Bisṭāmī (d. 875), but when the state ends the intellect knows that it was a state that was not the reality of unification (*ḥaqīqat al-ittiḥad*) but the ambiguity of unification (*shubha 'l-ittiḥād*). The possessor of this state has been annihilated (*faniya*) from himself and annihilated from his annihilation (*faniya 'an fanā'ihi*) because he has lost all consciousness of himself.

> In relationship to the one immersed in it, this state is called "unification" (*ittiḥād*), according to the language of metaphor (*majāz*), or is called "declaring God's unity" (*tawḥīd*) in the language of reality (*ḥaqīqa*).[29]

Al-Ghazālī quotes a poem here attributed to Ṣāḥib b. 'Abbād (d. 995):

> The glass is clear, the wine is clear,
> the two are similar, the affair confused,
> As if there is wine and no glass,
> or glass and no wine.[30]

And he adds, "There is a difference between saying, 'The wine is the cup' and 'It is *as if* the wine is the cup.' "[31] It was just this kind of ambiguous statement which troubled critics like Ibn Taymiyya who rejected the distinction between the reality and the metaphor of unification (*ittiḥād*) and therefore could only see these ideas as heresies, a denial of God's complete transcendence. Ibn Taymiyya believed that this denial was at the root of both the ecstatic utterances of the early Ṣūfīs and their philosophizing successors, hidden beneath the deliberate ambiguity of Ṣūfī terminology and style. Ibn 'Arabī describes the state of bewilderment (*hayra*) which occurs in the mystic when he realizes the ambiguity of existence, but Ibn Taymiyya declares this merely confusion, the result of the logical absurdities of the mystic's thinking.[32] In the *Mishkāt al-anwār*, al-Ghazālī anticipates this criticism, expressing his concern that what he has said will be misunderstood and suggests that those who cannot grasp this kind of knowledge should avoid it:

> It may be that some people will fall short of understanding the innermost meaning of these words. Hence, they will understand the words, "God is with everything, just as light is with the things," to mean that He is in each place – high exalted and holy is He from being ascribed to place! Probably the best way not to stir up such imaginings is to say that He is before everything, that He is above everything and that He makes everything manifest. Yet, in the knowledge of those who possess insight, that which makes manifest cannot be separate from that which is manifest. This is what we mean by our saying that "He is with everything." Moreover, it is not hidden from you that the manifester is above and before everything made manifest, although it is with everything in a certain respect. However, [the manifester] is with [everything] in one respect and before it in another respect, so you should not suppose that this is a contradiction. Take an example from sensory objects, which lie at your level of knowledge: Consider how the movement of a hand is both with the movement of its shadow and before it. He whose breast cannot embrace knowledge of this should abandon this type of science. There are men for each science, and "the way is eased for each person to that for which he was created."[33]

For ordinary people the declaration of God's unity (*tawḥīd*) is "There is no god but God," but for the elect the declaration of God's unity is "There is no he but He."[34]

The *Mishkāt al-anwār* represents a type of Ṣūfī writing which uses the language of philosophy and theology to describe a view of reality based on the Ṣūfī experience of annihilation (*fanā'*) and subsistence (*baqā'*). Although Ibn 'Arabī has often been considered the originator of this theoretical form of Ṣufism, the *Mishkāt al-anwār* demonstrates that al-Ghazālī was clearly his precursor.[35] Elsewhere, al-Ghazālī did address the types of theological issues which are the primary focus of al-Rāzī's commentary on the Light Verse, but these are not his concerns in the *Mishkāt al-anwār*. His concerns are also different from the purely philosophical approach of Ibn Sīnā in his interpretation of the Light Verse found in *Fī ithbāt al-nubuwwāt*. Like al-Rāzī, Ibn Sīnā declares physical light the "essential" meaning of light and the use of the term "light" in the Qur'ānic phrase

God is the light of the heavens and the earth "metaphorical," a linguistic stance opposite to that of al-Ghazālī.

> I say: *light* is an equivocal term (*mushtarak*) partaking of two meanings, one essential (*dhātī*) and the other metaphorical (*mustaʿār*). The essential stands for the perfection of the transparent inasmuch as it is transparent, as Aristotle said. The metaphorical meaning is to be understood in two ways: either as the good, or as the cause that leads to the good. Here, the sense is the metaphorical one in both meanings. I mean that God, the Exalted, is in Himself the good and the cause of everything good."[36]

In this respect, Ibn Sīnā has more in common with exoteric exegesis on this verse than with al-Ghazālī's interpretation, because he assumes that the meaning of the term "light" can be easily understood. For al-Ghazālī, in contrast, the true meaning of "light" contains a secret regarding the ambiguous status of man's existence. Al-Ghazālī links this particular understanding of man's relationship to God to problems of Qur'ānic interpretation both here and in his discussion in the *Iḥyāʾ ʿulūm al-dīn* of the meaning of the Qur'ānic verse *You did not throw when you threw but God threw* (8:17). The verse was revealed after the Battle of Badr and refers to a moment in the battle when the Prophet threw dust at the enemies of the Muslims.

> The external sense (*ẓāhir*) of this verse is clear but the truth of its meaning is obscure (*ghāmiḍ*) since it both affirms and negates the throwing. This is contradictory in the external sense unless one understands that he threw from one point of view and did not throw from another point of view, and from the point of view in which he did not throw God threw... The reality of this is taken from the vast ocean of the knowledges of unveiling (*ʿulūm al-mukāshafāt*). The external sense of the commentary will be of no use.[37]

The similitude of His/his light is as a niche

While the phrase *God is the light* was interpreted both metaphorically and literally, the phrase *the similitude of His/his light is as a niche* and the various elements of this niche was understood by all commentators as a metaphor, but a metaphor whose referents are ambiguous. Al-Rāzī lists ten different interpretations that can be grouped according to whether these words refer to God, Muḥammad, or the believer.[38] Although al-Rāzī includes interpretations from later commentators, all three referents can be found in the earliest interpretations transmitted from the Companions and the Followers. Al-Rāzī's preferred interpretation, as it was al-Ṭabarī's, is that the extended metaphor of the niche serves the purpose of describing a pure and perfect light, thereby describing, by analogy, the perfection of God's guidance. *His light* may also refer to the Qur'ān. Another interpretation suggests that the words mean Muḥammad, just as the Qur'ān 33:46 describes Muḥammad as *a light-giving lamp*. Muqātil (d. 767) is quoted as saying that it is a similitude for the light of faith in the heart of Muḥammad, so the *niche* is like the loins of 'Abd Allāh, Muḥammad's father; the *glass* the body of Muḥammad; and the *lamp* faith or prophecy in Muḥammad's heart. Or the *niche* can be compared to Ibrāhīm, the *glass* to Ismā'īl, the *lamp* to the body of Muḥammad, and the *tree* to prophecy and the message.

Whereas these interpretations identify the elements of the niche as referring to God's guidance or Muhammad, the other interpretations cited by al-Rāzī understand this part of the verse as referring to the believer. One interpretation suggests that the *light* is knowledge of God and the religious laws in the heart of the believer. The evidence for this interpretation is in Qur'ān 39:22, *Is he whose breast God has opened up to Islam so that he has a light from his Lord*... and verse 14:1, *in order that you might bring mankind out of the darkness into the light*. The interpretations of al-Ghazālī and Ibn Sīnā, which understand the *niche* as referring to the human perceptual faculties are summarized. Al-Rāzī then quotes a Ṣūfī interpretation which states that the *niche* is the breast, the *glass* is the heart, the *lamp* is knowledge, and the *blessed tree* is the angels and their inspirations which are *neither of the east nor west* because they are spiritual (*rūḥāniyya*). The oil from this tree *would well-nigh shine even if no fire touched it* because of the plentitude of their different types of knowledge and the powerfulness of their understanding of the secrets of the kingdom (*malakūt*) of God. Al-Rāzī adds critically, "It is obvious here that the thing compared (*mushabbah*) is not the thing compared therewith (*al-mushabbih bihi*)."[39]

Al-Rāzī does not explain why he finds this particular interpretation unacceptable. Al-Qurṭubī is clearer in his commentary that the issue is one of understanding the proper use of language. He states that metaphorical definitions of light are part of standard Arabic speech and gives examples of such from Arabic poetry to show that the statement *God is the light* refers to He who brings all things into existence, including light. He adds that the mistake of corporealists (*mujassima*) is that they follow the external sense of the verse and *aḥādīth* which seem to suggest that God *is* a light.[40] Metaphor, then, is part of the language of the Qur'ān. This does not mean, however, that words and expressions can be interpreted in ways that go beyond the metaphors that are a part of standard Arabic speech. Al-Qurṭubī quotes his teacher's critique of an interpretation of the elements of the *niche* similar to one of the interpretations al-Rāzī cites.

> Al-Qāḍī Abū Bakr b. al-'Arabī said: It is strange that there was a jurist who said that this is a similitude which God has struck for Ibrāhīm and Muḥammad, and for 'Abd al-Muṭṭalib and his son 'Abd Allāh...'Abd al-Muṭṭalib is likened to the *niche* in which there is a candle that is the *glass* that is like 'Abd Allāh. Muḥammad is like the *lamp*, meaning that he is from their loins, so that he is like *a glittering star* which is Jupiter.

> *Lit from a blessed tree* means the inheritance of prophecy from Ibrāhīm who is the *blessed tree*, meaning pure in faith (*ḥanifiyya*). *Neither of the east nor the west*, neither Jewish nor Christian. *Whose oil would well-nigh shine even if no fire touched it*. [The jurist] says, "Ibrāhīm would well nigh speak from revelation before it was revealed to him." *Light upon light*. Ibrāhīm then Muḥammad.
>
> Al-Qāḍī said: All of this is an abandonment of the obvious sense (*ẓāhir*) and nothing in the process of creating metaphors (*tamthīl*) prevents one from expanding it.[41]

Al-Qurṭubī's teacher is drawing attention to what he perceives to be the danger inherent in metaphors, their openness to endless interpretation. Yet he also states that metaphor in the Qur'ān is necessary because man can only understand that of which he already has some knowledge, namely himself and his world.

> This verse is a similitude which God has struck for His light. It is only possible to strike a similitude for His exalted light as an exhortation to His creation by some part of His creation, because men, due to their limitations, can only understand by means of themselves. If that were not so, no one would know God except He Himself.[42]

Still confusing here, however, is the definition of the boundaries of acceptable metaphorical interpretation. Ibn Taymiyya states that the use of analogy (*qiyās*) in interpretation is acceptable if the analogies produced are in agreement with other Qur'ānic verses, sound *ḥadīth*, and *salafī* interpretations. In his commentary on this passage of the Light Verse, he quotes a Ṣūfī interpretation which he deems acceptable.

> Among the sayings of the gnostics (*'ārifūn*) is that *the light* is that which illuminates the hearts of the sincere by its declaration of God's unity and illuminates the innermost hearts (*asrār*) of the lovers by its confirmation. It is said that it is that which enlivens the hearts of the gnostics by the light of its knowledge and the souls of the worshippers by the light of its worship.[43]
>
> This is the talk of some shaykhs who speak in a manner of admonition without verifying [what they say]. Shaykh Abū 'Abd al-Raḥmān in *Taḥqīq al-tafsīr*[44] mentions allusions (*ishārāt*), some of which provide useful lessons and some of which come from invalid or rejected transmitted material. The allusions of the Ṣūfī shaykhs can be divided into allusion by state (*ishāra ḥāliyya*), which are their allusions by means of hearts – and it is this by which they characterized – but this is not the case here; and allusions connected to teachings such as they take from the Qur'ān and the like. These allusions are in the category of consideration

> (*i'tibār*), analogy (*qiyās*), and appending that which is not in a text to that which is in the text (*ilḥā mā laysa bi-manṣūṣ bi 'l-manṣūṣ*). These are like the consideration and analogy that jurists use in legal judgements. But the Ṣūfī shaykhs use them for inspiration (*targhīb*) and warning (*tarhīb*), virtuous deeds and degrees of men, and things like that.[45] If the allusion is considerative (*i'tibāriyya*) by virtue of a sound type of analogy (*qiyās*), it is good and acceptable. If the analogy is weak, it is judged accordingly. If it is a distortion (*taḥrīf*) of the words beyond their [acceptable] interpretation, it is the type of sayings of the *qarāmiṭa*,[46] *bāṭiniyya* and *jahmiyya*.[47]

Ibn Taymiyya, then, finds metaphorical interpretations beyond those transmitted from the Companions and the Followers acceptable provided they can be verified as sound by the Qur'ān, *aḥādith* and *tafsīr* from the Companions and Followers, a process of verification he suggests the Ṣūfīs rarely do.

Ṣūfī interpretations of *the similitude of His/his light is as a niche*

Ibn Taymiyya identifies an important point here. Ṣūfī commentaries rarely refer directly to the commentaries of the Companions and Followers of the Prophet, but this fact should not be taken to mean that they were unaware or critical of them. One of the earliest recorded Ṣūfī interpretations on the Light Verse, attributed to Ja'far al-Ṣādiq, reflects and expands upon all the *salafī* interpretations of *the similitude of His/his light* in its detailing of a long list of the varied manifestations of God's light and the hierarchy of those who possess it: God, Muḥammad, and the believers.

> The lights are different. The first of them is the light of the protection of the heart, then the light of fear, then the light of hope, then the light of recollection, then vision by the light of knowledge, then the light of modesty, then the light of the sweetness of faith, then the light of Islam, then the light of doing beautiful acts (*iḥsān*), then the light of blessing, then the light of grace, then the light of benefits, then the light of generosity, then the light of affection, then the light of the heart, then the light of comprehension, then the light of awe, then the light of bewilderment, then the light of life, then the light of intimacy, then the light of uprightness, then the light of humility, then the light of tranquility, then the light of grandeur, then the light of majesty, then the light of power, then the light of might, then the light of divinity, then the light of oneness, then the light of singularity, then the light of eternity, then the light of endless time, then the light of eternity without beginning or end, then the light of permanence, then the light of sempiternity, then the light of subsistence (*baqā'*), then the light of universality, then the light of He-ness (*huwiyya*).

> Each of these lights has a people, a state (*ḥāl*) and a place (*maḥall*), and all of them are part of the lights of God (*al-ḥaqq*) that God has mentioned in his words, *God is the light of the heavens and the earth*. Each one of His servants is drinking from one of these lights and perhaps has a portion of two or three lights. These lights will not become complete for anyone except Muṣṭafa[48] because he stands with God by virtue of being rendered sound in servanthood and love. He is a light and is in a light from his Lord (*huwa nūr wa huwa min rabbihi ʿalā nūr*).[49]

The language in this interpretation can be compared to an interpretation of *the blessed olive tree neither of the east nor of the west* and *light upon light* related from the Companion Ubayy b. Kaʿb. Here, the believer is compared to a tree that receives just the right amount of light just as the believer is protected from life's vicissitudes by the strength which God gives him.

> He balances four characteristics: if he receives he is grateful; if he is afflicted he is patient; if he expresses an opinion he is fair; and if he speaks he is truthful. Among other men he is like a living man walking amidst the graves of the dead. *Light upon light*. He freely moves about in five different kinds of light. His speech is light, his action is light, his private affairs are a light, his public affairs[50] are a light, and his ultimate destination will be the light on the Day of Resurrection in the Garden.[51]

What distinguishes Ṣūfī commentaries, however, is not only their expanded use of the metaphor of light but also a seemingly literal way of understanding this light, as in al-Tustarī's description of the role of light in the creation of Muḥammad and the believers. In his commentary on the Light Verse, al-Tustarī suggests that *the similitude of His/his light* refers to Muḥammad. He also quotes al-Ḥasan al-Baṣrī as saying that what is meant is the heart of the believer. The creation of the lights of Muḥammad and the believers is described in al-Tustarī's comments on Qur'ānic verse 7:172, a verse which describes the primordial covenant between God and man.

> *When your Lord took from the children of Ādam their seed (dhuriyya) and caused them to bear witness concerning themselves, "Am I not your Lord?" They said, "Yes, we bear witness." That was so that you would say on the Day of Resurrection, "We ignored this."*

In his commentary on this verse, al-Tustarī describes three types of seeds representing future mankind. The first type of seed was Muḥammad who was created directly from God's light.

> God Most High, when he wished to create Muhammad (the blessings and peace of God upon him), manifested some of his light. When it attained the veil of majesty, it bowed down in prayer before Allah. Allah

> created from the position of prayer a great column like a glass of light, as both his interior and exterior. In it is the *'ayn* (very being, essence, source, eye) of Muhammad, God's blessings and peace upon him. He stood in service before the lord of the two worlds for one thousand years with the dispositions of faith, the beholding of faith, the unveiling of certitude, and the witness of the lord.[52]

The second type of seed was Ādam who was created from the light of Muḥammad. The third type of seed was mankind, the children of Ādam, who were created either from the light of Muḥammad or the light of Ādam. Those who are guides, who are desired (*murādūn*) were created from the light of Muḥammad, while those who are seekers (*murīdūn*) were created from the light of Ādam.[53] Mankind is created directly or indirectly from Muḥammad's light and will return to the divine light from which he was created.[54]

The lights of God interpreted as Muḥammad and the believers are also mentioned in the writings of al-Ḥallāj. In the first chapter of his *Kitāb al-ṭawāsīn*, al-Ḥallāj repeats many aspects of the theory of Muḥammad's light of al-Tustarī, who was his teacher for a brief period of time.[55] In the fragments recorded of al-Ḥallāj's Qur'ānic commentary, the focus is on light as representing the qualities of the believer.

> He compared the heart to a candle whose water is certainty and whose oil is patience and the sincerity which develops from it, and whose wick is trust in God and whose light is contentment. If it is characterized by this quality, the flavor of life can be found in its light.[56]
>
> God made submission (*islām*) a light for His people, and faith a light for His people, and assent (*taṣdīq*) a light in the heart of the believer. Knowledge (*'ilm*), intelligence (*'aql*) and insight (*baṣīra*) are lights. All of the moral traits (*akhlāq*) of the believers are lights. All of the acts of worship are lights and the nearness of the servants to God is in proportion with their lights.[57]

God is both "the light of light" (*nūr al-nūr*)[58] and "the illuminator (*munawwir*) of your hearts until you come to know and find (*wajadtum*)."[59] At this point the believer becomes full of light.

> In the head is the light of revelation (*waḥy*) and in the two eyes is the light of intimate dialogue with God, and in the ears is the light of certainty, and in the tongue is the light of clarity, and in the breast is the light of faith, and in the humours of the body (*ṭabā'i'*) is the light of glorifying God. When something catches fire from these lights it overwhelms the other light and incorporates it into its authority. When it has subsided the authority of that light returns and you are increased by what happened. When everything catches fire, it becomes *light upon light. God guides whom He wills to His light.*[60]

Another distinctive element of these early Ṣūfī interpretations of the Light Verse is the comparison made between the macrocosm of the universe and the microcosm of man, a type of analogical thinking which becomes even more pervasive in the later commentaries of al-Kāshānī and al-Nīsābūrī. Ibn ʿAṭāʾ, al-Ḥallāj's contemporary, explains what it is that God illuminates in *the heavens and the earth.*

> God adorned (*zayyana*) the heavens with the twelve signs of the zodiac, and they are the Ram, the Bull, the Twins, the Crab, the Lion, the Ears of Corn (Virgo), the Scales, the Scorpion, the Archer, the Sea Goat, the Water Bearer, and the Fish. He adorned the hearts of the believers with twelve characteristics: the mind, attention, explanation, intelligence, knowledge, certainty, understanding, insight, the life of the heart, hope, fear and life. As long as these signs of the zodiac exist the world will be in order and abundance. Similarly, as long as these characteristics exist in the heart of the Gnostic (*ʿārif*), there will be the light of the gnostic and the sweetness of worship.[61]

Al-Wasītī shows how the microcosm, man, is illuminated directly by God.

> God created the spirits (*arwāḥ*) before the bodies (*ajsād*). He illuminated them by His attributes (*ṣifāt*) and addressed them by means of His essence (*dhāt*), so they are illuminated and receive light by means of the light of His sanctity (*qudus*). He told of it in His words *God is the light of the heavens and the earth* because He is the illuminator (*munawwir*) of the spirits (*arwāḥ*) by the perfection of His light.[62]

The interrelationship between the corporeal (*jismānī*) and the spiritual (*rūḥānī*) forms the basis of the cosmology and hermeneutical theory that al-Ghazālī develops in his *Mishkāt al-anwār*. As discussed in Part I of this work, the theory states that what exists in one world serves as a similitude for what exists in the other and that the similitudes of the Qurʾān can be understood by understanding the relationship between these two worlds. Al-Ghazālī gives many examples of this, one of the most significant being that of man. Man was created "in the form of the Merciful," an allusion to a *ḥadīth* which al-Ghazālī understands as referring to man as a microcosm of the universe.

> God showed beneficience to Adam. He gave him an abridged form (*ṣūrat mukhtaṣar*) that brings together every sort of things found in the cosmos. It is as if Adam is everything in the cosmos, or an abridged transcription (*nuskha mukhtaṣar*) of the world.[63]

The *Mishkāt al-anwār* is divided into three parts. The first part is the discussion of the mystery of understanding *God is the light of the heavens and the earth.* The second part describes the two elements necessary for this understanding.

One of them is the hermeneutical theory of using similitudes which we have already discussed. The other is the structure of man himself and the relationship between the corporeal and spiritual worlds within him. This is described, according to al-Ghazālī, in the similitude of the elements of the niche, which represent the layers (*ṭabaqāt*) of the spirits (*arwāḥ*) of the human clay (*al-ṭīnat al-bashariyya*) and the degrees (*marātib*) of their lights.[64] Unlike most Ṣūfī commentators, Al-Ghazālī is careful to link his interpretation to *salafī* interpretations, in this case those of Ibn Mas'ūd, whom he quotes as saying, "*the similitude of his/His light* in the heart of the believers is like *a niche*," and Ubayy b. Ka'b, whom he quotes as saying, "*the similitude of* a light in the heart of one who has faith."[65]

According to al-Ghazālī, the first of the "luminous human spirits" (*al-arwāḥ al-bashariyya al-nūrāniyya*) is the sensory spirit (*al-rūḥ al-ḥassās*) which is found in animals and infants. It is like the niche because its lights come out of the different openings of the body such as the two eyes, ears, and nostrils, etc. The second is the imaginal spirit (*al-rūḥ al-khayālī*) which is capable of remembering and is found in older children, adults, and some animals. It is like glass, a dense substance which can be purified to channel light. The third is the rational spirit (*al-rūḥ al-'aqlī*) which comprehends meanings outside of the senses and imagination and is found only in human beings. It is like the lamp. The fourth is the reflective spirit (*al-rūḥ al-fikrī*) which combines part of the rational knowledge to derive a higher form of knowledge. It is like the tree because it begins from this root and then branches out. The fifth is the sanctified prophetic spirit (*al-rūḥ al-qudsī al-nabawī*) which belongs only to the prophets and some friends of God (*awliyā'*) and is beyond the intellect (*'aql*). It is the *oil which would well-nigh shine even if no fire touched it* because there are those among the friends of God who could almost do without the help of the prophets, and there are prophets who could almost do without the help of the angels.[66]

The third part of the *Mishkāt al-anwār* applies al-Ghazālī's understanding of the Light Verse to classify different types of people, by means of an interpretation of the *ḥadith* "God has seventy veils of light and darkness. If He were to unveil them, the glories of His face would burn up everyone whose eyes perceived Him." The third part synthesizes the points made in the first two parts by demonstrating how the perceptions of the lower spirits of man lead to faulty conclusions regarding the nature of God. Al-Ghazālī defines three kinds of people who are veiled from the truth in various ways.

To summarize his categories briefly, the first type are atheists (*mulḥida*) veiled by darkness; they include materialists and egotists, the latter being further subdivided into hedonists, predators, materialistic people, and status seekers.

The second type are those people who are veiled by light and darkness. Their veils correspond to the levels of the spirit that al-Ghazālī has described as the elements of the *niche*. Some of them are veiled by sensory darkness, meaning that they can only understand God as an object perceived by the senses. The objects which they perceive as divinities range from precious substances such as gold or silver, to beautiful human beings, to fire, the stars or the sun, or unlimited light.

More advanced than those are individuals veiled by imaginal darkness, who can only understand God as an imagined being sitting on a throne, having a body, existing in a certain place, etc. Finally, there are those who are veiled by the darkness of faulty rational comparisons who can only understand God in relation to their own attributes.[67]

The third type are those veiled by lights.[68] Among these are those who understand that God's attributes cannot be compared to those of humans. More advanced would be those who recognize God as the Mover (*muḥarrik*) of the furthest celestial sphere which envelops the lower celestial spheres moved by angels. Most advanced are those who recognize that the "Mover" must still only be an angel obeying the Lord who "is a mover of everything by means of command (*'amr*), not direct contact."[69] Those who have arrived (*wāṣilūn*) have found God to be beyond any of these descriptions. Like Ibrāhīm, they recognize that all their previous understandings of God are faulty.

> Therefore, they have turned their faces from the one who moves the heavens, from the one who moves the furthest celestial body, from the one who commands moving them, to Him who originates the heavens, originates the furthest celestial body, and originates the one who commands moving the heavens. They have arrived at an existent thing that is incomparable with everything that their sight had perceived. Hence, the august glories of His face – the First, the Highest – burn up everything perceived by the sights and insights of the observers. Thus, they find Him too holy for and incomparable with all that we described earlier.[70]

Some who reach this stage remain as perceivers and yet what they perceive completely disappears. Others, the elect of the elect (*khawāṣṣ al-khawāṣṣ*), cease to observe themselves as well; in other words, the perceiver himself disappears, as in *Everything is being annihilated except His face* (28:88).[71] This self-disclosure of God (*tajallī*) occurs in stages for some, as was the case with Ibrāhīm, and for others all at once, as was the case with Muḥammad.[72]

Al-Ghazālī's interpretation of the *niche* was clearly influenced by Ibn Sīnā's interpretation in *Al-Ishārāt wa'l-tanbīhāt*,[73] but while the similarities between the two interpretations are undeniable, al-Ghazāli makes significant modifications. While the five elements described in Ibn Sīnā's version are all parts of the intellect (*'aql*) which only man possesses, al-Ghazālī's version calls the faculties "spirit" (*rūḥ*) which opens up the metaphor to include all types of perception, even those shared with animals.[74] This change enables al-Ghazālī to classify faulty notions of God based on whether the possessor of those beliefs is bound by the limitations of animal or human perceptions.

Al-Kāshānī's interpretation of the Light Verse suggests a familiarity with the interpretations of both al-Ghazālī and Ibn Sīnā. He explains the elements of the niche as the integrated physical and spiritual elements of man which combine to enable him to achieve perfection. The *niche* represents the dark body (*jasad*) which is illuminated by the *lamp* of the spirit (*rūḥ*). The *glass* represents the heart which is both illuminated by the spirit and illuminates things other than itself.

> The *glass* is likened to *a glittering star* because of its openness, its extreme luminosity, its high position, and the plenitude of its rays, as this is the state (*ḥāl*) of the heart (*qalb*).[75]

The *glass* of the heart is *lit from a blessed olive tree* which is the sanctified soul (*al-nafs al-qudsiyya*) whose faculties grow up out of the earth of the body through the space of the heart to the heaven of the spirit. Its fruits are morals, works, and perceptions. Every kind of mystic knowledge and states are dependent upon it. It is *neither of the east nor the west* because "the soul is more subtle and luminous than the body and more dense than the spirit." Its *oil* is preparedness (*istiʿdād*) which *would well-nigh shine even if no fire*, the Active Intelligence (*al-ʿaql al-faʿʿāl*) *touched it.*[76]

Al-Nīsābūrī's commentary on the niche is interesting in that it gives two different levels of interpretation, one of which corresponds to the "world of horizons" and the other of which corresponds to the "world of souls."[77] The first interpretation refers to the macrocosm, the Cosmos.

> The *niche* is the world of bodies (*ajsām*). The *glass* is the Throne, the *lamp* is the Footstool, and the tree is the Tree of the Kingdom (*malakūt*) which is the inward part (*bāṭin*) of the world of bodies. It rises neither to the east of eternity and timelessness nor to the west of annihilation (*fanāʾ*) and nonexistence. Rather it is created for the everlastingness in which annihilation never occurs.
>
> *Whose oil*, which is the world of spirits (*arwāḥ*), *would well-nigh shine*, i.e., become manifest from nonexistence into the world of engendered form (*ʿālam al-ṣūrat al-mutawallida*) by means of the pairing (*iztidwāj*) of the world of the unseen with [the world] of witnessing *even if no fire*, the fire of the divine power, *touched it* and that is because of the nearness of its character to existence.
>
> *Light upon light*. The first is the light of the merciful attribute and the second is the light of the Throne, as in His saying, *The Merciful sat upon the throne* (20:5). His words, *God guides whom He wills to his/His light* is an allusion (*ishāra*) to the fact that the emanation (*fayḍ*) of the light of mercifulness is divided amongst everything which God wills to bring into existence from the Throne to that which is under the earth.[78]

The second interpretation refers to the microcosm, man. Like his predecessors, al-Nīsābūrī understands the different elements of the niche as referring to the various faculties of man which must be developed in order to achieve perfection, a state in which man realizes the nature of the mysterious relationship between God and man. While a significant portion of the *Mishkāt al-anwār* is devoted to the explanation of this concept, al-Nīsābūrī merely alludes to it through the famous *ḥadīth* of supererogatory acts, a *ḥadīth* understood by Ṣūfīs as referring to the states of annihilation (*fanā'*) and subsistence (*baqā'*).[79]

> The *niche* is the body, the *glass* is the heart, the *lamp* is the innermost heart (*sirr*), and the *tree* is the tree of spirituality (*al-rūḥāniyya*) which has been created for subsistence (*baqā'*) as has been described.[80] The *oil* is the human spirit (*al-rūḥ al-insāniyya*) which is profoundly receptive to the light of gnosis (*'irfān*) and the *fire* is the fire of God's self-disclosure (*tajallī*) and guidance in eternity. When it is combined with the light of the intellect (*'aql*) it becomes *light upon light*. When the *lamp* of the innermost heart (*sirr*) of *whom He wills* becomes illuminated by the light of timelessness, the *glass* of the heart and the *niche* of the body become illuminated. Their rays emerge from the aperture of the physical senses (*ḥawāss*) and the earth of humanity (*al-bashariyya*) is illuminated, just as He said, *the earth will shine with the light of its Lord* (39:69). This is the station (*maqām*) of the *ḥadith*, "I am his hearing, his seeing..."[81]

Al-Nīsābūrī's interpretation seems to suggest that, having experienced annihilation (*fanā'*) and subsistence (*baqā'*), the perfected man is both illuminated by the light he receives through the fire of God's self-disclosure (*tajallī*) and in turn illuminates others by this light which emerges from the "aperture of the physical senses (*ḥawāss*)."

In the interpretations of Ibn Sīnā, al-Ghazālī, al-Kāshānī and al-Nīsābūrī, each and every element of the Qur'ānic verse is explained by a single term. The similarities and differences in the resulting interpretations can be seen in Table 9.1. Another approach seen in Ṣūfī interpretations of the Light Verse has more in common with that of the interpretation of Ja'far al-Ṣādiq previously quoted. Here, the words open up to larger meanings rather than one-to-one correspondences and often refer to states in the believer. The believer is both created from light and engaged in an ongoing process of receiving light. To reach the higher states of *light upon light* the believer must be determined in his resolve to avoid man's natural tendency towards laziness, to allow himself to respond to the different states through which he travels, using the tension within and between them to motivate himself to continue in his exertions. This is how the phrase *neither of the east nor the west* was understood by Ja'far al-Ṣādiq:

> Neither the fear which imposes despair nor the hope which brings about delight. One should stand between fear and hope.[82]

Al-Qushayrī writes,

> The allusion (*ishāra*) in it is to the fact that the fear in their hearts should not be separate from the hope so that one would come close to despair. Neither should their hope be separate from fear so that one would come close to complacence. Rather the two should be balanced so that one

Table 9.1 A comparison of interpretations of the elements of the niche in the Light Verse (Qurʾān 24:35)

	Ibn Sīnā	*Al-Ghazālī*	*Al-Kāshānī*	*Al-Nīsābūrī*	
				Macrocosm	*Microcosm*
niche	material intellect (*ʿaql hayūliyya*)	sensory spirit (*rūḥ ḥassās*)	Body (*jasad*)	world of bodies (*ajsām*)	Body (*jasad*)
glass	habitual intellect (*ʿaql bi'l-malaka*)	imaginal spirit (*rūḥ khayālī*)	heart (*qalb*)	the throne	heart (*qalb*)
lamp	actual intellect (*ʿaql bi'l-fiʿl*)	rational spirit (*rūḥ ʿaqlī*)	Spirit (*rūḥ*)	the footstool	innermost heart (*sirr*)
tree	Contemplation (*fikra*)	reflective spirit (*rūḥ fikrī*)	holy soul (*nafs qudsiyya*)	the tree of the kingdom (*malakūt*)	the tree of spirituality (*rūḥāniyya*)
oil	Conjecture (*ḥads*)	holy spirit (*rūḥ qudsī*)	Preparedness (*istiʿdād*)	world of spirits (*arwāḥ*)	human spirit (*rūḥ insāniyya*)
fire	Active Intellect (*ʿaql faʿʿāl*)	(not specified)	Active Intellect (*ʿaql faʿʿāl*)	divine power (*qudra ilāhiyya*)	God's self-disclosure (*tajallī*)

> does not prevail over the other. Their awe (*hayba*) should come together with their intimacy (*uns*), their contracted state (*qabḍ*) with their expanded state (*basṭ*), their consciousness (*ṣaḥw*) with their effacement (*maḥw*), their subsistence (*baqā'*) with their annihilation (*fanā'*), their performance of the courtesies (*ādāb*) of the religious law with their realization of the all-comprehensive reality (*jawām'i'l-ḥaqīqa*).[83]

The believer's states are part of a dynamic process which combines both the believer's efforts and God's grace. *Light upon light* appears to him in his different states until he reaches a stage where words can no longer describe what has been unveiled to him. Al-Qushayrī is usually thought of as a moderate Ṣūfī, but what he describes at the end of this passage appears to hint at something like the concept of the unity of God as interpreted in al-Ghazālī's *Mishkāt al-anwār*.

> It is said that the effect of the light of the heart is the continuance of a state of agitation which does not allow one to remain lazy. One comes to his journey by the use of his reflection (*fikr*) and God nourishes him by the light of the success He grants until none of the obstacles to spiritual effort (*ijtihād*) can hold him back, neither love of leadership, nor the inclination to evil, nor indulgence. When the truth of one's forgetfulness is disclosed and vision takes hold of his situation, knowledge will be most certainly obtained. Then he will continue to increase in certainty (*yaqīn*) upon certainty based on what he sees in the interaction of contraction (*qabḍ*) and expansion (*basṭ*). The reward and compensation is in the increase of unveiling (*kashf*) upon the increase in effort and the obtainment of ecstasy (*wajd*) when performing the litany (*wird*).
>
> Then after it there is the light of interaction (*mu'āmala*), then the light of the mutual waystation (*munāzala*), and the broad daylight of the connection (*muwāṣala*). The suns of the declaration of unity (*tawḥīd*) shine and there are no clouds in the sky of their secrets and no fog in its air. God said, *light upon light, God guides whom He wills to His light.*
>
> It is said that the light of appeal (*muṭālaba*) appears in the heart and prompts its owner to settle his account. When he has seen his record and his prior disobedience, the light of examination (*mu'āyana*) comes to him and he reverts to blaming himself and drinks cups of remorse. Then he rises up from this by persistence in his goal and purification from what remained with him from the times of his lassitude. When he has become upright in that which was revealed by the light of observation (*murāqaba*), then he knows that God watches over him. After this is the light of beholding (*muḥāḍara*) which are flashes (*lawā'iḥ*) that appear in the innermost hearts (*sarā'ir*). Then after that is the light of unveiling (*mukāshafa*) and that is by means of the self-disclosure (*tajallī*) of the attributes (*ṣifāt*). Then after it is the light of witnessing (*mushāhada*) and his night becomes day, his stars moons, and his moons full moons, and his full moons suns.

> Then after this are the lights of the declaration of oneness (*tawḥīd*) and at the same time disengagement (*tajrīd*) is realized by the qualities of single-mindedness (*tafrīd*). Then no expression (*'ibāra*) can encompass it and no allusion (*ishāra*) can comprehend it. Explanations at that point become silent, evidence is effaced and the witnessing of another is absurd. This is the point *when the sun will be wrapped up, when the stars will become dull, when the mountains will be set moving, and when the pregnant camels will be neglected* (81:4) and *when the heavens will be split asunder* (84:1) and *split open* (82:1). All of these are different parts of the universe and that which was from nonexistence in them will end up in nonexistence. That which subsists through them is other than them and that which exists through them is other than them. Unity (*aḥadiyya*) is exalted, everlastingness is sublime, perpetuity (*daymūmiyya*) is sanctified, and the divinity is unblemished.[84]

Al-Qushayrī breaks through the common understanding of the metaphor of light here by focusing on its qualities of energy and movement. Rather than accepting the simple equivalence of light as guidance, he gives us the unusual image of light as something agitating to the heart. What al-Qushayrī is talking about becomes less clear as he moves from the heart to the innermost secret (*sirr*, pl. *sarā'ir)* and he gives up on language entirely when it comes to the state of annihilation.

Al-Maybudī's commentary also recalls the interpretation of Ja'far al-Ṣādiq, in his comments on the lights of Muḥammad and the believer.

> Know that the inner lights are different in their respective degrees. The first is the light of submission (*islām*) and with the submission is the light of sincerity. Another light is faith (*imān*) and with faith is the light of truthfulness. Another light is doing beautiful acts (*iḥsān*) and with doing beautiful acts is the light of certainty. The splendor of submission is in the light of sincerity and the splendor of faith is in the light of truthfulness and the splendor of doing beautiful acts is in the light of certainty. These are waystations (*manāzil*) on the path of the religious law and stations (*maqāmāt*) of the general believers. There is another light and state (*ḥāl*) as well for the people of truth (*ahl al-ḥaqīqat*) and the brave youths (*javān-mardān*) of the way, the light of perspicacity (*firāsat*) and with perspicacity is the light of unveiling (*mukāshifat*). There is also the light of uprightness and the light of witnessing (*mushāhadat*). There is also the light of declaring God's unity (*tawḥīd*) and with declaring God's unity there is the light of nearness (*qurbat*) in the presence of "withness" (*'indiyyat*).
>
> Until the servant has been in these stations, he will be captive to his own way. From here the allurement of God (*ḥaqq*) begins again, a divine attraction (*jadhba*) which unites and connects the lights, the light of grandeur, the light of majesty, the light of subtlety, the light of beauty,

the light of awe, the light of jealousy, the light of nearness, the light of divinity, and the light of he-ness (*huwiyyat*). These are those of which the Lord of the Worlds said, *light upon light*.

The situation reaches the point where servanthood (*'ubūdiyyat*) becomes invisible in the light of lordship (*rubūbiyyat*). In all the world these lights have only reached perfection and nearness to the possessor of majesty in the Arab Muṣṭafā. Everyone has a part of these but he has the whole because he is entirely perfect, the totality of beauty and the *qibla* of virtues.[85]

The similitude of his light. One group of commentators has said that the pronoun "his" refers to Muṣṭafā, since his character was light, his robe of honor light, his lineage light, his birth light, his witnessing light, his interactions light, and his miracle light. He himself was in his own essence *light upon light*. His superiority was such that in his face was the light of mercy, in his eyes the light of admonition, in his speech the light of wisdom, in the space between his shoulders the light of prophecy, in his palms the light of munificence, in his feet the light of service, in his hair the light of beauty, in his disposition the light of humility, in his breast the light of contentment, in his secret the light of purity, in his essence the light of obedience, in his obedience the light of declaring the unity of God (*tawḥīd*), in his declaring the unity of God the light of realization (*taḥqīq*), in his realization the light of God's good fortune (*tawfīq*), in his silence the light of exaltation, in his exaltation the light of declaring surrender (*taslīm*). A poem:

A sword of Indian steel drawn from amongst the swords of God.[86]

Al-Maybudī combines this style of interpretation with the relating of *aḥādīth* and traditions from the Companions and the Followers of the Prophet which illustrate the light possessed by believers. More so than any of the other commentators studied here, al-Maybudī uses and develops the literary quality of this material. The first *ḥadīth* he cites is an appealing anecdote from the Prophet concerning the superior light of those believers who have suffered the most.

It is related that Abū Sa'īd al-Khudrī[87] said: I was among a group of poor emigrants, some of whom were veiling others from their nakedness. We were listening to the recitation of the Qur'ān. The Prophet came up and stood over us. The reciter saw him and became silent. He greeted him, saying, "What are you doing?" We said, "O Messenger of God, the reciter is reciting to us and we are listening to his recitation." The Messenger of God said, "Praise be to God who has made those in my community towards whom I have been commanded to make myself patient." Then he sat down amidst us in order to occupy himself with us... The faces [of the poor emigrants] became illuminated... The Prophet said, "Rejoice you who have nothing! You will enter the garden in perfect light before the wealthy believers by half of a day whose reckoning will be five hundred years."[88]

The next *ḥadīth* which al-Maybudī cites is, "God created His creation in darkness, then cast some of His light upon them."[89] Al-Maybudī expands the imagery of the *ḥadīth* and links the primordial event it describes to the possibility of states in the believer in this world.

> The similitude of this light is such that Muṣṭafā has said, "God created the creation in darkness then sprinkled upon them some of His light." Mankind was a handful of dust remaining in their own darkness, a darkness whose quality had become bewilderment, remaining unaware in the veil of creation. Everything in the pre-eternal heavens received the rain of the lights of eternity. The dust became narcissus, the stone became the jewel, the color of the heavens and the earth followed in each other's footsteps. It is said that the quality of "dustness" is everything which is darkness but a quality is everything which should be bright and pure. A subtle substance (*laṭīfa*) became joined to that quality, and the expression for that subtle substance is found in "He sprinkled upon them some of His light." They asked, "O Messenger of God, what are the signs of this light?"[90] He said, When the light is made to enter the heart, the breast expands." When the standard of the just sultan enters the city, no seat remains for the crowd. When the breast becomes open with the divine light, the aspiration (*himma*) becomes high, the sad becomes tranquil, and the enemy the friend. Dispersion becomes union (*jam'*) in the heart, the carpet of subsistence (*baqā'*) is spread out while the mat of annihilation (*fanā'*) is rolled up, and the cloister of the anxiety is bolted while the garden of union (*wiṣāl*) is opened.[91]

Al-Maybudī's last illustration is a long story which he says is taken from the traditions concerning an unnamed scholar among the Followers of the Prophet. The scholar had been captured while participating in one of the military campaigns against the Roman army and remained among the Romans for some time. One day he was present with some 30,000 Romans who had gathered in the desert to hear a bishop who came out of his monastery once every four years to give advice to the people. The bishop ascended the pulpit but stood there without speaking. Finally he told his audience that he was unable to speak to them because of the Muslim amongst them. The people did not know who this was and the Muslim was afraid to identify himself, but the bishop was able to find him by looking closely into the faces of the people. He asked him to come and speak with him.

> [The narrator of this tale said]: He said to me, "You are a Muslim?"
>
> I said, "Yes, I am a Muslim."
>
> He said, "Are you among those who are knowledgeable or ignorant?"
>
> I said, "Regarding that which I know I am knowledgeable and that which I do not know I am a student. I am not one of the ignorant."

He said, "I have three questions I would like to ask you and have you answer."

I said, "I will give you the answers on the condition that you tell me how you recognized me and on the condition that I may ask you three questions." The two made a pact and a promise.

[The narrator continued.] Then the bishop put his mouth to my ear and softly whispered in a voice hidden from the Romans, "I knew you by the light of your faith. I recognized the light of faith and unity in you which shone from your face." Then in a loud voice he questioned me. "Your messenger has said to you that Paradise is a tree of which every lofty chamber is a branch. What is the similitude of that in the world?"

I said, "The similitude of that tree in the world is the sun, with an orb every ray of which is a branch."

The bishop said, "You have spoken truly." He asked the second question: "Your messenger said that the people of Paradise consume food and drink but no defilement comes out of them. What is the similitude of that in the world?"

I said, "The embryo in the womb of its mother who eats but does not defecate."

The bishop said, "You have spoken truly." He asked the third question. "The messenger of God said that on the Day of Resurrection every morsel, atom and grain of alms will be like a great mountain on the Scales. What is the similitude of that in the world?"

I said, "When the sun rises at daybreak or sets in the evening it causes the ruins of a house which is in reality short to appear tall."

The bishop said, "You have spoken truly."

Then the Muslim asked him, "What is the number of the doors of the Gardens?"

He said, "Eight."

He said, "What are the numbers of the doors of Hell?"

He said, "Seven."

He said, "What is it that is written on the door of the Garden?"

The Muslim said that when he asked this of him, the bishop was unable to give an answer. The Romans called out to him to give an answer so that this stranger would not say that the bishop did not know. The bishop said, "If this answer is forced, it will not bode well for the belt (*zunnār*)[92] and the cross." He tore open his belt and threw down his cross and said in a loud voice, "It is written on the door of the Garden that there is no God but God and Muḥammad is the messenger of God!"[93]

When the Romans heard this they began to throw rocks and insults at the bishop. The bishop wept and called out to tell the people that 700 angels were coming to carry 700 martyrs to their deaths, and it did come to pass that 700 Romans joined the bishop that day in becoming Muslims and were killed by their fellow Romans. Al-Maybudī tells us that

> the point of this tale is that the light of one believer who declared the unity of God shone amongst the handful of fighters and infidels so that the bishop saw and did what he did.[94]

In this story the inner light of the believer is not merely a metaphor for faith, but a perceptible light which can be seen, at least by some.

What unites the very different styles of the Ṣūfī commentaries cited here is the way in which they avoid using the word "light" in this Qur'ānic verse as a simple metaphor for "guidance" or something similar. The issue, as Izutsu explains in an article on metaphorical thinking in Iranian Ṣūfism, has to do with the relationship between language and one's understanding of reality. Aristotle defines metaphor in his *Poetics* as a linguistic sign functioning in a dual role by pointing simultaneously to a literal or conventional meaning and to another figurative meaning or non-conventional. Izutsu suggests that this is a problematic definition for Ṣūfīs because, for them, what would ordinarily be the figurative meaning is, in fact, the more literal or "real" meaning and correspondingly, the conventional meaning is the more figurative. He is not saying that Ṣūfīs never use metaphors in the Aristotelian sense of the term, but he distinguishes these from what he calls "archetypal metaphors" like light and darkness. Archetypal metaphors are not artificially or artistically created but rather are the result of mystic experience. When the mystic experiences spiritual light, he is not perceiving something similar to light, but rather sees a light far more powerful and "real" than physical light. The mystic does not choose a metaphor to describe his visionary experience; the metaphor or symbol does not point to something other than itself but rather is an indicator of its own self and the mystic has merely perceived this reality. Seen from the outside, the mystic's description of this reality appears to be a metaphor, but this is only because the observer has not grasped the true nature of things.[95]

The use of the word "light" in the manner described by Izutsu does seem to occur in many of the Ṣūfī interpretations cited here. However, the interpretations are best characterized as expressing more than one type of language use, by both an acceptance and elaboration of the meaning of "light" as "guidance" and a description of another, more literal, meaning similar to the Prophet's statement, "I see a light." The acceptance of interpretations based on this literal understanding of "light" will depend on the reader's acceptance or rejection of subjective mystical experience.

CONCLUSION

Although the styles of the Ṣūfī commentaries studied here are quite different, there is a shared hermeneutical base of assumptions concerning the nature of the Qurʾānic text, the way in which knowledge of its meanings is acquired, and the nature of the self who seeks understanding. The first of these assumptions is that the Qurʾān is a multi-layered and ambiguous text open to endless interpretation, a concept most frequently illustrated by the metaphor of the ocean and its treasures. However, this insistence upon the infinite possibilities of the text is not considered license justifying the production of any and all interpretations. The fact that the ocean can be a dangerous place corresponds, in this metaphor, to the dangers that Ṣūfīs identify in attempting to understand God's words. Al-Ghazālī, as we have seen, suggests that those who are not good swimmers should not even try. Al-Simnānī's use of the *ḥadīth* prohibiting interpretation by mere personal opinion (*raʾy*) locates the possibility for error at each level of interpretation.

The problem that open-ended interpretation presents is seen as both spiritual and political by Ṣūfīs in that it comprises both a fundamental danger to one's eternal soul and a more immediate danger in this world from other Muslims who consider Ṣūfī interpretations as a distortion of the true meanings of the Qurʾānic text. Al-Ghazālī's defense of Ṣūfī interpretation in his *Fayṣal al-tafriqa* is an attempt to protect Ṣufīs from the serious legal reprisals connected to the charge of disbelief (*takfīr*). The weaknesses of his arguments in this book result from the fact that he attempts to rebut his opponents on their own terms rather than questioning their basic assumptions. His strongest argument, found in the *Iḥyāʾ ʿulūm al-dīn*, is the simplest, namely that restricting the meaning of the Qurʾān to what has been transmitted from the Companions and Followers amounts to an unacceptable restriction of the Qurʾān's potentiality. Although most obvious in al-Ghazālī, the political tension that Ṣūfī interpretations created is apparent in other writings studied here as well, in the use of the terms "common people" (*ʿawāmm*) and "elite" (*khawāṣṣ*), a somewhat defensive dichotomy reflecting judgment on if not outright disdain for those who disagree with Ṣūfī concepts and methodology. The references to the Ibn Masʿūd *ḥadīth* and the traditions from ʿAlī and Jaʿfar al-Ṣādiq serve to legitimize the Ṣūfī approach by showing its conformity with the views of the Companions and Followers.

The second shared assumption of Ṣūfī interpretation concerns knowledge which is obtained by means other than the study of the transmitted interpretive tradition and rational thought. According to Ibn Taymiyya, the weakness of Ṣūfī interpretation is its reliance on subjective knowledge[1] and consequent vulnerability to error. Ibn Taymiyya's insistence on the importance of referring all interpretations to the Qur'ān and the words of the Prophet and his Companions and Followers is not so much a rejection of all knowledge by interior experience – although he does reject the validity of ecstatic states – but a rejection of the privileging of that experience over other, more public forms of knowledge. In contrast, the Ṣūfīs studied here use the language and discourse of the more publicly debatable areas of philosophy, theology, and the transmitted tradition, but always with the underlying assumption that knowledge of the deeper meanings of the Qur'ān is an essentially private experience. Unlike the revelations sent to the prophets, the knowledge which comes to individuals directly from God (*'ilm ladunī*) is not necessarily beneficial to disclose, a fact illustrated in the story of Mūsā and al-Khaḍir: Al-Khaḍir refuses to explain himself to Mūsā until they part. The communication between the two, which in Ṣūfī interpretations is understood as suggestive of the master–disciple relationship, is oral and private rather than written and public. In his comments on the Qur'ān 3:7, al-Qushayrī states that those who receive knowledge of the deeper meanings of the Qur'ān say what they have been commanded to say and, likewise, keep silent when commanded to do so.

The third assumption upon which Ṣūfī interpretation rests concerns the nature of the self seeking understanding of the meanings of the Qur'ān. Interpretation based on interior experience is ever changing because the self is in constant flux as it moves through different states and stations. In his interpretation of *light upon light*, al-Qushayrī describes the heart as agitated by light; knowledge is received by means of a series of interactions between the guidance sent to the self and the efforts it sends out. The subjectivity of the states and stations the self moves through make them unverifiable to anyone other than the individual experiencing them, paving the way to criticisms such as that of Ibn al-Jawzī who dismisses these states altogether as "a delirium without any basis."[2] The problem of outside verification of the knowledge obtained by means of states is acknowledged by the Ṣūfīs as well; while acknowledging the reality of these states generally they also acknowledge the possibility of individual delusion and error. Qur'ānic interpretations based on experience are problematic because they may be misunderstood by those who have not experienced a similar state, as well as by the interpreter himself if he misunderstands the nature of his own experience.

In order to see things as they truly are, the attitude of the self and the efforts it makes are as important as the states it experiences. Mūsā's long and tiring journey searching for the wise man al-Khaḍir and the frustration and confusion he experiences being with him is repeatedly referred to in Ṣūfī commentaries as a journey of discipline, of learning proper behavior (*ta'dīb*). As al-Ghazālī explains in his *Jawāhir al-Qur'ān*, it is arrogance to think that knowledge of the Qur'ān's deeper meanings can come without intense and persistent spiritual disciplines and efforts. In addition to the toil of the journey, there is a further demand placed on Mūsā, himself a prophet, of unquestioning acceptance of al-Khaḍir's bizarre and troubling actions, a requirement he is unable to fulfill. Maryam's story, on the other hand, represents the self who does possess the necessary attitude of complete and utter subservience towards God and His will, an attitude which in turn frees her from concern for anything else. The most important and difficult kind of knowledge to obtain, then, for the Ṣūfīs is a kind of knowledge that comes not from the strivings of the intellect but, rather, as the result of God's grace and a deeper kind of struggle within man. In his *Kitāb al-luma*ʿ Abū Naṣr al-Sarrāj characterizes this struggle in a corporeal way as the sacrifice of one's very lifeblood.

While the hermeneutics of these works is similar, the language and methods of discourse used are very different. Allegoresis is the most controversial type of Ṣūfī interpretation because it appears to abandon the obvious sense of Qurʾānic verses. The strictures against abandoning the obvious sense are behind al-Ghazālī's various attempts to justify and define acceptable interpretation, and to explain the theory of correspondences between the spiritual and the material world, and between the macrocosm of the universe and the microcosm of man. The method seems artificial when it consists of lists of these equivalences but substantive when the correspondences are more fully described and developed.

This kind of allegoresis, or finding correspondences (*taṭbīq*) as al-Kāshānī calls it, is different from symbolic Ṣūfī interpretations which arise from and remain with the tangible imagery and narratives of the Qurʾān. Here, the sensorial and emotional aspects of the text are emphasized and engaged with in kind: light illuminates, fire burns, and flood waters rage while people have doubts, desires, and longings. Symbolic interpretation uses both concrete and affective language, making use of metaphor, poetry, wordplay, narrative, and myth in a way that is unique among Qurʾānic commentaries. This is not to say that this kind of language use does not appear in other commentaries; al-Ṭabarī and others, for example, cite pre-Islamic and early Islamic poetry frequently in order to explain the meanings of obscure or ambiguous words, but the purpose is etymological while the affective and aesthetic elements of the poetry is ignored. Similarly, anecdotes, narratives, and homilies are very much part of the style of the early traditions transmitted from the Companions and Followers of the Prophet and continued to be cited in many commentaries. Al-Qurṭubī is a good example of a commentator who very much appreciates the appealing and entertaining qualities of this material, ignoring his otherwise rigorous standards of authentication to include it. But new stories, such as those told about Ṣūfī shaykhs, and new homilies, such as al-Maybudī's discussion of the journeys of Mūsā, are rare in this genre, perhaps considered more appropriately confined to the area of preaching. In Ṣūfī interpretation, poetry, metaphor, storytelling, and myth are accepted wholeheartedly, and if anything, take precedence over more explanatory language. The connection between other genres of Ṣūfī writing and the Qurʾān becomes clearer when one recognizes that these kinds of language acts represent an integral part of the Ṣūfī response to the Qurʾānic text.

As important as allegoresis and symbolic interpretation are in Ṣūfī commentaries, Ṣūfī interpretations characterized by close attention paid to words and phrases are equally prominent. Sometimes this takes the form of "rigorous fidelity to the text" as Chodkiewski defines it in the writings of Ibn 'Arabī. In the texts studied here, the fact that al-Khaḍir switches pronouns in speaking to Mūsā, from "*I wanted*" to "*We wanted*" to "*Your Lord wanted*" is considered highly significant and commented on accordingly. The approach can also be meditative and didactic, as in the attention paid to unusual words such as *'ilm ladunī* and *muḥarrar*. Unlike the allegorical approach, which raises concerns about reading alien concepts into the Qur'ānic text, this approach remains very much within the text. Many of these interpretations, like the symbolic interpretations, constitute a literary form of commentary that has not always been recognized as such.

APPENDIX

Commentators on the Qur'ān

To contextualize the work of Ṣūfī commentators, several commentaries have been referred to throughout this study. The following provides brief biographical information and descriptions of the style and contents of these commentaries.

Al-Ṭabarī

Abū Ja'far Muḥammad b. Jarīr al-Ṭabarī was born in Ṭabaristān in northern Iran but spent most of his life in Baghdād, where he died in 923.[1] According to one story, he first arrived in Baghdād hoping to study with Aḥmad b. Ḥanbal but found that he had recently died. Al-Ṭabarī himself attempted to establish a separate school of law based on his own principles, but apparently it was not distinct enough from Shāf'ism to survive his death. Instead, his fame rests upon two monumental works: his history of the world, *Mukhtaṣar ta'rīkh al-rusul wa'l-mulūk wa'l-khulafā'*, and his Qur'ānic commentary, *Jāmī' al-bayān 'an ta'wīl āy Qur'ān*. The commentary marks the beginning of the classical period of Qur'ānic commentaries, and is important for the vast amount of information it contains from the earliest sources of Islam.

In the edition used for this study, the *Jāmi' al-bayān* comprises thirty parts printed in twelve volumes.[2] Al-Ṭabarī usually begins his exegesis by paraphrasing a verse with the use of synonyms, prefaced by the phrase, "He (God) says" (*yaqūla*) or "He (or it) means" (*ya'nī*). He then provides philological information on the verse, including variant readings, definitions and etymologies of problematic words, and solutions to grammatical difficulties. The comments are based on named or unnamed reciters of the Qur'ān (*al-qurrā'*), Arabists (*ahl al-'arabiyya*), grammarians (*naḥwiyyūn*), and evidence from Arab speech patterns (*taqūlu al-'arab*) and poems. After establishing the basic meaning of the text, al-Ṭabarī addresses intratextual and extratextual problems of meaning, noting differences of opinion. The sources that al-Ṭabarī uses to solve these problems of meaning are the Qur'ān itself, the *aḥādīth* of the Prophet, and the exegetical Traditions attributed to his Companions and Followers. Al-Ṭabarī's commentary is often referred to as the first and foremost example of "interpretation by the transmitted tradition" (*tafsīr bi'l-ma'thūr*) because of the enormous quantity of *aḥādīth* and

Traditions which he includes. When quoting *aḥādīth* he often gives numerous versions with different chains of transmission (*asānīd*). He also supplies the full chain of transmission for Traditions related from the Companions and Followers, chains which end with al-Ṭabarī himself.[3] After quoting the *aḥādīth* and Traditions, al-Ṭabarī usually expresses his preferred interpretation, sometimes providing his reasoning, and sometimes not.

Al-Zamakhsharī

Abū'l-Qāsim Maḥmūd b. 'Umar al-Zamakhsharī was born in the province of Khwārazm south of the Aral Sea and died there in 1144 after years of studying and teaching which took him to such cities as Baghdad and Mecca.[4] He was a particularly sought after teacher in the areas of Arabic grammar and philology. His best known work is his *tafsīr*, *Al-Kashshāf 'an ḥaqā'iq al-tanzīl*, a work which was greatly admired and quoted for its linguistic insights while censured for its Mu'tazilī views. 'Abd Allāh b. 'Umar al-Bayḍāwī (d. 1286 or 1293) produced a commentary entitled *Anwār al-tanzīl wa-asrār al-ta'wīl* which is mostly an abridged version of al-Zamakhsharī's work purged of its suspect theology. Fakhr al-Dīn al-Rāzī appears to have used *Al-Kashshāf 'an ḥaqā'iq al-tanzīl* as a basis for his own commentary,[5] as did al-Nīsābūrī.[6]

Al-Zamakhsharī's commentary comprises four volumes.[7] He is far more selective than al-Ṭabarī in the *aḥādīth* and Traditions he chooses to include; those he does cite are often quoted anonymously and without any chain of transmission (*isnād*), introducted merely by "it has been said" (*qīla*) or "it has been related" (*ruwiya*). The result is little repetition and a far more condensed style, although he demonstrates an interest, like al-Ṭabarī, in expanding Qur'ānic narratives by providing details such as names of people and places, and story background. Johns has noted al-Zamakhsharī's fondness for this material, and the similarity between his accounts and those found in al-Tha'labī's *Qiṣaṣ al-anbiyā'*.[8] More so than al-Ṭabarī, al-Zamakhsharī makes the occasional tentative step towards homiletics by suggesting lessons to be learned from certain Qur'ānic verses.

Al-Zamakhsharī's commentary is punctuated by the questions that he asks of the text using classic *kalām* speech: "For if you were to say..." (*fa-in qulta*), "I would say..." (*qultu*). The questions pertain to linguistic, narrative, or theological issues. His discussions of linguistic issues are more involved and subtle than al-Ṭabarī's, and are often used to support theological concerns, namely, the rejection of anthropomorphic interpretations and the affirmation of the miraculous nature (*i'jāz*) of the Qur'ān.

Fakhr al-Dīn al-Rāzī

Abū 'Abd Allāh Muḥammad b. 'Umar b. al-Ḥusayn Fakhr al-Dīn al-Rāzī was born in the Persian town of Rayy five years after the death of al-Zamakhsharī. The years after finishing his studies were difficult ones, as his outspokenness provoked the antagonism of Mu'tazilīs and Karrāmiyya[9] in the areas through which he traveled. He finally found patronage, wealth, and prestige in Heart where he spent most of his life before dying in 1210.[10] Although still a thorn in the side of some, al-Rāzī was a popular preacher and sought after teacher. He seems to have possessed a genuine piety combined with both intellectual virtuosity and an abrasive personality. He is often labeled a philosopher–theologian because of his interest in both areas of Islamic thought.

Al-Rāzī's connection to Ṣūfism is unclear. We know that Ibn 'Arabi sent him a letter inviting him to consider the differences between mystical and rational knowledge.[11] According to several biographical sources, he is said to have met the Ṣūfī teacher Najm al-Dīn Kubrā and asked to become his disciple, but the outcome of this meeting is uncertain. Wherever al-Rāzī's ultimate loyalties lie, his interest in philosophy, theology, and Ṣūfism are all apparent in his *tafsīr*, which is known as either *Mafātiḥ al-ghayb* or *Kitāb al-tafsīr al-kabīr*, and is considered his most important work. Ibn Taymiyya scoffed at the work, saying that it contained everything except *tafsīr*, whereas its admirers insisted that it contained everything else in addition to *tafsīr*. It is an encyclopedic work, similar in length to al-Ṭabarī's *tafsīr*.

Al-Rāzī usually begins his discussion of a verse by examining its place within the larger context of the *sūra* or the Qur'ān as a whole, finding evidence of the inimitability (*i'jāz*) of the Qur'ān in the ordering and sequencing of its verses. After addressing such contextual issues, al-Rāzī sometimes points out the lessons to be learned by a verse before proceeding to his summaries of the transmitted exegetical Traditions. Like al-Zamakhsharī, he does not always identify the *salafi* sources for this material, but he is more likely to present the full range of interpretations. Al-Rāzī is inclined to draw attention to the majority opinion particularly when he is about to disagree with it. He also demonstrates his independence from traditional exegetical discourse by including such authorities as Ibn Sīnā and Abū Ḥāmid al-Ghazālī, although the traditional authorities he cites far outweigh the nontraditional.

Al-Rāzī uses al-Zamakhsharī's *Al-Kashshaf 'an ḥaqā'iq al-tanzīl* as a basis for his philological and grammatical comments, although in an abridged form and not uncritically.[12] Al-Rāzī addresses the theological issues raised by the Qur'ānic text far more insistently and comprehensively than al-Zamakhsharī, and he searches for answers in a far more expanded intellectual universe, calling upon the ideas of Mu'tazilīs, philosophers, and Ṣūfīs in addition to their more orthodox Sūnnī counterparts. Structurally, he conducts these discussions by dividing his commentary on individual verses into various "issues" (*masā'il*), "questions" (*as'ila*), "aspects" (*wujūh*), "topics" (*mabāḥith*), and "parts" (*aqsām*), an arrangement his biographer al-Ṣafadī says he was the first one to use.[13]

Al-Qurṭubī

Abū 'Abd Allāh Muḥammad b. Aḥmad b. Abī Bakr b. Faraj al-Anṣārī al-Khazrajī al-Andalusī al-Qurṭubī was born on the other side of the classical Muslim world, in Spain, although, like his predecessors, he traveled widely in his studies before settling in Egypt where he died in 1272.[14] He was an expert not only in *tafsir*, but also *ḥadīth* and Mālikī law. The best known of his works is his Qur'ānic commentary entitled *Al-Jāmiʿ li-aḥkām al-Qur'ān wa'l-mubayyin li-mā taḍammana min al-sunna wa-āyāt al-furqān*. It is approximately the same size as the commentaries of al-Ṭabarī and al-Rāzī, comprising twenty slim volumes.[15]

Al-Qurṭubī's commentary is renowned for the large number of *aḥādīth* he includes therein, many of which are not found in al-Ṭabarī. Al-Ṭabarī limits his *aḥādīth* and Traditions to those which directly comment on Qur'ānic verses, whereas al-Qurṭubī includes others as well which are thematically related. While he is sometimes meticulous in addressing the authenticity of this material, he makes surprisingly frequent use of the more controversial *isrāʾīliyāt* material found in the works of Abū Isḥāq al-Thaʿlabī (d. 1036).[16]

Al-Qurṭubī also makes extensive use of the works of post-*salafī* exegetes, demonstrating the virtuosity of a keen mind well aware of the complex issues which divided these exegetes as well as the Muslim community at large, and he often displays a jurist's desire to define the boundaries of acceptable thought and practice. Like al-Rāzī, he frequently divides his commentary according to the issues (*masā'il*) raised by one or more verses, although he does not resort to anything like al-Rāzī's extensive subdivisions and his writing style is far more straightforward and clear. Al-Qurṭubī is markedly less interested in theological issues than al-Rāzī; of greater concern to him are the legal ramifications of the Qur'ānic text. His mastery of the many disciplines employed in *tafsīr*, however, is undeniable, and Calder has suggested that is was al-Qurṭubī who most fully realized the possibilities of the genre.[17]

Ibn Taymiyya

Taqī al-Dīn Aḥmad b. Taymiyya was a Ḥanbalī theologian and jurist who led an eventful life as an outspoken activist.[18] Born in Ḥarrān, Syria in 1263, he was forced at the early age of five to flee with his family from the Mongols to Damascus where he lived most of his life. Coming from a family of renowned Ḥanbalī scholars, he took over his father's directorship of the *Sukkariyya* mosque and *madrasa* at the age of twenty and later taught at the oldest Ḥanbalī *madrasa* in Damascus, the *Ḥanbaliyya*.

Ibn Taymiyya's long career of controversial activism began at the age of thirty when he was briefly imprisoned for organizing a protest against the authorities' inaction with regards to a prominent Christian accused of insulting the Prophet. As was to be the case in the many incarcerations to follow, he spent his time in prison writing, producing his first great work. In the years that followed, Ibn Taymiyya's influence grew as he exhorted the people of Damscus to *jihād* against the Mongols and their Shīʿī supporters, and as he accompanied the fighting armies. Apparently unconcerned with his own safety or well-being, Ibn Taymiyya wrote treatise after treatise attacking any doctrine or practice, however popular, which he felt degraded the original, pure message of Islam. The objects of his polemics included *kalām*, philosophy, popular saint worship, antinomian Ṣūfīs, the followers of Ibn 'Arabī, and Shī'īs. He died in a prison in Damascus in 1328.

Ibn Taymiyya's relationship to Ṣūfism is complicated. He appears to have been a member of the *Qādariyya* order[19] and wrote of his respect for several individual Ṣūfīs.[20] However, he was fiercely opposed to many aspects of Ṣūfī doctrine and practice based on his assessment of their heretical nature. The extent of Ibn Taymiyya's criticism is such that, using his creedal criteria, few of the major writings of Ṣūfism would be considered sound. Nonetheless, he seems to have desired to reform the tradition from within by carefully separating the sound from the false in both Ṣūfī doctrine and practice. He writes approvingly of the moral and ethical focus of Ṣūfī writings while rejecting what he perceives to be faulty conclusions regarding the nature of the relationship between man and God. These faulty conclusions, according to Ibn Taymiyya, are the result of turning away from the teachings of the Prophet and the pious first generations (*salaf*), substituting their wisdom with the inferior tools of *kalām* and philosophy, and concepts based on excessive emotional states.[21]

Ibn Taymiyya managed to write profusely on many different subjects, producing creeds, legal judgments, polemical and exegetical works. In the last category, he wrote the hermeneutical work *Muqaddima fī uṣūl al-tafsīr* and commentaries on a few Qur'ānic *sūra*s and *āyāt*. These commentaries reflect the epistemological principle laid out in his *Muqaddima* that knowledge is either the result of authentic transmission (*naql muṣaddaq*) or verifiable deduction (*istidlāl muḥaqqaq*). Although Ibn Taymiyya is most often associated with the term "transmitted interpretation" (*tafsīr bi'l-ma'thūr*), it is the use of deduction (*istidlāl*) which is most striking in his exegesis. Al-Ṭabarī's commentary on *Sūrat al-Ikhlāṣ* consists of about four pages of transmitted material from the first generations of Muslims (*salaf*). This material is expanded to almost 300 pages in Ibn Taymiyya's commentary with his original arguments and reformulations, all firmly based on *salafī* views.[22] Ibn Taymiyya's exegetical works read more like treatises than line by line commentary.

The style is quite different than the famous commentary of Ibn Taymiyya's student, Ibn Kathīr (d. 1373), *Tafsīr al-Qur'ān al-'aẓīm*. While Ibn Kathīr explicitly adopts the methodology of Ibn Taymiyya, even copying a portion of his *Muqaddima* into his introduction,[23] he is much more sparing in his use of deduction in his commentary, confining himself almost exclusively to the process of sifting through the transmitted material and selecting what he deems most authentic. When he ventures beyond this, it is usually to serve as a spokesperson for the more independent thought of his teacher.

GLOSSARY OF TERMS

Terms related to human faculties

ʿaql Intellect, reason.
istiʿdād The preparedness or aptitude of individual human souls.
***laṭāʾif* (s. *laṭīf*)** (1) Subtle interpretations of the Qurʾān or (2) subtle faculties in humans.
nafs Soul.
al-nafs al-ammāra The demanding soul.
al-nafs al-lawwāma The blaming or reproachful soul.
al-nafs al-muṭmaʾinna The soul at peace.
qalb Heart.
rūḥ Spirit.
sirr Secret or innermost heart.

Terms related to knowledge or ways of seeking knowledge

***adab* (pl. *ādāb*)** Disciplined and refined ways of acting and speaking.
dhawq Tasting.
***ḥāl* (pl. *aḥwāl*)** State.
ijtihād The process of seeking understanding of the Qurʾān based on an individual's independent investigation and judgment.
ilhām Inspiration.
ʿilm al-aḥwāl Knowledge that comes from spiritual states.
ʿilm badīhī Intuitive knowledge of self-evident truths.
ʿilm ḍarūrī Necessary knowledge (as opposed to acquired knowledge); knowledge that comes without the need for reflection or examination of proofs; sensory knowledge.
***ʿilm kasbī* (or *iktisābī*)** Knowledge that is acquired through study.
ʿilm ladunī Knowledge that comes to individuals directly from God.
kashf The process of obtaining knowledge by "unveiling."
riyāḍa Spiritual discipline.
waḥy A kind of revelation that is not restricted to prophets.

Terms related to the interpretation and interpreters of the Qur'ān

bāṭin The inner or esoteric meaning of Qur'ānic verses.

bāṭiniyya A derogatory name used to describe those who reject the exoteric sense of Qur'ānic verses.

ḍarb al-mithāl The creating of similitudes or parables; making analogies.

***ḥadīth* (pl. *aḥādīth*)** The sayings of the Prophet Muḥammad.

ishāra Allusion; a silent signal or gesture.

laṭā'if (1) Subtle interpretations of the Qur'ān or (2) subtle faculties in humans.

majāz Figurative expression or metaphor.

muḥkamāt Clear and unambiguous verses in the Qur'ān.

mutashābihāt Ambiguous verses in the Qur'ān that can be interpreted in different ways.

muṭṭala' A high place from which one can view things clearly, meaning either (1) the vantage point from which one views the Resurrection or (2) one of four aspects of the Qur'ān described in a *ḥadīth.*

al-rāsikhūn fi'l-'ilm *Those firmly rooted in knowledge* who are qualified to interpret the Qur'ān.

al-salaf al-sāliḥ The pious first generations after the Prophet Muḥammad whose comments on the meaning of the Qur'ān form the basis of the exegetical tradition.

tafsīr Commentary on the Qur'ān.

tafsīr bi'l-ma'thūr Commentary on the Qur'ān based on the *aḥādīth* and the interpretations of the pious first generations (*al-salaf al-sāliḥ*).

tafsīr bi'l-ra'y A term usually used to refer to blameworthy commentary on the Qur'ān based on mere opinion, but also sometimes used to refer positively to exegesis based on reasoning.

taṭbīq To make or find correspondences between two things.

ta'wīl A term originally synonymous with *tafsīr* but which came to mean (1) interpretation of anthropomorphic or other Qur'ānic verses that are ambiguous in meaning or (2) esoteric interpretation of the Qur'ān.

'ulamā' Religious scholars.

ẓāhir (1) The obvious or apparent sense of Qur'ānic verses or (2) the exoteric meaning of the Qur'ān.

NOTES

INTRODUCTION

1 I. Goldziher, *Die Richtungen der islamischen Koranauslegung*, Leiden: E.J. Brill, 1952, pp. 180–262.
2 Ibid., p. 180.
3 L. Massignon, *Essai sur les origins du lexique technique de la Mystique Musulmane*, Paris: J. Vrin, 1968.
4 P. Nwyia, *Exégèse Coranique et Language Mystique*, Beirut: Dar El-Masreq, 1970.
5 The experiential methodology of the early Ṣūfīs is noted as well in the study of Sahl al-Tustarī by G. Böwering, *The Mystical Vision of Existence in Classical Islam*, Berlin: Walter De Gruyter, 1980 and P. Heath's analysis of Ibn 'Arabī in "Creative Hermeneutics: A Comparative Analysis of Three Islamic Approaches," *Arabica*, 36, 1989, pp. 173–210.
6 H. Corbin, *Creative Imagination in the Sufism of Ibn 'Arabī*, Princeton, NJ: Princeton University Press, 1969.
7 T. Izutsu, *Creation and the Timeless Order of Things*, Ashland, OR: White Cloud Press, 1994.
8 W. Chittick, *Imaginal Worlds: Ibn al-'Arabī and the Problem of Religious Diversity*, Albany, NY: SUNY Press, 1994.
9 Ibid., pp. 25–6.
10 F. Rahman, "Dream, Imagination, and *'Ālam al-mithāl*," in *The Dream and Human Societies*, eds G.E. Grunebaum and R. Caillois, Berkeley, CA: University of California Press, 1966, p. 415.
11 L. Lewisohn, *Beyond Faith and Infidelity*, Richmond, Surrey: Curzon Press, 1995, 19, 175–6.
12 H. Dabashi, "Historical Conditions of Persian Sufism during the Seljuk Period," in *Classical Persian Sufism: From its Origins to Rumi*, ed. Leonard Lewisohn, London: Khaniqahi Nimatullahi Publications, 1993, pp. 137–74.
13 M. Sells, "The Bewildered Tongue: The Semantics of Mystical Union in Islam," in *Mystical Union in Judaism, Christianity, and Islam*, eds M. Idel and B. McGinn, New York: Continuum, 1996, p. 88.
14 J.C.Bürgel, *The Feather of Simurgh: The "Licit Magic" of the Arts in Medieval Islam*, New York: New York University Press, 1988.
15 C. Ernst, *The Shambhala Guide to Sufism*, Boston, MA: Shambhala, 1997, pp. 18–31.

1 THE QUR'ĀN AS THE OCEAN OF ALL KNOWLEDGE

1 Quoted in Abū Naṣr al-Sarrāj, *Kitāb al-luma' fī taṣawwuf*, London: Luzac, 1963, p. 73.
2 Quoted in Al-Ghazālī, *Ihyā' 'ulūm al-dīn*, Beirut: Al-Dār al-Kutub al-'Ilmiyya, 1989, vol. 5, p. 99; and Rūzbihān al-Baqlī's *'Arā'is al-bayān*, vol. 1, Lucknow, 1898, p. 3.

3 Said to be an elixer used to change silver into gold.
4 Al-Ghazālī, *Jawā'ir al-Qur'ān wa duraruh*, Beirut: Dār al-Afāq al-Jadīda, 1983, pp. 8–9. There is an English translation of this work by Abul Quasem, *The Jewels of the Qur'ān*, London: Kegan Paul International, 1983.
5 Al-Kāshānī, *Ta'wīlāt*, published as *Tafsīr al-Qur'ān al-karīm* and attributed incorrectly to Ibn 'Arabī, Beirut: Dār al-Yaqẓat al-'Arabiyya, 1968, vol. 1, p. 3.
6 In verses such as Qur'ān 6:120, 6:151, 7:33, 31:20, 57:3.
7 For biographical information on al-Ṭabarī, see the Appendix.
8 Al-Ṭabarī, *Jāmi' al-bayān 'an ta'wīl āy al-Qur'ān*, Egypt: Muṣṭafā al-Bābī al-Halabī, 1954–7, p. 12. There is an English translation of al-Ṭabarī's introduction to his *tafsīr* in *The Commentary on the Qur'ān*, translated by J. Cooper, Oxford: Oxford University Press, 1987. The *ḥadīth* of Ibn Mas'ūd is also recorded in *Al-Musnad al-Ṣaḥīḥ 'alā 'l-taqāsīm wa'l anwā'* of Abū Bakr Muḥammad b. Ḥibbān (d. 965), Beirut: Mu'assasāt al-Risālā, 1984–91, vol. 1, p. 243.
9 Al-Ṭabarī, *Jāmi' al-bayān*, vol. 1, pp. 11–42.
10 'Umar b. al-Khaṭṭāb (d. 644), the second caliph.
11 Al-Ṭabarī, *Jāmi' al-bayān*, vol. 1, p. 32. Lane understands the meaning of *muṭṭala'* in this saying of 'Umar as the "place whence one will look down on the day of resurrection," *Arabic-English Lexicon*, vol. 2, Cambridge: The Islamic Texts Society, 1984, p. 1870.
12 For an analysis of the different ways in which the word *ta'wīl* in used in the Qur'ān, see Tabatabai's "The Concept of Al-Ta'wil in the Qur'ān," *Message of Thaqalayn* 2, 1995, 21–40.
13 Al-Tustarī, *Tafsīr al-Tustarī*, Beirut: Dār al-Kutub al-'Ilmiyya, 2002, p. 16. A similar interpretation, cited later, is attributed to 'Alī (d. 661).
14 G. Böwering, *The Mystical Vision of Existence in Classical Islam: The Qur'ānic Hermeneutics of the Ṣūfī Sahl al-Tustarī*, Berlin: Walter De Gruyter, 1980, p. 232.
15 Abū Ṭālib al-Makkī, *Qūt al-qulūb*, Cairo: Dār al-Rashād, 1991, p. 102.
16 Al-Ghazālī, *Iḥyā'*, vol. 5, p. 129.
17 Rūzbihān, *'Arā'is al-bayān fī ḥaqā'iq al-Qur'ān*, vol. 1, pp. 2–3.
18 Al-Nīsābūrī, *Gharā'ib al-Qur'ān wa raghā'ib al-furqān*, Cairo: Muṣṭafā al-Bābī al-Ḥalabī, 1962–70, vol. 1, p. 26.
19 Ibid.
20 Al-Kāshānī, *Ta'wīlāt*, p. 4.
21 Al-Simnānī, *Tafsīr najm al-Qur'ān*, quoted in J. Elias, *The Throne Carrier of God*, Albany, NY: SUNY Press, 1995, pp. 107–8. The English translation here is that of Elias based on his reading of manuscript editions of al-Simnānī's *Tafsīr* in Istanbul and Damascus.
22 Ibid., 108. Elias is paraphrasing al-Simnānī here.
23 The cosmological terms which al-Simnānī uses in his interpretation have a long history in Ṣūfism and can be traced to several sources (see L. Gardet's "'Ālam al-Djabarūt, 'Ālam al-malakūt, 'Ālam al-mithāl" and R. Arnaldez's "Lāhūt and Nāsūt," in *The Encyclopaedia of Islam*, new ed, Leiden: Brill, 1960–2002). Elias suggests that al-Simnānī may have been the first to use these terms consistently in a hierarchial fashion (Elias, *The Throne Carrier of God*, pp. 154–7). The word "Kingdom" (*malakūt*) is Qur'ānic (6:75, 7:185, 23:88, and 36:83), and the word "Omnipotence" (*jabarūt*) occurs in the *aḥādīth*, but with meanings not clearly related to levels of existence. The terms "humanity" (*nāsūt*) and "divinity" (*lāhūt*) are not used in either the Qur'ān or the *aḥādīth*. The Ṣūfī al-Ḥallāj (d. 922) used these terms, perhaps adopting them from Arab Christians or Imāmī theologians (Arnaldez, vol. 5, p. 613). Abū Ṭālib al-Makkī used all four of these terms along with a fifth realm of Ipseity (*hāhūt*) (C. Glassé, *The Concise Encyclopedia of Islam*, San Francisco, CA: Harper and Row, 1989, pp. 128–32). The five realms were also discussed by the followers and systematizers of Ibn 'Arabī's thought in what was called the Five Divine Presences (*al-ḥaḍarāt al-ilāhiyyat al-khams*) (W. Chittick, "The Five Divine Presences," *The Muslim World*, 72, 1982, 107–28).

24 Both men are claimed in most of the lineages of Ṣūfī orders, and are considered to be the first and sixth imams by the Ismā'īlī and Twelver Shī'īs.
25 Rūzbihān, *'Arā'is al-bayān fī ḥaqāi'q al-Qur'ān*, vol. 1, p. 4. Al-Sulamī quotes a slightly different version in his *Ḥaqā'iq al-tafsīr* (Beirut: Dār al-Kutub al-'Ilmiyya, 2001, vol. 1, p. 22–3).
26 Abū Ṭālib al-Makkī, *Qūt al-qulūb*, p. 94; Al-Ghazālī, *Iḥyā'*, vol. 5, p. 87.
27 Al-Ghazālī, *Iḥyā'*, vol. 5, pp. 93–4, 129; The version of this tradition in al-Sulamī and Rūzbihān is a little different: "It is related from Abū Juḥayfa (d. 693) that he asked 'Alī whether he had any revelation (*waḥy*) from the Messenger of God other than the Qur'ān. 'Alī said, 'By the One who created the seed and the breath of life, no, except for that God gives a servant understanding of His Book' " (Al-Sulamī, *Ḥaqā'iq al-tafsīr*, vol. 1, p. 20 and Rūzbihān, *'Arā'is al-bayān fī ḥaqāi'q al-Qur'ān*, vol. 1, p. 3).
28 Abū Ṭālib al-Makkī, *Qūt al-qulūb*, p. 101; Al-Ghazālī, *Iḥyā'*, vol. 5, pp. 129–30.
29 Al-Ghazālī, *Iḥyā'*, vol. 5, pp. 135.
30 Al-Sulamī, *Ziyādāt ḥaqā'iq al-tafsīr*, Beirut: Dār al-Mashriq, 1986, p. 2; Rūzbihān's version substitutes verification (*taḥaqquq*) for *taḥqīq* (*'Arā'is al-bayān fī ḥaqāi'q al-Qur'ān*, vol. 1, p. 14).
31 Ibid.
32 Al-Sulamī, *Ḥaqā'iq al-tafsīr*, vol. 1, p. 22 and Rūzbihān, *'Arā'is al-bayān fī ḥaqāi'q al-Qur'ān*, vol. 1, p. 4. In Al-Sulamī's version, *'ibāra* reads *'ibāda*, which makes less sense.

2 THE QUR'ĀNIC TEXT AND AMBIGUITY: VERSE 3:7

1 Abū Ja'far al-Ṭabarī, *Jāmi' al-bayān 'an ta'wīl āy al-Qur'ān*, Egypt: Muṣṭafā al-Bābī, al-Ḥalabī, 1954–7, vol. 3, pp. 172–5. For a discussion of various medieval definitions of the *mutashābihāt*, see L. Kinberg's "*Muḥkamāt* and *Mutashābihāt* (Koran 3/7): Implication of a Koranic Pair of Terms in Medieval Exegesis," *Arabica*, 35, 1988, 143–72.
2 Al-Ṭabarī, *Jāmi' al-bayān*, vol. 3, pp. 174–5.
3 Ibid., vol. 3, pp. 173–4.
4 Abū'l-Qāsim al-Qusharyī, *Laṭā'if al-ishārāt*, vol. 1, Cairo: Dār al-Kutub al-'Arabī, 1980, vol. 3, p. 232.
5 Rashid al-Din al-Maybudī, *Kashf al-asrār wa 'uddat al-abrār*, Tehran: Amīr Kabīr, 1982–3, vol. 3, p. 34.
6 Rūzbihān al-Baqlī, *'Arā'is al-bayān fī ḥaqā'iq al-Qur'ān*, Lucknow, 1898, vol. 1, pp. 68–9.
7 See E.W. Lane, *Arabic-English Lexicon*, vol. 2, Cambridge: Islamic Texts Society, 1984, p. 2648.
8 Scholars of Rūzbihān's writings have translated the term *iltibās* in different ways. In his *En Islam Iranien*, Corbin translates it as "amphibolie," Paris: Gallimard, 1972. C. Ernst finds this "an excessively abstract overtranslation" which "fails to convey the sense of the root L-B-S as 'clothing'." He prefers the phrase "clothing with divinity," "when the context makes it clear that *iltibās* means a theophany clothed in visible form" (*Ruzbihan Baqli: Mysticism and the Rhetoric of Sainthood in Persian Sufism*, Richmond, UK: Curzon Press, 1995, p. 104, n. 56). In 'Abd al-Razzāq al-Kāshānī's glossary of Ṣūfī technical terms (*A Glossary of Sufi Technical Terms*, London: Octagon Press, 1991, p. 45), *al-labs*, the noun derived from the first form verb *labasa*, is defined as "the elemental form (*al-ṣurāt al-'unsuriyya*) that clothes (*talbisu*) spiritual realities (*al-ḥaqā'iq al-rūḥāniyya*). He also cites the following Qur'ānic verse containing the verb *labasa*, a verse which replies to the unbelievers who ask why an angel is not sent down to them:

> *If We had made him [the Messenger] an angel, We would have made him [appear] as a man and We would have certainly confused* (labasnā) *them just as they are already in confusion* (yalbisūna).
>
> (6:9)

9 Al-Kāshānī, *Ta'wīlāt*, published as *Tafsīr al-Qur'ān al-karīm* and attributed incorrectly to Ibn 'Arabī, Beirut: Dār al-Yaqẓat al-'Arabiyya, 1968, vol. 1, p. 167.
10 See W. Chittick, *The Sufi Path of Knowledge: Ibn al-'Arabi's Metaphysics of Imagination*, Albany, NY: SUNY Press, 1989, pp. 89–94.
11 Al-Ṭabarī, *Jāmi' al-bayān*, vol. 3, pp. 174–5; Abū Hāmid Muḥammad Al-Ghazālī, *Al-Mustaṣfā min 'ilm al-uṣūl*, Beirut: Mu'assasāt al-Risāla, 1997, p. 203; Al-Qurṭubī, *Al-Jāmi' li-aḥkām al-Qur'ān wa'l-mubayyin li-mā taḍammana min al-sunna wa-āyāt al-furqān*, Beirut: Dār al-Kutub al-'Arabī, 1980, vol. 4, p. 18.
12 Al-Ṭabarī, *Jāmi' al-bayān*, vol. 3, p. 175.
13 Ibid.
14 Ibid., vol. 3, p. 183
15 Ibid., pp. 178–80. This is one of three interpretations al-Ṭabarī lists for *those in whose hearts is a turning away*.
16 For biographical information on al-Zamakhsharī, see the Appendix.
17 Maḥmūd b. 'Umar Abū'l-Qāsim al-Zamakhsharī, *Al-Kashshāf 'an ḥaqā'iq al-tanzīl*, Egypt: Muṣṭafā al-Bābī al-Ḥalabī, 1966, vol. 1, p. 412.
18 For biographical information on Fakhr al-Dīn al-Rāzī, see the Appendix.
19 Fakhr al-Dīn al-Rāzī, *Al-Tafsīr al-kabīr*, Beirut: Dār Iḥyā al-Turāth al-'Arabī, 1980, vol. 7, pp. 183–4.
20 Ibid., vol. 7, p. 184–5. See also al-Zamakhsharī, *Kashshāf 'an ḥaqā'iq al-tanzīl*, vol. 1, p. 412.
21 Fakhr al-Dīn al-Rāzī, *Al-Tafsīr al-kabīr*, vol. 7, pp. 181–2.
22 Ibid., vol. 7, p. 186.
23 Ibid., pp. 187–91.
24 Ibid., p. 191.
25 Abū Hāmid Muḥammad al-Ghazālī, "The Canons of Ta'wil," translated by N. Heer in *Windows on the House of Islam: Muslim Sources of Spirituality and Religious Life*, ed. John Renard, Berkeley, CA: University of California Press, 1998, p. 53.
26 Ibid., p. 54.
27 For biographical information on Ibn Taymiyya, see the Appendix.
28 See B. Abrahamov's "Ibn Taymiyya on the Agreement of Reason with Tradition" (*Muslim World*, 82, 1992, 256–72), which discusses Ibn Taymiyya's response to al-Rāzī in his *Dar' ta'āruḍ al-'aql wa'l-naql*.
29 Abū Ḥāmid Muḥammad al-Ghazālī, *Iljām al-'awāmm 'an 'ilm al-kalām*, Beirut: Dār al-Kitāb al-'Arabī, 1985, p. 60.
30 Ibid., pp. 67–8.
31 Al-Qushayrī, *Laṭā'if al-ishārāt*, vol. 1, p. 232.
32 Ibid., p. 233.
33 Ibid.
34 Rūzbihān, *'Arā'is al-bayān*, vol. 1, p. 69.
35 Ibid., pp. 69–70.
36 As mentioned earlier, al-Rūzbihān uses the term "verifiers" (*muḥaqqiqūn*) to refer to theologians. Al-Kāshānī is following the usage of Ibn 'Arabī: "In general the Shaykh al-Akbar applies the term 'Verifiers' (*al-muḥaqqiqūn*) to the highest category of the friends of God. They follow no one's authority (*taqlīd*), since in themselves they have 'verified' (*taḥqīq*) and 'realized' (*taḥaqquq*) – through unveiling and finding – the truth (*ḥaqq*) and reality (*ḥaqīqa*) of all things, i.e. the Real Himself (*al-ḥaqq*)." (W. Chittick, *Sufi Path of Knowledge*, p. 389, n. 11.)
37 Al-Kāshānī, *Ta'wīlāt*, vol. 1, p. 167.
38 The word *rabbāniyyūn* appears in the Qur'ān in 3:79, 5:44, and 5:63. Sībawayh defines the *rabbānī* as one who devotes himself to the knowledge of the Lord exclusively (see Lane, *Arabic-English Lexicon*, vol. 1, pp. 1006–7 and M. Asad, *The Message of the Qur'ān*, Gilbraltar: Dar al-Andalus, 1980, p. 79, n. 62). Al-Tustarī appears to be

coining the words *nūrāniyyūn* and *dhātiyyūn* using the same Arabic word form. Cf. G. Böwering, who translates these three words as "those who perceive God as Lord," "those who perceive God as Light," and "those who perceive God as Essence" (*The Mystical Vision of Existence in Classical Islam: The Qur'ānic Hermeneutics of the Ṣufī Sahl at-Tustarī*, Berlin: Walter De Gruyter, 1980, p. 228). See also Böwering on al-Tustarī's commentary on 3:79 in the same work, pp. 228–9.

39 Abū Muḥammad Sahl b. 'Abd Allah Al-Tustarī, *Tafsīr al-Tustarī*, Beirut:Dār al-kutub al 'Ilmiyya, 2002, p. 46. Qur'ānic verse 18:65 refers to the wise man Mūsā meets on a journey, identified in the *ḥadīth* as al-Khaḍir.

40 The phrase occurs in the Qur'ān sixteen times. See H. Kassis' *Concordance of the Qur'ān*, Berkeley, CA: University of California Press, 1983, pp. 732–3.

41 Lane, *Arabic-English Lexicon*, vol. 2, p. 2643.

42 *Qishr* (pl. *qushūr*) is a word that is used for an outer covering such as the husk of wheat, the shell of nuts, or the rind of fruit.

43 Al-Kāshānī, *Ta'wīlāt*, vol. 1, p. 168.

44 The Day of the Covenant is a concept understood from Qur'ānic verse 7:172: *When your Lord took the seeds of their future progeny from the loins of the children of Ādam and made them testify regarding themselves, "Am I not your Lord?"* (*alastu bi-rabbikum*) *They said, "Yes, we testify." Lest you say on the Day of Resurrection, "We were not aware of this."* According to A. Schimmel, "The goal of the mystic is to return to the experience of the 'Day of *Alastu*,' when only God existed, before He led future creatures out of the abyss of not-being and endowed them with life, love, and understanding so that they might face Him again at the end of time," (*Mystical Dimensions of Islam*, Chapel Hill, NC: University of North Carolina Press, 1975, p. 24).

45 Al-Nīsābūrī, *Al-Gharā'ib al-Qur'ān wa raghā'ib al-furqān*, Cairo: Muṣṭafā al-Bābī al-Ḥalabī, 1962–70, vol. 3, p. 138.

3 UNCOVERING MEANING: KNOWLEDGE AND SPIRITUAL PRACTICE

1 Abū Naṣr al-Sarrāj (d. 988), so far as we know, was the author of only one book, *Kitāb al-luma 'fī 'l-taṣawwuf*, a highly influential work which served both as a defense of Ṣūfism and a manual for its followers. It was used by al-Qushayrī for his *Risāla* and al-Ghazālī for his *Iḥyā' 'ulūm al-dīn* (P. Lory, "Al-Sarrādj," in *The Encyclopedia of Islam*, eds C.E. Bosworth, E. vab Donzel, W.P. Heinrichs, and G. Leconnte, Leiden: E.J. Brill, new ed. 1960–2002).

2 Abū Naṣr al-Sarrāj, *Kitāb al-luma' fī 'l-taṣawwuf*, London: Luzac, 1963, pp. 13–4. The Arabic text of *Kitāb al-luma'* is edited by R.A. Nicholson and followed by his abridged English translation. The *Kitāb al-luma'* has also been translated into German by R. Gramlich as *Schlaglichter über das Sufitum*, Stuttgart: Franz Steiner Verlag, 1990.

3 Abū Naṣr al-Sarrāj, *Kitāb al-luma'*, pp. 13–4.

4 Ibid., pp. 14–5.

5 Ibid., p. 15.

6 Abū Ḥāmid Muḥammad al-Ghazālī, *Jawāhir al-Qur'ān wa duraruh*, Beirut: Dār al-Afāq al-Jadīda, 1983, pp. 32–3.

7 Al-Sulamī, *Ṭabaqāt al-ṣūfiyya*, ed. Sharība, Cairo, 1372, p. 119 (quoting a saying from Abū Hafṣ al-Ḥaddād, d. 880 or 884), cited in G. Böwering, "The *Adab* Literature of Classical Sufism: Anṣarī's Code of Conduct," in *Moral Conduct and Authority: The Place of Adab in South Asian Islam*, ed. B. Daly Metcalf, Berkeley, CA: University of California Press, 1984, p. 67.

8 Abū Naṣr al-Sarrāj, *Kitāb al-luma'*, p. 73.

9 Abū Ṭālib al-Makkī, *Qūt al-qulūb*, Cairo: Dār al-Rashād, 1991, p. 97; Abū Ḥāmid Muḥammad Al-Ghazālī, *Iḥyā' 'ulūm al-dīn*, Beirut: Al-Dār al-Kutub al-'Ilmiyya, 1989,

vol. 5, p. 122; Abd al Razzāq Al-Kāshānī *Ta'wīlāt* (*Ta'wil al-Qur'ān*), published as *Tafsīr al-Qur'ān al-karīm* and attributed incorrectly to Ibn 'Arabī, Beirut: Dār al-Yaqẓat al-'Arabiyya, 1968, p. 4.

10 Abū Ṭālib al-Makkī, *Qūt al-qulūb*, p. 95; Al-Ghazālī, *Iḥyā'*, vol. 5, pp. 85–6.

11 Abū Naṣr al-Sarrā, *Kitāb al-luma'*, p. 80. This three stage approach to reading the Qur'ān also appears in Abū Ṭālib al-Makkī's *Qūt al-qulūb* in a somewhat different version, pp. 96–7; and in al-Ghazālī, *Iḥyā'* vol. 5, pp. 121–2.

12 Abū Ṭālib al-Makkī, *Qūt al-qulūb*, p. 100; Al-Ghazālī, *Iḥyā'*, vol. 5, p. 123.

13 Abū Ṭālib al-Makkī, *Qūt al-qulūb*, p. 97; Al-Ghazālī, *Iḥyā'*, vol. 5, pp. 122–3.

14 Al-Kāshānī, *Ta'wīlāt*, vol. 1, p. 4; Al-Kāshānī's version of the tradition from Ja'far al-Ṣādiq echoes the *ḥadīth* from Ibn Mas'ūd. It is said that Ja'far fell down in a faint during prayer and when asked about it he said, "I kept on repeating the verse until I heard it from the Speaker of it and I saw that which comes to me sometimes from the secrets of the realities of the depths (*buṭūn*), the lights of the splendors of the heights (*muṭṭala'āt*) beyond what is attached to externals (*ẓawāhir*) or limits (*ḥudūd*) with a clearly delineated limit (*ḥadd*)," pp. 4–5.

15 R. Gramlich's German translation of the *Qūt al-qulūb* entitled *Die Nahrung der Herzen* details each passage borrowed by al-Ghazālī in his *Iḥyā' 'ulūm al-dīn*, Stuttgart: Franz Steiner Verlag, 1992–5.

16 Abul Quasem has translated this portion of the *Iḥyā' 'ulūm al-dīn* in *The Recitation and Interpretation of the Qur'ān*, London: Kegan Paul International, 1982.

17 Al-Ghazālī, *Iḥyā'*, vol. 5, pp. 25–79.

18 Ibid., pp. 80–3; Cf. Abū Ṭālib al-Makkī, *Qūt al-qulūb*, pp. 97–8.

19 Literally, "bring to his heart (*yuḥḍiru fī qalbihi*)."

20 Al-Ghazālī, *Iḥyā'*, vol. 5, pp. 84–5.

21 Ibid., pp. 85–7.

22 Ibid., pp. 87–92.

23 Al-Qushayrī, *Laṭā'if al-ishārāt*, Cairo: Dār al-Kutub al-'Arabī, 1968–71, vol. 1, p. 232.

24 Al-Ghazālī, *Iḥyā'*, vol. 5, pp. 92–100.

25 'Abd Allāh b. al-'Abbās (d. *c.*687) is the Companion of the Prophet most often quoted in commentaries on the Qur'ān.

26 Mujāhid b. Jubayr al-Makkī (d. 722) was a student of Ibn 'Abbās and is one of the best-known commentators from the Meccan school of the Followers.

27 Al-Ghazālī, *Iḥyā'*, vol. 5, pp. 100–7.

28 Ibid., pp. 107–10.

29 Ibid., pp.110–21.

30 Ibid., pp. 121–4. Cf. Abū Ṭālib al-Makkī, *Qūt al-qulūb*, pp. 96–7.

31 Al-Ghazālī, *Iḥyā'*, vol. 5, pp. 124–7. Just as al-Ghazālī reworked the material for this passage of his *Iḥyā'* from Abū Ṭālib al-Makkī's *Qūt al-qulūb*, the material was rewritten once again and included in the Persian *Javāhir al-tafsīr* of Husayn Va'iz-i Kashifi (d. 1504–5). Never mentioning al-Ghazālī by name, Kashifi selected, changed, and added poetry to his translation and embellishment of al-Ghazālī's ten external courtesies and ten inner practices for reading and understanding the Qur'ān (K. Sands, "On the Popularity of Husayn Va'iz-i Kashifi's *Mavahib-i 'aliyya*: A Persian Commentary on the Qur'an," *Iranian Studies*, 36, 2003, pp. 474–5)

4 METHODS OF INTERPRETATION

1 Abū Naṣr al-Sarrāj, *Kitāb al-luma' fī'l-taṣawwuf*, ed. Reynold A. Nicholson, Gibb Memorial series, no. 22, London: Luzac, 1963, p. 90.

2 Ibid., pp. 90–1.

3 Ibid., p. 91.

4 Ibid.
5 Ibid.
6 Abū Ḥāmid Muḥammad al-Ghazālī, *Al-Ghazālī: The Niche of Lights, A parallel English Arabic Text Translated, Introduced, and Annotated* by David Buchman, Provo, UT: Brigham Young University Press, 1998, p. 25. The edition used here contains a complete English translation by D. Buchman that faces the Arabic text. The translations given here are my own unless otherwise specified. Another English trans. is that of W.H.T. Gairdner, *Al-Ghazzālī's Mishkat al-anwar*, Lahore: Sh. Muhammad Ashraf, 1991.
7 Al-Ghazālī, *Al-Ghazālī: The Niche of Lights*, p. 29.
8 Ibid., pp. 25–6.
9 Ibid., p. 27.
10 The reference is to Qur'ānic verses 6:76–9: *When the night covered (Ibrāhīm), he saw a star. He said, "This is my Lord," but when it set he said, "I do not love that which sets." When he saw the moon appear, he said, "This is my Lord," but when it set he said, "If my Lord does not guide me, I will surely be among the people who lose their way." When he saw the sun appear, he said, "This is my Lord. This is the greatest." But when it set, he said, "O my people, I am free of your polytheism. Surely, I have turned my face to the One who created the heavens and the earth, in pure faith. I will never be one of the polytheists."*
11 Al-Ghazālī, *Al-Ghazālī: The Niche of Lights*, pp. 27–8.
12 *Has the story of Mūsā reached you? When he saw a fire and said to his family, "Wait. I perceive a fire. Maybe I can bring you a firebrand from it or find some guidance at the fire." Then, when he came to it, a voice was heard, "O Mūsā, surely I am your Lord. So take off your shoes in the holy valley Ṭuwā* (20: 9–12).
13 Al-Ghazālī, *Al-Ghazālī: The Niche of Lights*, p. 30.
14 Ibid., pp. 29–32.
15 Abū Ḥāmid Muḥammad al-Ghazālī, *Jawāhir al-Qur'ān wa duraruh*, Beirut: Dār al-Afāq al-Jadīda, 1983, p. 33.
16 M. Abul Quasem points this out in his translation of the *Jawāhir al-Qur'ān* (*The Jewels of the Qur'ān*, London: Kegan Paul International, 1982, p. 57, n. 112). The passage from al-Zamakhsharī's *Al-Kashshāf 'an ḥaqā'iq al-tanzīl* (Egypt: Muṣṭafā al-Bābī al-Ḥalabī, 1966–8) is found in vol. 3, pp. 445–6.
17 W. Chittick, *The Sufi Path of Knowledge: Ibn al-'Arabi's Metaphysics of Imagination*, Albany, NY: SUNY Press, 1989, pp. 199–202.
18 W. Chittick, *Imaginal Worlds: Ibn al-'Arabi and the Problem of Religious Diversity*, Albany, NY: SUNY Press, 1994, pp. 67–73.
19 Ibid., pp. 73–76; Chittick, *Sufi Path of Knowledge* pp. 231, 245.
20 W. Chittick, *Imaginal Worlds*, pp. 76–7.
21 W. Chittick, *Sufi Path of Knowledge*, p. 199.
22 Ibid., p. 244–50; M. Chodkiewicz, *An Ocean Without a Shore: Ibn Arabi, the Book and the Law*, Albany, NY: SUNY Press, 1993, p. 35.
23 The distinction made by Abū Naṣr al-Sarrāj between the method of understanding (*fahm*) and the method of allusion (*ishāra*) seems to have been ignored by later Ṣūfīs, for whom allusion (*ishāra*) described all Ṣūfī commentary. This is particularly apparent in al-Qushayrī's commentary entitled *Laṭā'if al-ishārāt*, where he uses the term continually, in spite of the fact that his commentary more closely corresponds to Abū Naṣr al-Sarrāj's method of understanding (*fahm*).
24 W. Chittick, *The Self-Disclosure of God: Principles of Ibn al-'Arabī's Cosmology*, Albany, NY: SUNY Press, 1998, pp. 118–19.
25 Ibid., pp. 398–9, n. 35.
26 Chodkiewicz, *An Ocean Without a Shore*, pp. 19–57; Chittick, *Sufi Path of Knowledge*, pp. 242–4.

27 Chodkiewicz, *An Ocean Without a Shore*, p. 37.
28 Ibid., pp. 19–20.
29 For a discussion of the different definitions of these terms as they were understood towards the end of the classical period, see Jalāl al-Din al-Suyūṭī, *Al-Itqān fī 'ulūm al-Qur'ān*, Lahore: Suhail Academy, 1980, pp. 173–4.
30 Nizām al-Din Al-Nīsābūrī, *Gharā'ib al-Qur'ān wa raghā'ib al-furqān*, ed. Ibrāhīm 'Aṭwah 'Iwaḍ, vol. 1 Cairo: Muṣṭafā al-Bābī al-Ḥalabī, 1962–70, p. 52. This section introduces his commentary on Surat al-Fātiḥa.
31 Prior to P. Lory's more extensive analysis of al-Kāshānī's commentary, Goldziher had suggested that *ta'wīl* was al-Kāshānī's word for the interpretation of passages whose literal meaning was obscure, and that *taṭbīq* was his word for the symbolic interpretation of passages whose unambiguous literal meaning remains intact. Lory, on the basis of his more complete reading of al-Kāshānī, states that al-Kāshānī used *ta'wīl* as the broader term for all forms of esoteric interpretation, and *taṭbīq* for the specific type of esoteric interpretation which uncovers the correspondences between Qur'anic symbols and man's spiritual psychology and development (I. Goldziher, *Die Richtungen der islamischen Koranauslegung*, Leiden: E.J. Brill, 1952, p. 243; P. Lory, *Les Commentaires ésotériques du Coran d'après 'Abd ar-Razzāq al-Qāshānī*, Paris: Les Deux Oceans, 1980, pp. 29–33).
32 By using the verb "to behold" (*iṭṭala'a*), al-Kāshānī is making a reference to the Ibn Mas'ūd *ḥadīth* regarding levels of meaning in the Qur'ān. The noun "lookout point" (*muṭṭali'*) used in this *ḥadīth* comes from the same root as the verb *iṭṭala'a*.
33 Al-Kāshānī, *Ta'wīlāt*, published as *Tafsīr al-Qur'ān al-karīm* and attributed incorrectly to Ibn 'Arabī, Beirut: Dār al-Yaqẓat al-'Arabiyya, 1968, vol. 1: 5.
34 Abū Naṣr al-Sarrāj, *Kitāb al-luma'*, pp. 107–8.
35 Abū Muḥammad b. abī Naṣr Rūzbihān al-Baqlī, *'Arā'is al-bayān fī ḥaqā'iq al-Qur'ān*, Lucknow, 1989, vol. 1, p. 3.
36 This *ḥadīth*, which is not mentioned in any of the canonical books of *ḥadīth*, appears to be a variation on the seven *ḥarfs* of the Qur'ān mentioned in the *ḥadīth* attributed to Ibn Mas'ūd and recorded by al-Ṭabarī.
37 'Alā al-Daula Al-Simnānī, "Muqaddima tafsīr al-Qur'ān li-'Alā' al-dawla al-Simnānī," ed. Paul Nwyia *Al-Abḥāth*, 26, 1973–77, pp. 146–57. Part of the *Muqaddima* has been analyzed by H. Corbin in *The Man of Light in Iranian Sufism*, trans. Nancy Pearson, Boulder, CO: Shambhala, 1978, pp. 121–31. J. Elias analyzes the concept of the seven subtle substances in *The Throne Carrier of God: The Life and Thought of 'Ala ad-dawla as-Simnani*, Albany, NY: SUNY Press, 1995, pp. 79–99.
38 Al-Simnānī, "Muqaddima tafsīr al-Qur'ān, p. 146.
39 Ibid., p. 147.
40 Ibid., p. 149–50.
41 Ibid., p. 152–4.

5 ATTACKING AND DEFENDING ṢŪFĪ QUR'ĀNIC INTERPRETATION

1 Quoted in al-Ṭabarī's Qur'ānic commentary *Jāmi' al-bayān 'an ta'wīl āy al-Qur'ān*, Egypt: Muṣṭafa al-Bābī al-Ḥālabī, 1954–7, vol. 1, p. 34.
2 Ibid.
3 Ibid., vol. 1, pp. 33–4, 41.
4 Ibid., p. 35.
5 Ibid., p. 41.

6 Abū Ḥāmid Muḥammad al-Ghazālī, Iḥyā' 'ulūm al-dīn, Beirut: Al-Dār al-Kutub al-'Ilmiyya, 1989, vol. 5, p. 136. This section is translated in its entirety in M. Abul Quasem's *The Recitation and Interpretation of the Qur'an: Al-Ghazāli's Theory*, London: Kegan Paul International, 1982.

7 Al-Ghazālī, *Iḥyā'*, vol. 5, p. 140.

8 Ibid., pp. 137–41.

9 Ibid., pp. 141–4.

10 Ibid., pp. 144–5.

11 For biographical information on al-Qurṭubī, see the Appendix.

12 Muḥammad b. Aḥmad 'Abd Allāh al-Anṣārī Al-Qurṭubī, *Al-Jāmi' li-aḥkām al-Qur'ān wa'l-mubayyin li-mā taḍammana min al-sunna wa-āyāt al-furqān*, vol. 1, Beirut: Dār al-Kutub al-'Arabī, 1968–71, pp. 33–4. In his article "Al-Ḳurṭubī" in *Encyclopedia of Islam*, new ed., R. Arnaldez compares the passage on the manner of reading the Book of God in the introduction to al-Qurṭubī's *tafsīr* to a passage in al-Ghazālī's *Iḥyā' 'ulūm al-dīn*, which is similar in style but not in content. Al-Qurṭubī's borrowing from al-Ghazālī here suggests he was working directly from the *Iḥyā'*, adapting parts of al-Ghazālī's writing to reflect his somewhat different point of view. The passage from al-Ghazālī is also copied without attribution in the introduction to al-Nīsābūrī's *Gharā'ib al-Qur'ān wa raghā'ib al-furqān*, Cairo: Muṣṭafā al-Bābī al-Ḥalabī, 1962–70, vol. 1, p. 57.

13 Al-Ghazālī, *Iḥyā'*, vol. 5, p. 129.

14 For Ibn al-Jawzī's connection to Ṣūfīsm see G. Makdisi's "The Hanbali School and Sufism," *Humaniora Islamica*, 2, 1974, 61–71.

15 Abū'l-Faraj Ibn al-Jawzī, *Mukhtaṣar kitāb talbīs Iblīs*, Beirut: Mu'assasāt al-Risāla, 1992, pp. 148, 268–79; There is a partial English translation of this work by D.S. Margoliouth entitled "The Devil's Delusion" in *Islamic Culture* in 10, 1936, pp. 229–68 and 11, 1937, pp. 393–403.

16 Ibn al-Jawzī, *Mukhtaṣar kitāb talbīs Iblīs*, p. 271.

17 Ibid., p. 274.

18 Ibid., p. 273.

19 Aḥmad Taqi al-Din Ibn Taymiyya, *Al-radd 'alā al-manṭiqiyyīn*, Bombay: Al-Maṭba'at al-Qayyima, 1949, pp. 509–10.

20 Ibid., pp. 510–11.

21 Ibid., p. 511. Ibn Taymiyya does not mention who said this.

22 The English translation here is that of T. Michel from his "Ibn Taymiyya's *Sharḥ* on the *Futūḥ al-ghayb* of 'Abd al-Qādir al-Jīlānī," *Hamdard Islamicus*, 4, 1981, p. 8.

23 Abū Isḥāq Aḥmad al-Tha'labi (d. 1045) wrote a book entitled *Qatlā 'l-Qur'ān* with the stories of men and jinn who died upon hearing a recitation of the Qur'ān. B. Wesimüller has prepared a critical edition and German translation of this text, *Die vom Koran Getöten: Aṭ-Ṯa'labīs Qatlā l-Qur'ān nach der Istanbuler und den Leidener Handscriften* with commentary (Würzburg: Ergon Verlag, 2002). See also Kermani's comments on the text, in which he emphasizes that the deaths are described as occurring not from bliss, but from an intense fear of God and His judgment *(Gott ist schön: Das ästhetische Erleben des Koran*, Munich: Verlag C.H. Beck, 1999).

24 Ibn al-Jawzī, *Mukhtaṣar kitāb talbīs Iblīs*, pp. 206–16.

25 This is T.E. Homerin's translation from "Ibn Taimiyya's *Al-Ṣūfiyah wa-al-fuqarā'*," *Arabica*, 32, 1985, 225–8.

26 The concept of ecstasy (*wajd*) is related to the concept of fanā' (annihilation), which Ibn Taymiyya discusses in detail in a number of his works. According to J. Pavlin, who has made a study of these works, Ibn Taymiyya does not reject the concept entirely but attempts to redefine it according to the pietism of the Hanbalī *madhab*. He describes three types of *fanā'*, a classification that separates those states and beliefs that he

judges to be praiseworthy from those that he considers to be deficient and blameworthy. ("The *Salafī*-ization of the *Fanā'*: Ibn Taymiyya and the Annihilation of the Self," Paper presented at the Midde East Studies Association Annual Meeting, Washington, DC, Nov. 19–22, 1999.)

27 Ibn al-Jawzī, *Mukhtaṣar kitāb talbīs Iblīs*, p. 150.

28 Ibid., pp. 149–51.

29 Ibid.

30 Ibn Taymiyya, *Muqaddam fī uṣūl al-tafsīr*, Cairo: Maktaba al-Turāth al-Islamiyya, 1988. For an English translation of this work, see *Muqaddam fī uṣūl al-tafsīr: An Introduction to the Principles of Tafseer*, trans. M. Ansari, Birmingham, UK: Al-Hidaayah Publishing, 1993. An excerpt of the work is also translated by J. McAuliffe in "Ibn Taymiyya: Treatise on the Principles of Tafsīr," *Windows on the House of Islam: Muslim Sources on Spirituality and Religious Life*, Berkeley, CA University of California Press, 1998, 35–43.

31 On al-Ghazālī's rejections of the Companions' opinions as *ḥujja*, see his *Al-Mustaṣfā min 'ilm al-uṣūl*, vol. 1, Beirut: Mu'assasāt al-Risāla, 1997, pp. 400–9.

32 Ibn Taymiyya, *Muqaddam fī uṣūl al-tafsīr*, pp. 93–102.

33 Ibid., pp. 46–7.

34 Ibid., pp. 46–7, 96–8, 100–2.

35 In "The Principles of Ibn Taymiyya's Qur'ānic Interpretation," D. Syafruddin suggests that it is not the hierarchy of sources that make Ibn Taymiyya's methodology unique, but rather the assumptions behind it (M.A. Thesis, Institute of Islamic Studies, McGill University, Montreal, 1994), pp. 113–8.

36 Ibn Taymiyya, *Muqaddam fī uṣūl al-tafsīr*, pp. 83–92. Although Ibn Taymiyya's criticism of al-Sulamī is somewhat mild here, G. Böwering states that Ibn Taymiyya issued highly critical judgments against his *tafsīr* in his *Fatāwā* ("The Qur'ān Commentary of al-Sulamī," *Islamic Studies Presented to Charles J. Adams*, ed. W.B. Hallaq and D.P. Little, Leiden: E.J. Brill, 1991, pp. 41–56), p. 52.

37 Al-Ghazālī, *Fayṣal al-tafriqa bayna al-Islām wa'l-zandaqa*, Dār al-Nashr al-Maghrabiyya, 1983. There is an English translation of this by R.J. McCarthy in *Freedom and Fulfillment*, Boston, MA: Twayne, 1980, pp. 45–174.

38 Two people who would disagree here with al-Ghazālī, for entirely different reasons are Ibn Taymiyya and Ibn 'Arabī. We have already mentioned that Ibn Taymiyya insists that the literal sense of the Qur'ānic text must never be abandoned because reason properly applied will never contradict the Qur'ān or authentic *aḥādīth* (B. Abrahamov, "Ibn Taymiyya on the Agreement of Reason with Tradition," *Muslim World*, 82, 1992, 256–72). Ibn 'Arabī also insists that the literal sense must never be abandoned, but for a different reason: perfect knowledge combines both the faculties of the intellect and imagination, both of which are needed to understand God's revelation (W. Chittick, *The Sufi Path of Knowledge: Ibn al-'Arabi's Metaphysics of Imagination*, Albany, NY: SUNY Press, 1998, pp. 199–202).

39 Al-Ghazālī, *Fayṣal al-tafriqa*, pp. 9–15.

40 Aḥmad ibn Ḥanbal (d. 855) was the founder of the Ḥanbalī School of Law. Al-Ghazālī states that there were three *aḥādīth* which Ibn Ḥanbal interpreted metaphorically, but cites only two of these interpretations. One example will suffice here. The Prophet said, "The believer's heart is between the two fingers of the Merciful." Ibn Ḥanbal interpreted these fingers as the touch of the angel and the devil, by means of which God upsets the hearts of men.

41 Traditions based on multiple transmission (*bi-tawātur*). Al-Ghazālī, *Fayṣal al-tafriqa*, pp. 18–21.

42 Ibid., pp. 23–5.

43 Ibid., pp. 21–3.

44 Al-Ghazālī, *Iḥyā'*, vol. 10, pp. 517–22.

45 *Al-Ghazālī, The Niche of Lights*, A Parallel English-Arabic text translated, introduced and annotated by David Buchman, Prov, UT: Brigham Young University Press, 1998, pp. 27–8.
46 Ibid., pp. 30, 32–4.
47 Ibid., p. 23.
48 Ibid., p. 28.
49 In his *Al-Ibāna ʻan uṣūl al-diyāna* (Beirut, 1994), al-Ashʻarī states that one must not abandon the literal sense of the Qurʾān without proof (*ḥujja*), pp. 105–6. This work has been translated into English by W.C. Klein (*Al-Ash'arī's Al-Ibānah ʻan ḥaqāʾiq al-tanzīl*, Egypt, 1966).
50 Mālik b. Anas (d. 796) is the imām of the school of Mālikīs.
51 Qurʾān 20:5.
52 *Istawā* is the verb used in Qurʾān 20:5, translated here as "sits firm."
53 Muwaffaq al-Din ʻAbd Allāh Ibn Qudāma, *Ibn Qudāma's Censure of Speculative Theology: An edition and translation of Ibn Qudāma's Taḥrīm an-naẓar fī kutub ahl al-kalām*, trans. G. Makdisi, London: Luzac, 1962, p. 30.
54 Al-Rāzī, *Al-Tafsīr al-kabīr*, Beirut: Dār Iḥyā, al-Turāth al-ʻArabī, 1980, vol. 7, pp. 187–8.
55 For the chronology of al-Ghazālī's works, see G.F. Hourani's "The Chronology of al-Ghazālī's Writings," *Journal of the American Oriental Society*, 79, 1959, 225–33.
56 Al-Ghazālī, *Iljām al-ʻawāmm ʻan ʻilm al-kalām*, Beirut: Dār al-Kitāb al-ʻArabī, 1985, pp. 60–68.
57 Al-Ghazālī, *Iḥyāʾ*, vol. 5, pp. 142–3. Cf. al-Qurṭubī, *Al-Jāmiʻli-aḥkām*, vol. 1, pp. 33–4 and al-Nīsābūrī, *Gharāʾib al-Qurʾān*, vol. 1, pp. 56–7.
58 When al-Qurṭubī quotes this passage from al-Ghazālī in the introduction to his own *tafsīr*, he adds a significant phrase, "it is prohibited because it is an analogy (*qiyās*) in language that is not permitted," Al-Qurṭubī, *Al-Jāmiʻ li-aḥkām*, vol. 1, p. 33.
59 According to Hourani, the *Mishkāt al-anwār* is generally considered to be a late work of al-Ghazālī's, based on its developed mystical doctrine. However, based on references within the writings of al-Ghazālī to his other works, it is unclear whether it was written before or after *Fayṣal al-tafriqa*. In any event, *Iḥyāʾ ʻulūm al-dīn* is considered the earliest book of the books discussed here.
60 Elsewhere, al-Ghazālī defines the *ḥashawiyya* as those "believing themselves bound to a blind and routine submission to the criterion of human authority and to the literal meaning of the revealed books" (*Iqtiṣād fīʾl iʻtiqād*, quoted in A.S. Halkin, "The Hashawiyya," *Journal of the American Oriental Society*, 54, 1934, 12). According to Halkin, the term was a derogatory term originally directed towards traditionalists (*aṣḥab al-ḥadīth*) and Ḥanbalīs themselves (Halkin, pp. 1–28).
61 Al-Ghazālī is saying that this tradition is either from the Prophet or from ʻAlī.
62 The root of this verb is the same as that for the noun "similitude" (*mithāl*). Literally, it could be translated as, "he made himself similar to."
63 Al-Ghazālī, *Mishkāt al-anwār*, pp. 32–3. "Taking heed" (*iʻtibār*) and "crossing over" (*ʻubūr*) come from the same root as dream or vision interpretation (*taʻbīr*).
64 ʻAlāʾ al-Dawla Al-Simnānī, "Muqaddima tafsīr al-Qur'ān li-'Alā al-dawla al-Simnānī," *Al-Abḥāth*, 1973–71, vol. 26, p. 151.
65 Ibid., pp.155–6. Some of the terms used here are difficult to understand without a broader overview of al-Simnānī's thought. Al-Simnānī is describing the descent of evermore subtle understandings of the Qur'ān, all of which may be denied at different spiritual levels. This descent can be understood in terms of his system of emanation, for which see J. Elias, *The Throne Carrier of God: The Life and Thought of 'Ala ad-dawla as-Simnani*, Albany, NY: SUNY Press, 1995, pp. 72–77.
66 Al-Simnānī, "Muqaddima tafsīr al-Qur'ān," p. 156.

6 ṢŪFĪ COMMENTATORS ON THE QUR'ĀN

1 Norman Calder, "Tafsīr from Ṭabarī to ibn Kathīr: Problems in the description of the genre, illustrated with reference to the story of Abraham," in *Approaches to the Qur'ān*, ed. G.R. Hawting and A.A. Shareef, London: Routledge, 1993, pp. 101–40.
2 Ibid., p. 101.
3 Calder includes orthography, lexis, syntax, rhetoric, and symbol/allegory in the category of instrumental structures; and prophetic history, theology, eschatology, law and Ṣūfism in the category of ideological structures (Ibid., pp. 105–6).
4 Ibid., pp. 134 and 134–5, nn. 2–3.
5 The Ṣūfī commentaries that address each *sūra* of the Qur'ān do not comment on each and every verse. Some are even more selective, such as the commentary of al-Ghazālī on the Verse of Light which addresses only one verse and one *ḥadīth*.
6 See I. Goldziher's chapter "Koranauslegung der islamischen Mystik" in his *Die Richtungen der islamischen Koranauslegung*, Leiden: E.J. Brill, 1952, pp. 180–262; and A. Rippin in his articles on "Tafsīr" for *The Encyclopedia of Islam*, new ed. and *The Encyclopedia of Religion*.
7 A. Habil, "Traditional esoteric commentaries on the Quran," in *Islamic Spirituality: Foundations*, ed. S.H. Nasr, New York: Crossroad, 1987, p. 25.
8 For the life and works of al-Tustarī, see G. Böwering, *The Mystical Vision of Existence: The Qur'ānic Hermeneutics of the Ṣūfī Sahl at-Tustarī*, Berlin: Walter De Gruyter, 1980, pp. 7–75.
9 Ibid., pp. 100–9. The edition used for this study was published under the title *Tafsīr al-Tustarī* in Beirut 2002. Although the editor, Muḥammad Bāsil 'Uyūn al-Sūd, has added notes identifying *aḥādith*, and authors and works cited, the text appears to be the same as the edition entitled *Tafsīr al-Qur'ān al-aẓīm* published in Cairo in 1911. Selected passages of this work have been translated into English by M. Sells in *Early Islamic Mysticism: Sufi, Qur'an, Mi'raj, Poetic and Theological Writings*, New York: Paulist Press, 1996, pp. 89–96.
10 G. Böwering, *Mystical Vision of Existence*, pp. 128–9.
11 Ibid., pp. 129–30, 262.
12 Ibid., p. 129.
13 Information on the life and works of al-Sulamī can be found in several of G.Böwering's works: "The Qur'ān Commentary of al-Sulamī," in *Islamic Studies Presented to Charles J. Adams*, eds W. Hallaq and D. Little, Leiden: E.J. Brill, 1991, pp. 41–6; "The Major Sources on Sulamī's Minor Qur'ān Commentary," *Oriens*, 35, 1996, pp. 35–56; *Mystical Vision of Existence*, pp. 110–2, and the introduction by Böwering to Al-Sulamī's *Ziyādāt ḥaqā'iq al-tafsīr (The Minor Qur'ān Commentary)*, Beirut: Dār al-Mashriq, 1986, pp. 15–21.
14 Al-Sulamī, *Ḥaqā'iq al-tafsīr*, ed. S. 'Umrān, Beirut: Dār al-Kutub al-'Ilmiyya, 2001.
15 L. Massignon copied the comments attributed to al-Hallāj in his *Essai sur les origins du lexique technique de la Mystique Musulmane*, Paris: J. Vrin, 1968, pp. 359–412 and P. Nwyia copied the comments attributed to Ja'far al-Ṣādiq in "Le Tafsir mystique attribué à Ja'far al-Ṣādiq," *Melanges De L'Universite Saint Joseph*, 1968, vol. 43, pp. 179–230. A few passages from the latter have been translated into English by M. Sells, *Early Islamic Mysticism*, pp. 75–89. A significant amount of material from the *Ḥaqā'iq al-tafsīr* is quoted in Rūzbihān al-Baqlī's commentary *'Arā'is al-bayān fī ḥaqā'iq al-Qur'ān*, Lucknow, 1898.
16 Al-Sulamī, *Ziyādāt ḥaqā'iq al-tafsīr* (*The Minor Qur'ān Commentary*).
17 Böwering, "The Major Sources of Sulamī's Minor Qur'ān Commentary," p. 39. The inclusion of material attributed to Ja'far al-Ṣādiq has intrigued scholars since Massignon first noted it in his *Essai* (pp. 201–6) because it raises the question of

the relationship between Ṣūfism and Shī'ism in the early stages of Islam. How much Ja'far al-Ṣādiq's approach to interpretation influenced both Ṣūfīs and Shī'īs is difficult to determine. Ṣūfī exegesis came to be characterized by symbolic and literary interpretation based on mystical experiences, but the hallmark of Shī'ī exegesis was allegorical interpretation which found hidden Qur'ānic references to 'Alī, Fāṭima, and their descendents. Only one of the manuscripts of Sulamī's *Ḥaqā'iq* contains anything like the latter, and this in only one passage which identifies five beings which received five of God's names: Muḥammad, 'Alī, Fāṭima, Ḥasan, and Ḥusayn (Sells, *Early Islamic Mysticism*, 77–8). On the basis of an analysis of the *isnads* given for Ja'far al-Ṣādiq's sayings in al-Sulamī's works and the absence of this material in any previous Ṣūfī works, Böwering concludes that al-Sulamī was the first Ṣūfī to incorporate the body of teachings attributed to Ja'far al-Ṣādiq into Ṣūfism. Ibn Taymiyya accused al-Sulamī of lying about what Ja'far al-Ṣādiq said. (M. al-Dhahabī, *Al-tafsīr wa'l-mufassirūn*, Cairo: Dār al-Kutub al-ḥadītha, 1967, p. 386.) Other Shī'ī sources were used earlier than al-Sulamī, such as the first four imams and other Shī'ī authorities quoted by al-Tustarī in his *tafsīr.* (Böwering, *Mystical Vision*, p. 67.) On the existence of mystical esotericism in early Shī'ism, see M. Amir-Moezzi, *The Divine Guide in Early Shī'ism: The Sources of Esotericism in Islam*, trans. D. Streight, Albany, NY: SUNY, 1994.

18 Böwering, "The Qur'ān Commentary of al-Sulamī," p. 52.

19 Böwering, "The Major Sources of Sulamī's Minor Qur'ān Commentary," p. 40.

20 Böwering, "The Qur'ān Commentary of al-Sulamī," p. 56, and *Mystical Vision*, p. 110.

21 Ibid., p. 51. Cf. *Mystical Vision*, pp. 136–7.

22 Nwyia, *Exégèse Coranique, et Language Mystique: Nouvel essaisur le lexique technique des mystiques musulmans*, Beirut: Dar El-Masreq, 1970, p. 178.

23 Quoted by I. Basyūnī in his introduction to al-Qushayrī's *Laṭā'if al-ishārāt*, p. 16.

24 Abū'l-Faraj Ibn al-Jawzī, *Mukhtaṣar kitāb talbīs Iblīs*, Beirut: Mu'assasāt al-Risāla, 1992, pp. 149–51, 280–2.

25 See Basyūnī's introduction to al-Qushayrī's *Laṭā'if al-ishārāt*, p. 16, and Böwering, "The Qur'ān Commentary of al-Sulamī," p. 52.

26 Information on the life and works of al-Qushayrī can be found in R. Ahmad, "Abu al-Qāsim al-Qushairī as a Theologian and Commentator," *Islamic Quarterly*, 12, 1968, 71–119; Basyūnī's introduction to al-Qushayrī's *Laṭā'if al-ishārāt*, pp. 19–27, and H. Halm's "Al-Ḳushayrī" in *The Encyclopedia of Islam*, new ed.

27 Al-Qushayrī, *Laṭā'if al-ishārāt.*

28 Ibid., Introduction by Basyūni, p. 42.

29 Ibid.

30 Ibid., pp. 43–4 and Ahmad, "Abu al-Qāsim al-Qushairī," pp. 60–5.

31 Ibid., pp. 47–9.

32 In his *Takrīj abyāt laṭā'if al-ishārāt l-imam al-Qushayrī wa dirāsat al-minhaj al-Qushayrī fī'l-istashād al-adab* (Cairo: Al-Sa'āda, 1986), A.A. Muṣṭafā states that al-Qushayrī borrows some 4,000 lines from Jāhiliyya and 'Abbāsid poetry, adapting them to his own themes and purposes by spiritualizing their sensual references.

33 Information on the life and works of al-Ghazālī can be found in M. Watt's "Al-Ghazālī" in *The Encyclopedia of Islam* and *The Encyclopedia of Religion*. For an excellent review of scholarly research on al-Ghazālī, see D. Buchman's introduction to *Al-Ghazālī: The Niche of Lights*, Provo, UT: Brigham Young University Press, 1998.

34 N. Heer, "Abū Ḥāmid al-Ghazālī 's Esoteric Exegesis of the Koran," in *Classical Persian Sufism: From its Origins to Rumi*, ed. L. Lewisohn, London: Khaneqahi Nimatullahi Publications, 1993, p. 235.

35 The edition used here is a parallel English-Arabic text with English translation by Buchman. An earlier English translation was published by W.H.T. Gairdner, Lahore: Sh.Muhammad Ashraf, 1991 (originally published in 1924).

36 Quoted in F. Kholeif's *A Study on Fakhr al-Dīn al-Rāzī and His Controversies in Transoxiana*, Beirut: Dar El-Machreq, 1966, p. 13.
37 Rashid al-Din al-Maybudī, *Kashf al-asrār wa-'uddat al-abrār*, ed. 'A.A. Hikmat, Tehran: Amīr Kabīr, 1982–3.
38 M.M. Rokni, *Laṭāyif-i az Qur'ān-i karīm*, Mashhad: Mu'assasah-i chāp va intisharāt-i āstān-I quds-I rāavi, 1996, pp. 31–6.
39 Al-Maybudī, *Kashf al-asrār*, vol. 1, p. 1. There are no independent extant copies of al-Anṣarī's commentary.
40 Ibid.
41 Böwering, *Mystical Vision*, p. 36.
42 Rokni, *Laṭāyif-i az Qur'ān-i karīm*, pp. 115–21. In addition to Rokni's work in Persian on Maybudī, Annabel Keeler will be publishing a monograph in English based on her PhD dissertation entitled "Persian Sufism and Exegesis: Maybudī's Commentary on the Qur'ān, the *Kashf al-asrār*" (University of Cambridge, 2001).
43 *Ṣābiqūn* is a Qur'ānic term used in verses 9:100, 23:61, 35:32.
44 A.J. Arberry, *Shiraz: Persian City of Saints and Poets*, Norman, OK: University of Oklahoma Press, 1960, p. 90. Information on the life and works of Rūzbihān can be found in C. Ernst, "Rūzbihān Baqlī" in *The Encyclopedia of Islam*, new ed. and *Rūzbihān Baqlī: Mysticism and the Rhetoric of Sainthood in Persian Sufism*, Richmond, UK: Curzon Press,1995, pp. 1–15; and L.Massignon, "La Vie et les oeuvres de Ruzbehan Baqli," in *Opera minora*, ed. Y. Moubarac, Beirut: Dār al-Ma'ārif, 1963, vol. 2, pp. 451–65.
45 Translated into English by C. Ernst in *The Unveiling of Secrets: Diary of a Sufi Master*, Chapel Hill, NC: Parvardigar Press, 1997; and analyzed in Ernst's *Rūzbihān Baqlī*.
46 Discussed by H. Corbin in *En Islam iranien*, Paris: Gallimard, 1972, vol. 3, pp. 45–64.
47 Discussed by C. Ernst as *Words of Ecstasy in Sufism*, Albany, NY: SUNY Press, 1985, pp. 14–21, 85–94.
48 Rūzbihān al-Baqlī, *'Arā'is al-bayān fī haqā'iq al-Qur'ān*, Lucknow, 1898.
49 A. Godlas, "Psychology and Transformation in the Sufi Qur'ān Commentary of Rūzbihān al-Baqlī," *Sufi Illuminations*, 1, 1996, p. 55, n. 4.
50 Quoted in C. Ernst, "The Symbolism of Birds and Flight in the Writings of Ruzbihan Baqli," in *The Legacy of Mediaeval Persian Sufism*, ed. L. Lewisohn, London: Khaneqahi Nimatullahi, 1992, p. 356.
51 Ibid., pp. 355–6.
52 Quoted in Ernst, *Rūzbihān Baqlī*, p. xi.
53 A. Schimmel, *Mystical Dimensions of Islam*, Chapel Hill, NC: University of North Carolina Press, 1975, p. 298.
54 See P. Lory, *Les Commentaires ésotériques du Coran d'après 'Abd ar-Razzāq al-Qāshānī*, Paris: Les Deux Oceans, 1980, pp. 20–2 and D.B. Macdonald, "'Abd al-Razzāq al-Kāshānī," *The Encyclopedia of Islam*, new ed.
55 On the term "school of Ibn 'Arabī" and the followers to which it refers, see W. Chittick, "The School of Ibn 'Arabī," *History of Islamic Philosophy*, ed. S.H. Nasr and O. Leaman, London: Routledge, 1996, vol. 1, pp. 510–23.
56 The edition used for this study was published as *Tafsīr al-Qur'ān al-karīm* and attributed to Ibn 'Arabī, Beirut, 1968. The authenticity of the work is discussed in P. Lory, *Les Commentaires ésotériques*, pp. 19–20 and J. Morris, "Ibn Arabi and His Interpreters. Part II (Conclusion): Influences and Interpretations," *Journal of the American Oriental Society*, 107, 1987, p. 101, n.73. Translations of portions of the commentary have been paraphrased and translated into English in M. Ayoub's *The Qur'ān and its Interpreters*, Albany, NY: SUNY Press, 1992 (but attributed to Ibn 'Arabī); and S. Murata's *The Tao of Islam: A Sourcebook of Gender Relationships in Islamic Thought*, Albany, NY: SUNY Press, 1992.
57 W. Chittick, *The Sufi Path of Knowledge: Ibn al-'Arabī's Metaphysics of Imagination*, Albany, NY: SUNY Press, 1998, pp. xvi–xx.

58 Morris, "Ibn 'Arabi and His Interpreters. Part II," 103–4.
59 Ibid., pp. 102–3.
60 Ibid., pp. 105. It is the philosophical underpinning of this kind of technique which R. Ahmad has in mind when he suggests that there are two types of Ṣūfi commentary, symbolic (*ishārī* or *ramzī*) and speculative (*naẓarī*), "Qur'ānic Exegesis and Classical Tafsir," *The Islamic Quarterly*, 12, 1968, 104–5.
61 Lory, *Les Commentaires ésotériques*, pp. 28–33.
62 Ibid., pp. 3–5. These passages have been translated in Part I. A French translation of the entire introduction can be found in Lory, pp. 149–53.
63 Information on the life and works of al-Nīsābūrī can be found in al-Dhahabī, *Al-Tafsīr wa'l-mufassirūn*, Cairo: Dār al-kutub al-ḥadītha, 1967, vol. 1, pp. 321–2.
64 Al-Nīsābūrī, *Gharā'ib al-Qur'ān wa raghā'ib al-furqān*, Cairo, 1962–70. Portions of this commentary have been paraphrased and translated into English in Ayoub, *The Qur'ān and Its Interpreters*.
65 Al-Nīsābūrī, *Gharā'ib al-Qur'ān*, vol. 30, p. 223.
66 J. Elias, *The Throne Carrier of God: The Life and Thought of 'Ala' ad-dawla as-Simnani*, Albany, NY: SUNY Press, 1995, pp. 203–6. Elias gives additional information for many of the manuscripts of these *tafsīrs*.
67 Cf. al-Suyūṭī's list of the fifteen types of knowledge required for the commentator, the last of which is "bestowed knowledge" (*'ilm al-mawhiba*), which is the knowledge that God bequeaths to those who act on what they know," *Al-Itqān fī 'ulūm al-Qur'ān*, Egypt, 1954–7, pp. 180–1.

7 QUR'ĀNIC VERSES 18:60–82: THE STORY OF MŪSĀ AND AL-KHAḌIR

1 A.J. Wensinck, in his article "al-Khaḍir" in *The Encyclopedia of Islam*, new ed., identifies the common elements as follows. In the Gilgamesh epic, Gilgamesh travels looking for his ancestor who lives at the mouth of the rivers and has been given eternal life. In the Alexander romance, Alexander is accompanied by his cook Andreas in his search for the spring of life. At one point in their difficult journey, Andreas washes a salted fish in a spring that causes it to come alive and swim away. Andreas jumps in after it and attains immortality. In the Jewish legend, the prophet Elijah travels with Rabbi Joshua ben Levi, with the condition that he accepts his actions unconditionally. Elijah performs a series of seemingly outrageous acts that are ultimately explained to the perplexed Joshua (vol. 4; pp. 902b–3a).
2 A.J. Wensinck, "Ilyās," *Shorter Encyclopedia of Islam*, p. 164b, following the earlier opinions of Y.L. Zunz, Abraham Geiger, and Israel Friedländer. For the references for these earlier opinions, see B.M. Wheeler, "The Jewish Origins of Qur'ān 18:65–82? Reexamining Arent Jan Wensinck, Theory," *Journal of the American Oriental Society*, 118, 1998, 155. This article has been rewritten into a chapter in Wheeler's *Moses in the Quran and Islamic Exegesis*, London: RoutledgeCurzon, 2002, pp. 10–36.
3 Wheeler, "The Jewish Origins of the Qur'ān 18:65–82?" pp. 153–71.
4 Abū Ja'far al-Tabarī, *Jāmi' al-bayān 'an ta'wīl āy Qur'ān*, vol. 15, Egypt: Muṣṭafa al-Bābī al-Halabī, 1954–7, p. 278.
5 Ibid., vol. 15, p. 277.
6 Ibid., p. 280.
7 Ibid.
8 Ibid., p. 283.
9 Ibid., pp. 278–9.
10 Ibid., p. 279.
11 Ibid., p. 281.

12 Al-Ṭabarī, *The History of al-Ṭabarī (Taʾrīkh al-rusul waʾl-mulūk): The Children of Israel*, vol. 3, p. 5. L. Massignon in "Elie et son rôle transhistorique, Khadiriya, en Islam" (*Opera Minora*, ed. Y. Moubarac, Beirut: Dār al-Maʿārif, 1963, vol.1, pp. 142–61), notes the common pairing of Khaḍir and Ilyās and the fact that they are sometimes even identified with one another in Muslim sources. He explores the role of al-Khaḍir in the devotional life of Muslims and finds his alleged immortality and sainthood, and his reported apparitions and acts of intercession functioning as a symbol of messianic hope for the poor and oppressed similar to the role of Elijah in Judaism and Christianity.

13 Al-Qurṭubī, *Al-Jāmiʿ li-aḥkām al-Qurʾān waʾl-mubayyin li-mā taḍammana min al-sunna wa-āyāt al-furqān*, Beirut: Dār al-Kutub al-ʿArabī, 1980, vol. 11, pp. 41–5.

14 H. Corbin, inspired by al-Khaḍir's role as a spiritual master in the life of Ibn ʿArabī and other Ṣūfīs, uses concepts from both Ṣūfism and Jungian analytical psychology to analyze the spiritual experience that he believes represents the act of recognizing oneself as a disciple of al-Khaḍir. He views al-Khaḍir as both a person and an archetype who leads each of his disciples throughout the ages to their own theophanies (*Creative Imagination in the Ṣūfism of Ibn ʿArabī*, trans. R. Manheim, Princeton, NJ: Princeton University Press, 1969, pp. 53–67).

15 C. Ernst, *The Shambala Guide to Sufism*, Boston, MA: Shambhala, 1997, p. 23.

16 The complete verse reads, *And your Lord revealed to the bees, "Take houses for yourselves from the mountains, trees, and from what they build."*

17 The complete verse reads, *And We revealed to the mother of Mūsā, "Nurse him, but when you are afraid for him, cast him into the river. Do not be afraid nor grieve, for We will return him to you and We will make him one of the messengers."*

18 Al-Sulamī, *Ziyādāt ḥaqāʾiq al-tafsīr* (*The Minor Commentary*), Beirut: Dār al-Mashriq, 1986, p. 84. Quoted in Rūzbihān al-Baqlī's *ʿArāʾis al-bayān fī ḥaqāiq al-Qurʾān* (Lucknow, 1898) without the chain of transmission (*isnād*), vol. 1, p. 592. This interpretation is not included in the edition of Al-Tustarī's *tafsīr* used for this study.

19 Al-Sulamī, *Ḥaqāʾiq al-tafsīr*, Beirut: Dār al-Kutub al-ʿIlmiyya, 2001, vol.1, p. 414 and Rūzbihān, *ʿArāʾis al-bayān*, vol. 1, p. 591. The use of the word *kashf* to describe the unveiling of certain realities has its basis in the Qurʾānic verses *You were heedless of this but now We have removed* (*kashafnā*) *your veil* (50:22) and *That which is imminent becomes imminent. No one but God can unveil* (*kāshifa*) *it* (53:57–58). In his *Risāla*, al-Qushayrī describes three stages of increasing nearness to the truth: presence of the heart before God's signs (*muḥāḍara*), unveiling (*mukāshafa*), and direct witnessing (*mushāhada*). For this and other examples of the term *kashf* in Ṣūfism, see L. Gardet's article "*Kashf*" in *The Encyclopedia of Islam*, new ed.

20 Abūʾl-ʿAbbās al-Qāsim b. Mahdī al-Sayyārī.

21 Al-Sulamī, *Ḥaqāʾiq al-tafsīr*, vol. 1, p. 414 and Rūzbihān, *ʿArāʾis al-bayān*, vol. 1, p. 591.

22 Al-Sulamī, *Ziyādāt ḥaqāʾiq al-tafsīr*, pp. 84–5.

23 Al-Qushayrī, *Laṭāʾif al-ishārāt*, Cairo: Dār al-Kutub al-ʿArabī, 1968–71, vol. 4, pp. 79–80.

24 Al-Rāzī, *Al-Tafsīr al-kabīr*, vol. 21, Beirut, 1980, p. 148.

25 Ibid.

26 The terms are found in Islamic theology as far back as the Ashʿarī scholars Abu Bakr al-Bāqallānī (d. 1013) and ʿAbd al-Qāhir b. Ṭāhir al-Baghdādī (d. 1037–8). See F. Rosenthal's *Knowledge Triumphant: The Concept of Knowledge in Medieval Islam*, Leiden: E.J. Brill, 1970, pp. 216–18, 227–30 and A.J. Wensinck's *The Muslim Creed: Its Genesis and Historical Development*, New York: Barnes and Noble, 1965, p. 250f.

27 Al-Rāzī, *Al-Tafsīr al-kabīr*, vol. 21, p. 149.

28 Al-Rāzī's use of the phrase "considerative types of knowledge (*al-ʿulūm al-naẓariyya*)" is confusing because he appears to be using it as a synonym for "necessary types of

knowledge (*al-'ulūm al-ḍarūriyya*)". It is possible that he is using the adjective *naẓarī* in its broadest sense to refer to consideration (*naẓar*) by the five physical senses and the intellect before it engages in the processes of inference or deduction. But then he uses the noun "consideration" (*naẓar*) in the opposite category, to describe an acquired form of knowledge. It is this second usage that is the more common, and the term speculative knowledge (*'ilm naẓarī*) is often used as a synonym for acquired (*muktasab* or *kasbī*) knowledge. See Rosenthal *Knowledge Triumphant*, pp. 216–18, 227–30 and Wensinck, *The Muslim Creed*, p. 250f.

29 Al-Rāzī, *Al-Tafsīr al-kabīr*, vol. 21, p. 150.

30 M. Watt, following Miguel Asin, does not consider *Al-Risālat al-laduniyya* to be an authentic work of al-Ghazālī. He quotes Asin's observation concerning the similarity between the work and the *Risāla fī'l-nafs wa'l-rūḥ* of Ibn 'Arabī: Asin judged the terminology and ideology of the latter work to be distinctly that of Ibn 'Arabī's and therefore judged *Al-Risālat al-laduniyya* as incorrectly attributed to al-Ghazāli. Watt judges the work as inauthentic on this basis and his own assessment that the work is uncharacteristic of al-Ghazālī's thought as demonstrated in works of indisputable authenticity. According to Watt, in *Al-Risālat al-laduniyya*, al-Ghazālī gives precedence to reason (*'aql*) over revelation, and he makes a distinction between revelation (*waḥy*) and inspiration (*ilhām*). The first idea is contrary to the precedence given to revelation in al-Ghazālī's *Al-Munqidh min al-ḍalāl* and the second idea is not discussed there or in the *Mishkāt al-anwār*, an omission Watt finds puzzling if this distinction was part of al-Ghazālī's belief ("The Authenticity of the Works Attributed to al-Ghazāli," *Journal of the Royal Asiatic Society*, 1952, pp. 33–4). In response to Asin's textual evidence, the mention of a treatise by al-Ghazālī on *'ilm ladunnī* in al-Rāzī's *tafsīr* demonstrates that a book on this topic attributed to al-Ghazālī existed before 1209, the year of al-Rāzī's death, at which time Ibn 'Arabī was in his early forties. It seems unlikely then, that Ibn 'Arabī's *Al-Risāla fī'l-nafs wa'l-rūḥ* could have been the source of the treatise mentioned here. The additional arguments made by Watt on the basis of the content of the *Risāla al-laduniyya* are not, in my opinion, sufficient to disprove the authenticity of the work. Al-Ghazālī is not elevating the human faculty of the intellect over revelation in *Al-Risāla al-laduniyya*, but rather the Universal Intellect. The distinction between revelation and inspiration is found in early Ṣūfism, so its adoption by al-Ghazālī is unsurprising and is not inconsistent with the ideas found in his *Iḥyā' 'ulūm al-dīn*.

31 Al-Ghazālī, *Al-Risālat al-laduniyya*, Cairo, n.d., pp. 19–26. A English translation of this treatise was done by M. Smith, "Al-Risālat Al-Laduniyya," *Journal of the Royal Asiatic Society*, 1938, 177–200, 353–74.

32 The notion of the Universal Soul (*al-nafs al-kullī*) and the Universal Intellect (*al-'aql al-kullī*) are found in the Neoplatonic teachings of Plotinus, as Smith points out in the introduction to her translation of this treatise, pp. 181–6. Al-Ghazālī understands these metaphysical concepts as the equivalent of the Qur'ānic terms "Tablet" (*lawḥ*) (Al-Ghazālī, *Al-Risālat al-laduniyya*, p. 25) and "Pen" (*qalam*) (Smith's introduction p. 196, n. 6).

33 Cf. Ibn Sīnā in his *Fī ithbāt al-nubuwwāt* (Beirut: Dār al-Nahār li'l-Nashr, 1968), where he writes, "Revelation is the emanation and the angel is the received emanating power that descends on the prophets as if it were an emanation continuous with the universal intellect" (p. 45; English translation taken from M. Marmura, "On the Proof of Prophecies and the Interpretation of the Prophets' Symbols and Metaphors," in *Medieval Political Philosophy: A Sourcebook*, eds. R. Lerner and M. Mahdi, Ithaca, NY: Cornell University Press, 1963, p. 115); for an analysis of Ibn Sīnā's ideas on the nature of prophecy and the Intellect as a cause of human thought, see H.A. Davidson's *Alfarabi, Avicenna, and Averroes, on Intellect: Their Cosmologies, Theories of the Active Intellect, and Theories of Human Intellect*, Oxford: Oxford University Press,

1992, pp. 83–94, 116–23). Davidson demonstrates the influence of Ibn Sīnā on al-Ghazālī's *Mishkāt al-anwār* (pp. 129–44), an influence that is also apparent in *Al-Risālat al-laduniyya*. Curiously, a copy of *Al-Risālat al-laduniyya* exists in a manuscript attributed to Ibn Sīnā in a library in Istanbul. It is listed as *Al-ʿIlm al-ladunī* in G.C. Anawati's comprehensive bibliography of works attributed to Ibn Sīnā (*Muʾallafāt Ibn Sīnā*, Cairo: Dār al-Maʿārif, 1950, p. 231) and has been published as such in H. ʿĀṣī's *Al-tafsīr al-Qurʾānī waʾl lughat al-ṣūfiyya fī falsafa Ibn Sīnā*, Beirut: Al-Muʾassasāt al-Jāmiʿiyya liʾl-Dirāsāt waʾl-Nashr waʾl-Tazīʿ, 1983. Neither Anawati nor ʿĀṣī mention that it is the same work as the work attributed to al-Ghazālī.

34 We have already seen that al-Ghazālī recommends in his *Fayṣal al-tafriqa* that the Ṣūfī who claims to be released from the obligations of religious law should be killed (Dār al-Nashr al-Maghrabiyya, 1983), p. 28.

35 Al-Qurṭubī, *Al-Jāmiʿ li-aḥkām al-Qurʾān*, vol. 11, pp. 40–1.

36 Ibid., vol. 11, pp. 28–32.

37 Material which al-Maybūdī uses as well in his discussion of the same topic in his *Kashf al-asrār wa ʿuddat al-abrār*, Tehran: Amīr Kabīr, 1982–3, vol. 20, p. 232, as part of his commentary on the miraculous and instantaneous transporting of the throne of the Queen of Sabaʾ to the court of Sulaymān (Qurʾān 27:38).

38 Fāris b. ʿĪsā al-Dīnawarī al-Baghdādī (d. 951).

39 Al-Sulamī, *Ḥaqāʾiq al-tafsīr*, vol. 1, p. 415 and Rūzbihān, *ʿArāʾis al-bayān* vol. 1, p. 593.

40 Abūʾl-Ḥusayn al-Ḥuṣrī (d. 981).

41 Al-Sulamī, *Ḥaqāʾiq al-tafsīr*, vol. 1, p. 415 and Rūzbihān, *ʿArāʾis al-bayān*, vol. 1, p. 593.

42 Al-Qushayrī, *Laṭāʾif al-ishārāt*, vol. 4, p. 78.

43 Ibid., vol. 4, p. 83.

44 Al-Thaʿlabī, *Qiṣaṣ al-anbiyāʾ: Musammā biʾl-ʿArāʾis al-majālis*, Egypt: Maktabat al-Jumhūriyya al-ʿArabiyya, 195?, p. 123.

45 Al-Thaʿlabī's *ʿĀrāʾis al-majālis* is considered to be the first independent collection of stories of the prophets (T. Nagel, "Kiṣaṣ al-Anbiyāʾ" in *The Encyclopedia of Islam*, new ed. and W.M. Thackston, Introduction to *The Tales of the Prophets of al-Kisaʾi*, Boston, MA: Twayne Publishers, 1978, p. xvi). This material from Jews and Christians was considered problematic fairly early on in the Muslim community. G. Newby has suggested that the *isrāʾīliyyāt* narratives included in al-Ṭabarī's *tafsīr* already represent "the remains of a moribund tradition" that found a more congenial home in the genre of *qiṣaṣ al-anbiyāʾ* because of its less exacting standards ("Tafsir Israʾiliyat," *Journal of the American Academy of Religion*, 47, 1979, 685–97). Al-Thaʿlabī's *tafsīr, Al-Kashf waʿl-bayān ʿan tafsīr al-Qurʾān*, was criticized for its use of the same kind of material. Ibn Taymiyya praised the exegete al-Baghawī (d. sometime between 1117 and 1122) for writing an abridged version of al-Thaʿlabī's *tafsīr* purged of the "inferior traditions and heretical opinions," thereby producing a *tafsīr* that Ibn Taymiyya judged superior to those of al-Zamakhsharī and al-Qurṭubī, two exegetes who quoted al-Thaʿlabī frequently (quoted in P.G. Riddell, "The Transmission of Narrative-Based Exegesis in Islam" in *Islam*: Essays on *Scripture, Thought and Society*, eds P.G. Riddell and T. Street, Leiden: E.J. Brill, 1997, p. 67).

46 R. Arnaldez states that al-Qurṭubī made very little use of this material ("Al-Ḳurṭubī" in *The Encyclopedia of Islam*, new ed., vol. 5, p. 531b), but the index to al-Qurtubī's *tafsir, Fahāris al-Jāmiʿ li-aḥkām al-Qurʾān* (Beirut: Dār al-Kutub al-ʿIlmiyya, 1988) cites something like 250 citations from al-Thaʿlabī alone, and as mentioned in the previous note, Ibn Taymiyya criticized al-Qurṭubī for using this material. One example of al-Qurṭubī's use of al-Thaʿlabī's material will demonstrate what is at issue here. It is a comment on Mūsā's reaction to al-Khaḍir's killing of the boy.

> When Mūsā said, "*Have you killed an innocent soul*...?," al-Khaḍir become angry. He ripped off the left shoulder of the boy and then peeled

> the skin off of it. There, on the bone of the shoulder, was written, 'An infidel who will never believe in God" (Al-Qurṭubī, *Al-Jāmiʿ li-aḥkām al-Qurʾān*, vol.11:21, Al-Thaʿlabī, Qiṣaṣ al-anbiyāʾ, p. 127).

This tradition would seem to warrant questioning because it contradicts the chronology of the Qurʾānic narrative in which al-Khaḍir refuses to explain his actions until they part. Al-Qurṭubī demonstrates his critical method with regard to traditions elsewhere in his *tafsīr*, but here he is silent, and one wonders whether his choice to include this material is based on his appreciation of the entertaining manner in which it is written. The genre of the stories of the prophets (*qiṣaṣ al-anbiyāʾ*) was closely connected to the preaching profession where the importance of keeping the attention of one's audience with a story well told was understood.

47 In his *Risāla* al-Qushayrī calls the station of desire (*irāda*) the first station of those who seek God (Principles of Sufism, trans. B. von Schlegell, Berkeley, CA: Mizan Press, 1992, p. 175).

48 Al-Maybudī, *Kashf al-asrār*, vol. 16, pp. 726–8.

49 Ibid., pp. 728–9.

50 Ibid., p. 729.

51 A reference to Qurʾān 89:27–8: *O soul at peace return to your Lord, well pleased and well-pleasing*. The Ṣūfīs believed in a potential progression of the soul from that which commands evil (*al-nafs al-ammāra*) as in Qurʾān 12:53, *truly the soul commands evil unless my Lord has mercy*, to the soul which blames (*al-nafs al-lawwāma*) as in Qurʾān 75:2, *Nay, I call to witness the blaming soul*, to the soul at peace (*al-nafs al-muṭmaʾinna*) (A. Schimmel, *Mystical Dimensions of Islam*, Chapel Hill, NC: University of North Carolina Press, 1975, p. 112). For al-Kāshānī's definition of these three stages see note 61.

52 Al-Maybudī, *Kashf al-asrār*, vol. 16, pp. 729–30.

53 The expression "the one who was carried (*maḥmūl*)" is also used in al-Qushayrī.

54 Rūzbihān, *ʿArāʾis al-bayān*, vol. 1, p. 590.

55 A reference to the Qurʾān 25:53, *It is He who has let forth the two seas. This one is sweet and thirst-quenching, and the other is salty and bitter, and* 35:12, *The two seas are not alike. This one is sweet, thirst-quenching and pleasant to drink and the other is salty and bitter.*

56 Al-Kāshānī, *Taʾwīlāt*, published as *Tafsīr al-Qurʾān al-karīm* and attributed incorrectly to Ibn ʿArabī, Beirut: Dār al-Yaqẓat al-ʿArabiyya, 1968, vol. 1, p. 766.

57 Al-Kāshānī, as has been mentioned, was a follower of the ideas of Ibn ʿArabī, but in this passage his allegiance to Ibn Sīnā is far more apparent. Ibn ʿArabī adopted some of Ibn Sīnā's terminology and concepts, but adapted them to his own thought far more extensively than al-Kāshānī does here; al-Kāshānī's interpretation of the Mūsā and al-Khaḍir story follows Ibn Sīnā's theories of the soul and knowledge closely. Summaries of these theories can be found in S.M. Afnan's *Avicenna: His Life and Works* (London: George Allen and Unwin, 1958), pp. 136–67 and P. Heath's *Allegory and Philosophy in Avicenna (Ibn Sina): With a Translation of the Book of the Prophet Muhammad's Ascent to Heaven*, Philadelphia: University of Pennsylvania Press, 1992, pp. 53–106.

58 Elsewhere al-Kāshānī uses the term Holy Spirit (*rūḥ al-qudus*) to describe al-Khaḍir (*Iṣṭilāḥāt al-ṣufiyya*, London: Octagon Press, 1991, p. 160). In Ibn Sīnā's terminology, the "holy intellect (*al-ʿaql al-qudsī*)" refers to a soul which is blessed with the highest level of intellectual aptitude, an aptitude reserved for prophets (Heath, *Allegory and Philosophy in Avicenna*, pp. 89–90).

59 Al-Kāshānī, *Taʾwīlāt*, vol. 1, p. 768–9. Ibn Sīnā also made spiritual discipline a prerequisite for obtaining higher knowledge in his *Al-Ishārāt waʾl-tanbīhāt* (Tehran, 1958), although he does not mention emulation of another nor does he use the term "heart (*qalb*)."

60 Ibn Sīnā understood the human soul as comprised of three parts: the vegetative (*nabātī*) or natural (*ṭabī'ī*) soul which governs the natural processes of the body; the animal (*ḥayawānī*) soul which governs instinctive and voluntary movement, the latter being based on desire or anger, and perception through five external and five internal senses; and the rational (*nāṭiqa*) soul, unique to man, which is made up of the practical (*'amalī*) and theoretical (*naẓarī*) intellects which enable men to seek moral and intellectual perfection (Afnan, *Avicenna*, pp. 136–9; Heath, *Allegory and Philosophy in Avicenna*, pp. 60–5).

61 Al-Kāshānī, *Ta'wilāt*, vol. 1, pp. 769, 772. We have already mentioned the different stages of the soul in al-Maybudī's allegorical interpretation. Al-Kāshānī defines these three stages as follows. "The commanding soul (*al-nafs al-ammāra*) is that which leans towards the bodily nature (*al-ṭabī'a al-badaniyya*) and commands one to sensual pleasures and lusts and pulls the heart (qalb) in a downward direction. It is the resting place of evil and the source of blameworthy morals and bad actions. God said, *truly the soul commands evil* (12:53). The blaming soul (*al-nafs al-lawwāma*) is that which has been illuminated by the light of the heart to the extent that it awakens from the habit of forgetfulness. It becomes watchful and begins to improve its state, wavering between the two directions of lordliness and creaturelinesss. Whenever something bad emanates from its unjust temperament, the light of divine awakening overtakes it and it begins to blame itself and to turn from it, asking for forgiveness and returning to the door of the Forgiving and the Compassionate. Because of this, God mentions it in oaths: *Nay, I call to witness the blaming soul* (75:2). The soul at peace (*al-nafs al-muṭma'inna*) is that whose illumination has been perfected by the light of the heart so that it has lost its blameworthy qualities and become shaped by praiseworthy morals. It has turned towards the direction of the heart altogether, following it in rising up to the abode of the world of holiness (*'ālam al-qudus*), freed from the abode of uncleanliness, diligent in acts of obedience, dwelling in the presence of the highest of degrees until its Lord addresses it, '*O soul at peace, return to your Lord, well pleased and well-pleasing. Enter among my servants and enter my Garden* (85:27–30)' of the absolute (*tajarrud*)" (*Iṣṭilāḥāt al-ṣufiyya*, pp. 77–8).

62 Al-Kāshānī, *Ta'wilāt*, vol. 1, pp. 770, 772.

63 Ibid., p. 770.

64 According to Ibn Sīnā, the rational soul is made up of the practical and theoretical faculties or intellects. The practical intellect mediates between the vegetal and animal souls and the theoretical intellect, using the rationality of the latter to control the appetites and passions of the former by fostering ethical behavior. The practical intellect deals with the particulars of the external material world while the theoretical intellect has the potential to understand universal concepts received from the Active Intelligence (*al-'aql al-fa''āl*), either through a slow process of applied logic or immediate intuition (*ḥads*), a potential which may or may not be actualized. Al-Kāshānī adopted Ibn Sīnā's conception of the practical and theoretical intellects (P. Lory, *Les Commentaires ésotériques du Coran d'après 'Abd ar-Razzāq al-Qāshānī*, Paris: Les Deux Oceans, 1980, p. 76) and viewed the Active Intelligence as the equivalent of the angel Gabriel or the Holy Spirit (*rūḥ al-qudus*) (p. 55).

65 Al-Kāshānī, *Ta'wilāt*, vol. 1, p. 773. Elsewhere, al-Kāshānī states that the heart (*qalb*) is what the philosopher (*al-ḥakīm*) calls the rational soul (*al-nafs al-nāṭiqa*) (*Iṣṭilāḥāt al-ṣufiyya*, p. 141).

66 Al-Nīsābūrī, *Gharā'ib al-Qur'ān wa raghā'ib al-furqān*, Cairo: Muṣṭafā al-Bābī al-Ḥalabī, 1962–70, vol. 16, p. 17.

67 Ibid., p. 18.

68 Al-Sulamī, *Ḥaqā'iq al-tafsīr*, vol. 1, p. 417; Rūzbihān, *'Arā'is al-bayān*, vol. 1, p. 595; Al-Maybudī, *Kashf al-asrār*, vol. 16, p. 730.

69 Ibid.

70 Cf. Ibn 'Aṭā's interpretation of *"We wanted"* where the "we" refers to al-Khaḍir and Mūsā.

71 Al-Maybudī adds a comment here: "For whoever is able to sacrifice his own qualities (*ṣifāt*) on the holy path, We will paint the secrets of the different types of knowledge of the real in his heart for *We taught him knowledge from Our very presence* (*min ladunnā*) (vol. 16, p. 728).
72 Rūzbihān understands this first station as one of mystical union, while al-Ḥallāj describes it as the total mastery (*istīlā'*) of God.
73 Ibid., vol. 1, p. 595.
74 M. Chodkiewicz, *An Ocean Without Shore: Ibn Arabi, the Book, and the Law*, Albany, NY: SUNY Press, 1993, pp. 30, 45.

8 QUR'ĀNIC VERSES ON MARYAM

1 J.I. Smith and Y. Haddad, "The Virgin Mary in Islamic Tradition and Commentary," *The Muslim World*, 79, 1989, p. 162.
2 H. Corbin, *Creative Imagination in the Sufism of Ibn 'Arabi*, trans. R. Manheim, Princeton, NJ: Princeton University Press, 1969, pp. 145, 153, 170; *The Man of Light in Iranian Sufism*, trans. N. Pearson, Boulder, CO: Shambhala, 1978, p. 131; and *Spiritual Body and Celestial Earth: From Mazdean Iran to Shī'ite Iran*, trans. N. Pearson, Princeton, NJ: Princeton University Press, 1977, p. 309.
3 Al-Ṭabarī, *Jāmi' al-bayān 'an ta'wīl āy Qur'ān*, Egypt: Muṣṭafā al-Bābī al-Halabi, 1954–7, vol. 3, p. 325.
4 Ibid., pp. 325–6; al-Zamakhsharī, *Kashshāf 'an ḥaqā'iq al-tanzīl*, vol. 1, Egypt: Muṣṭafā al-Bābī al-Ḥalabi, 1966–8, p. 425; al-Qurṭubī, *Al-Jāmi' li-aḥkām al-Qur'ān*, vol. 4, Beirut: Dār al-kutub al-'Arabī, 1980, pp. 65–6.
5 Al-Sulamī, *Ḥaqā'iq al-tafsīr*, vol. 1, Beirut: Dār al-Kutub al-'Ilmiyya, 2001, p. 98 and Ja'far al-Ṣadiq, "Le Tafsir Mystique attribute a Ga'far Sadiq," *Melanges De L'Universite Saint Joseph*, 43, 1968, p. 192.
6 Al-Tustarī, *Tafsīr al-Tustarī*, Beirut: Dār al-Kutub al-'Ilmiyya, 2002, p. 48.
7 Al-Qushayrī, *Laṭā'if al-ishārāt*, Cairo: Dār al-Kutub al-'Arabi, 1968–71, vol. 1, p. 249.
8 Quoted in F. Rosenthal, *The Muslim Concept of Freedom Prior to the Nineteenth Century*, Leiden: E.J. Brill, 1960, p. 110.
9 Ibid., p. 111.
10 In his *Kitāb al-ta'arruf*, Abū Bakr al-Kalābādhī mentions Abū Bakr Qaḥṭubī as a Ṣūfī who wrote a book on the sciences of allusion (*The Doctrine of the Sufis Kitāb al-ta'rruf li-madhhab ahl al-taṣawwuf*, trans. A. Arberry, Cambridge: Cambridge University Press, 1977), p. 13.
11 Al-Maybudī, *Kashf al-asrār wa 'uddat al-abrār*, Tehran: Amīr Kabīr, 1982–3, pp. 109–10.
12 A discussion based on the *ḥadīth* saying that many men have reached perfection but among women, only these four.
13 Al-Ṭabarī, *Jāmi' al-bayān*, vol. 3, pp. 263–4.
14 Al-Qurṭubī, *Al-Jāmi' li-aḥkām al-Qur'ān*, vol. 4, pp. 82–4.
15 Rūzbihān, *'Arā'is al-bayān fī ḥaqā'iq al-Qur'ān*, Lucknow, vol. 1, p. 1898, p. 83.
16 Ibid., vol. 12, p. 333.
17 See Qur'ān 7:54, 13:2, 16:12, 22:65 and 31:20, etc.
18 See Qur'ān 2:116, 30:26, and 33:35, etc.
19 A. Schimmel, *Mystical Dimensions of Islam*, Chapel Hill, NC: University of North Carolina Press, 1975, p. 112 and S. Murata, *The Tao of Islam: A Sourcebook of Gender Relationships in Islamic Thought*, Albany: SUNY Press, 1992, pp. 313–4.
20 Al-Ṭabarī, *Jāmi' al-bayān*, pp. 3:241–7.
21 Al-Qushayrī, *Laṭā'if al-ishārāt*, vol. 1, p. 250 and al-Maybudī, *Kashf al-asrār*, vol. 2, p. 111. This quote also appears in al-Qushayrī 's *Risāla*, where al-Qushayrī states that

he heard it from his teacher, Abū ʿAlī al-Daqqāq (Rosenthal, *Muslim Concept of Freedom*, p. 112).

22 Rūzbihān, *ʿArāʾis al-bayān*, vol. 1, pp. 80–1.
23 Al-Qushayrī, *Laṭāʾif al-ishārāt*, vol. 1, p. 251.
24 Ibid., vol. 1, p. 250.
25 Rūzibhān, *ʿArāʾis al-bayān*, vol. 1, p. 81.
26 Al-Kāshānī, *Taʾwīlāt*, published as *Tafsīr al-Qurʾān al-karīm* and attributed incorrectly to Ibn ʿArabī, Beirut: Dār al-Yaqẓat al-ʿArabiyya, 1968, vol. 1, p. 182.
27 Al-Nīsābūrī, *Gharāʾib al-Qurʾān wa raghāʾib al-furqān*, Cairo: Muṣṭafā al-Bābī al-Ḥalabī, 1962–70, vol. 3, p. 186.
28 Ibid.
29 Al-Sulamī, *Ḥaqāʾiq al-tafsīr*, vol. 1, Beirut: Dār al-Kutub al-ʿIlmiyya, 2001, p. 98 and Jaʿfar al-Ṣādiq, *Le Tafsir Mystique*, p. 192.
30 Al-Qushayrī, *Laṭāʾif al-ishārāt*, vol. 1, p. 251.
31 Ibid., p. 251.
32 Rūzbihān, *ʿArāʾis al-bayān*, vol. 1, p. 81.
33 Ibid.
34 Al-Qushayrī, *Laṭāʾif al-ishārāt*, vol. 1, p. 252.
35 Ibid.
36 Al-Maybudī, *Kashf al-asrār*, vol. 2, p. 111.
37 Al-Nīsābūrī, *Gharāʾib al-Qurʾān*, vol. 3, p. 186.
38 Al-Ṭabarī, *Jāmiʿ al-bayān*, vol. 16, p. 71.
39 Al-Qushayrī, *Laṭāʾif al-ishārāt*, vol. 4, p. 97.
40 Jaʿfar al-Ṣādiq, *Le Tafsir Mystique*, p. 208.
41 Rūzbihān, *ʿArāʾis al-bayān*, vol. 2, p. 8 and quoted anonymously in al-Sulamī, *Ḥaqāʾiq al-tafsīr*, vol. 1, p. 424.
42 Al-Maybudī, *Kashf al-asrār*, vol. 6, p. 42.
43 Ibid., vol. 2, p. 89.
44 For a discussion of the idea of preparedness (*istiʿdād*) in the thought of Ibn ʿArabī, see W. Chittick, *The Sufi Path of Knowledge: Ibn al-ʿArabi's Metaphysics of Imagination*, Albany, NY: SUNY Press, 1989, pp. 91–4. For the concept as discussed in the thought of Ṣadr al-Dīn Qunawī (d. 1274) and Saʿīd al-Dīn Farghānī (d. 1296), see S. Murata, *The Tao of Islam*, pp. 107ff.
45 Translated by S. Murata, *The Tao of Islam*, pp. 275–6.
46 Translated by S. Murata, *The Tao of Islam*, p. 43.
47 Al-Kāshānī, *Taʾwīlāt*, vol. 2, p. 89.
48 Ibid., p. 670.
49 Rūzbihān, *Arāʾis al-bayān*, vol. 2, p. 7.
50 Ibid.
51 Ibid.
52 Ibid., vol. 1, p. 69.
53 Quoted in Corbin, *Creative Imagination*, p. 272.
54 Schimmel, *Mystical Dimensions*, p. 290.
55 H. Corbin, *En Islam Iranien*, vol. 2, Paris: Gallimard, 1972, pp. 9–146 and Rūzbihān, *Le Jasmin des Fideles d'amour* (*Kitab-e ʿAbhar al-ʿashiqin*), trans. H. Corbin and M. Mo'in, Teheran: L'Institute Franco-Iranien, 1958, p. 114.
56 Rūzbihān, *Arāʾis al-bayān*, vol. 2, p. 7.
57 Quoted in and translated by C. Ernst, *Words of Ecstasy in Sufism*, Albany, NY: SUNY Press, 1985, p. 27. The material from al-Ḥallāj that Rūzbihān is commenting on is, "I wonder at You and me. You annihilated me out of myself into You. You made me near to Yourself, so that I thought that I was You and You were me." The quote from al-Ḥallāj is from his *Diwān* and Rūzbihān's comments are from his *Sharḥ-i shaṭḥiyāt*.

9 QUR'ĀN 24:35 (THE LIGHT VERSE)

1 I. Goldziher, *Die Richtungen der islamischen Koranauslegung*, Leiden: E.J. Brill, 1952, pp. 180–5.
2 Al-Ṭabarī, *Jāmi' al-bayān 'an ta'wīl āy Qur'ān*, Egypt, 1954–7, vol. 18, p. 135. God is called "the Guide (*hādī*)" in Qur'ānic verses 22:54 and 25:31.
3 Al-Ṭabarī, *Jāmi' al-bayān*, vol. 18, p. 135.
4 Al-Rāzī, *Al-Tafsīr al-kabīr*, Beirut, 1980, vol. 23, p. 224; al-Qurṭubī, *Al-Jāmi' li-aḥkām al-Qur'an*, Beirut: Dār al-Kutub al-'Arabī, vol. 12, p. 257.
5 Al-Ṭabarī, *Jāmi' al-bayān*, vol. 18, p. 135.
6 Al-Zamakhsharī, *Al-Kashshāf 'an ḥaqā'iq al-tanzīl*, Egypt, 1966, vol. 3, p. 67.
7 See the section on the attributes of God in L. Gardet's article, "Allāh" in *Encyclopedia of Islam*, new ed.
8 Al-Rāzī, *Al-Tafsīr al-kabīr*, vol. 7, pp. 181–2.
9 Al-Rāzī appears to have used al-Zamakhsharī's *al-Kashshāf 'an ḥaqā'iq al-tanzīl* as a basis for his philological and grammatical comments, although in an abridged form and not uncritically (Ceylan, *Theology and Tafsir in the Major Works of Fakhr al-Dīn al-Rāzī*, Kuala Lumpur: International Institute of Islamic Thought and Civilization, 1996, pp. 16, 19–20; A.H. Johns, "Solomon and the Queen of Sheba: Fakhr al-Dīn al-Rāzī's Treatment of the Qur'ānic Telling of the Story," *Abr-Nahrain*, 24, 1986, 76–80.
10 Al-Rāzī, *Al-Tafsīr al-kabīr*, vol. 7, pp. 223–4.
11 Qur'ān 2:257, *God is the friend of those who believe. He brings them out of the shadows into the light*; 6:122, *Why, is he who was dead and We gave him life and made a light for him like him who is in the depths of darkness from which he cannot come out?*; and 42:52, *But We made it a light by which We guide those whom We will of Our servants.*
12 Al-Rāzī, *Al-Tafsīr al-kabīr*, vol. 23, p. 224.
13 Ibid., vol. 23, pp. 224–30.
14 F. Rosenthal understands al-Rāzī's exegesis as a rebuttal to al-Ghazālī's view (*Triumphant Knowledge: The Concept of Knowledge in Medieval Islam*, Leiden: E.J. Brill, 1970, p. 160), but this reading does not take into account the fact that al-Rāzī states that there is no contradiction between his own preferred view and that of al-Ghazālī.
15 W. Heinrichs, "On the Genesis of the *Ḥaqīqa-Majāz* Dichotomy," *Studia Islamica*, 59, 1984, 136–7 and "Contacts Between Scriptural Hermeneutics and Literary Theory," *Zeitschrift für Geschichte der Arabisch-Islamischen Wissenschaften*, 7, 1991–2, 256–7.
16 Al-Rāzī, *Al-Tafsīr al-kabīr*, vol. 7, pp. 181–231 and *Sharḥ asmā' Allāh ta'āla wa'l-ṣifāt*, Cairo: Maktaba al-Kulliyāt al-Azhariyya, 1976, pp. 346–8.
17 Ibn Taymiyya *Al-tafsīr al-kabīr*, Beirut: Dār al-Kutub al-'Ilmiyya, 1988, vol. 5, p. 422.
18 This is what the Ash'arīs and Ḥanbalīs called themselves because they believed that they alone affirmed God's attributes.
19 The *jahmiyya* were an early sect said to have been founded by Jahm b. Ṣafwān (d. 746) who, like the Mu'tazila, denied the distinct existence of God's attributes and therefore resorted to their interpretation (*ta'wīl*).
20 Ibn Taymiyya, *Al-Tafsīr al-kabīr*, vol. 5, p. 421. Cf. al-Rāzī, in his *Sharḥ al-asmā'*: Know that light is the name of that mode of being (*kayfiyya*) which has darkness as its opposite, and it is impossible that God (*al-ḥaqq*) could be that for several reasons. The first is that this mode of being comes and goes but it is inconceivable that God (*al-ḥaqq*) could be like that. The second reason is that bodies (*ajsām*) are alike in corporeality but different with regards to light and darkness, so that light is a mode of being in need of a body in which to exist, but the Necessary Existent (*wājib al-wujūd*) could never be like that. The third reason is that light is the contrary to darkness, and far be it from God to have an opposite or an antagonist. The fourth reason is that

God said, *the similitude of His light*, so He attributed light to Himself. If He were a light then this attribution of a thing to Himself would be inconceivable. Therefore, God is not a light, nor is He a thing qualified by this mode of being because this mode of being can only be understood as established in bodies, pp. 346–7. See also al-Razī's *Al-Tafsīr al-kabīr*, vol. 23, p. 223.

21 Ibn Taymiyya, *Al-Tafsīr al-kabīr*, vol. 5, p. 430.

22 Ibid., p. 429.

23 Ibid., pp. 435–8, 440.

24 Ibn Taymiyya's view on the Light Verse bears further investigation. According to J. Pavlin, in his *Bughtat al-Murtadd* Ibn Taymiyya refers to the *hadīth* that says, "His veil is light," to justify interpreting the word "light" and to reject the literal reading that equates God with light ("The Medieval Debate over Quranic Hermeneutics: Ibn Taymiyyah's Discussion of al-Ghazali's Metaphysics in the *Bughtat al-Murtadd*, Paper presented at the American Academy of Religion Annual Meeting, Atlanta, GA, Nov. 22–25, 2003).

25 D. Buchman has done an admirable job of locating the Ṣūfī maxims and *aḥādith* in *Mishkāt al-anwār*. See his translations for these references, which will not be repeated here.

26 Al-Ghazālī, *Al-Ghazālī: The Niche of Lights*, trans. D. Buchman, Provo, UT: Brigham Young University Press, 1998, pp. 1–2. The English translations of *Mishkāt al-anwār* quoted in this chapter are those of Buchman, although I have added some of the transliterated Arabic.

27 Ibid., p. 4.

28 Ibid., pp. 5–13.

29 Ibid., p. 18.

30 Ibid.

31 Ibid.

32 For these and other criticisms Ibn Taymiyya made of the Ṣūfīs, see W. Chittick, "Rūmī and *waḥdat al-wujūd*" in *Poetry and Mysticism in Islam: The Heritage of Rūmī*, eds. A. Banani, R. Hovannisian, and G. Sabagh, Cambridge: Cambridge University Press, 1984, pp. 85–7; A. Knysh, *Ibn 'Arabī in the Later Islamic Tradition: The Making of a Polemical Image in Medieval Islam*, Albany, NY: SUNY Press, 1999, pp. 87–111; and T. Michel, *A Muslim Theologian's Response to Christianity: Ibn Taymiyya's Al-Jawab al-Sahih*, Delmar: Caravan, 1984, pp. 5–14, 24–39.

33 Al-Ghazālī, *The Niche of Lights*, p. 24.

34 Ibid., p. 20.

35 For example, G. Böwering writes, "Ibn al-'Arabī's theory transformed the early Ṣufis' psychological experience of mystical union into an ontological speculation on the unity of being, propelling the idea of *tawḥīd* to a dynamic conclusion" ("Ibn al-'Arabī's Concept of Time," in *God is Beautiful and He Loves Beauty*, Bern: Peter Lang, 1994), p. 75. In his "Bewildered Tongue: The Semantics of Mystical Union in Islam," Sells remarks that "The move from the *dialogical* language of union found in Hallaj and Bistami to the mystical *dialectic* of Ibn 'Arabī need not be seen, as it often has been seen, as a decadent movement from genuine experience to intellectual abstraction… Mystical union transforms philosophical and other objective or scientific discourse, even as the philosophical language offers a new dimension of critical self-awareness and logical precision to the mystical" (in *Mystical Union in Judaism, Christianity, and Islam*, eds M. Idel and B. McGinn, New York: Continuum, 1996), p. 116. One of Ibn 'Arabī's critics, Sa'd al-Dīn Taftāzānī (d. 1389 or 1390), acknowledged an outward similarity between the metaphysical views of al-Ghazālī and Ibn 'Arabī and his followers, but insisted that a closer examination of their works demonstrated the orthodoxy of the former and errors of the latter. He criticized Ibn 'Arabī and his followers for distorting the Ṣūfī concepts of annihilation (*fanā'*) and subsistence (*baqā'*), mistakenly

understanding subjective mystical experience as indicative of the objective reality of things (Knysh, *Ibn 'Arabi in the Later Islamic Tradition*, pp. 150–3). The differences between the metaphysical theories of al-Ghazālī and Ibn 'Arabī is an area which warrants further investigation, but the fact remains that al-Ghazālī preceded Ibn 'Arabī in making ontological statements based on mystical experience and adopting philosophical and theological language and terminology to systematize the view of reality alluded to in earlier Ṣūfī statements and writings.

36 Ibn Sīnā, *Fī ithbāt al-nubuwwāt li-Ibn Sīnā*, Beirut: Dār al-Nahār li'l-Nashr, 1968, p. 49. The English translation here is M. Marmura's, "On the Proof of Prophecies and the Interpretation of the Prophets' Symbols and Metaphors," in *Medieval Political Philosophy: A Sourcebook*, ed. R. Lerner and M. Mahdi, Ithaca, NY: Cornell University press, 1963, p. 116.

37 Al-Ghazālī, *Iḥyā' 'ulūm al-dīn*, vol. 5, Beirut: Al-Dār al-Kutub al-'Ilmiyya, 1989, pp. 173–4. W. Chittick indicates that this same verse drew the attention of Ibn 'Arabī who cites it more often than any other verse to show what Chittick calls the "radical ambiguity of existence," *The Sufi Path of Knowledge: Ibn al-'Arabī's Metaphysics of Imagination*, Albany, NY: SUNY Press, 1989, pp. 113–4.

38 Al-Rāzī, *Al-Tafsīr al-kabīr*, vol. 23, pp. 232–5.

39 Ibid., p. 235.

40 Al-Qurṭubī, *Al-Jāmi' li-aḥkām al-Qur'ān*, vol. 12, p. 206. The *aḥādīth* al-Qurṭubī is referring to here are those quoted in Ibn Taymiyya's discussion of the Light Verse: "O God, praise be to You, light of the heavens and the earth and what is in them," and the Prophet's reply to the question of how he saw his lord, "I see a light."

41 Ibid., p. 263.

42 Ibid., p. 264.

43 Ibn Taymiyya, *Al-Tafsīr al-kabīr*, vol. 5, p. 422. Cf. al-Rāzī: The portion of the servant in [God's name "light"]: Know that the light of the heart is an expression for knowledge of God who said, *Anyone for whom God does not appoint a light has no light* (24:40). The shaykhs have said that light is that which illuminates the hearts of the sincere by its declaration of God's unity and illuminates the innermost hearts of the lovers by its confirmation. It is said that it is that which beautifies human beings by giving form (*taṣwīr*) and the innermost hearts (*asrār*) by illumination. It is said that it is that which enlivens the hearts of the Gnostics by the light of its knowledge and enlivens the souls of the worshippers by the light of its worship (*Sharḥ al-asmā'* p. 348).

44 Ibn Taymiyya is referring to Abū 'Abd al-Raḥmān al-Sulamī's *Ḥaqā'iq al-tafsīr*.

45 Ibn Taymiyya's choice of words here shows that he is following the teachings of Aḥmad b. Ḥanbal with regards to using material that is judged weak in transmission. Elsewhere Ibn Taymiyya quotes Ibn Ḥanbal as saying, " 'If a tradition deals with *ḥalāl* and *ḥarām* (legal matters), we are strict regarding chains of transmission; and if it deals with *targhīb* and *tarhīb* we are lenient.' Ibn Taymiyya points out that this is one of the reasons why the *'ulamā* use *al-ḥadīth al-ḍa'īf* (weak tradition) for *faḍā'il al-'amal* (virtuous deeds). By so doing, they do not intend, however, to make them the basis of legally suggested deeds (*istiḥbāb*), for *istiḥbāb* is an Islamic legal matter that should be based on an Islamic legal argument (*dalīl shar'ī*)," (D. Syafruddin, "The Principles of Ibn Taymiyya's Quranic Interpretation, M.S. Thesis, Institute of Islamic Studies, McGill University, Montreal, 1994, p. 68); the quote from Ibn Ḥanbal is found in Ibn Taymiyya's *Majmū' fatāwā Ibn Taymiyya: al-ḥadīth*, Beirut, 198–, vol. 18, p. 65).

46 The *qarāmiṭa* was a movement appearing in the late ninth century which combined esoteric doctrines and practices with programs for social justice.

47 Ibn Taymiyya, *Al-Tafsīr al-kabīr*, vol. 5, p. 423.

48 One of the epithets of Muḥammad which means "the chosen one."

49 Al-Sulamī, *Ḥaqā'iq al-tafsīr*, vol. 2, Beirut: Dār al-Kutub al-'Ilmiyya, 2001, p. 47; Ja'far al-Ṣādiq, "Le Tafsir Mystique attribute a Ga'far Sadiq," *Melanges De L'Universite Saint Joseph*, 43, 1968, pp. 211–12; and Rūzbihān, *'Arā'is al-bayān* vol. 2, p. 84.

50 The Arabic in al-Ṭabarī here literally means, "entrance" (*madkhal*) and "exit" (*makhraj*). Al-Rāzī writes that al-Rab'ī asked Abū'l-'Āliya (d. 708–9 or 714) about these words and he replied that they meant one's private and public affairs (*sirruhu wa 'alāniyatahu*), 23:237.

51 Al-Ṭabarī, *Jāmi' al-bayān*, vol. 18, p. 138.

52 Al-Tustarī, *Tafsīr al-Tustarī*, Beirut: Dār al-Kutub al-'Ilmiyya, 2002, pp. 40–1. The English translation here is that of M. Sells, *Early Islamic Mysticism: Sufi, Qur'an, Mi'raj, Poetic and Theological Writings*, New York: Paulist Press, 1996, p. 11.

53 Al-Tustarī, *Tafsīr al-Tustarī*, p. 69. The full English translation of this passage can be found in M. Sells, *Early Islamic Mysticism*, pp. 93–4 and is discussed in G. Böwering, *The Mystical Vision of Existence in Classical islam: The Qur'ānic Hermeneutics of the Ṣūfī Sahl at-Tustarī*, Berlin: Walter De Gruyter, 1980, pp. 153–4.

54 On the basis of his reading of al-Tustarī's entire Qur'ānic commentary, Böwering summarizes al-Tustarī's vision of the relationship between God, Muḥammad, and man as follows: "God is light that issues forth in its radiance and articulates itself in the primordial light of Muḥammad the primal man and archetypal mystic. This divine light pervades the whole universe of this-worldly and other-worldly realities and represents the hidden marrow of their existence... The primordial Muḥammad represents the crystal which draws the divine light upon itself, absorbs it in its core (the heart of Muḥammad), projects it unto mankind in the Qur'ānic scripture, and enlightens the soul of mystic man... Man issues as an infinitely small particle of divine light in pre-existential eternity and achieves his final fulfillment as he is engulfed by the divine light in post-existential eternity" (*Mystical Vision*, pp. 264–5). The concept of the Muḥammadan light (*nūr Muḥammadī*) was a controversial one, with some scholars such as al-Ghazālī and Ibn Taymiyya rejecting the notion of Muḥammad's pre-existence, interpreting instead the primordial creation of Muḥammad as referring only to his predestination. A less controversial term which later Ṣūfīs adopted to describe Muḥammad's primordial nature was the Muḥammadan reality (*ḥaqīqa Muḥammadiyya*), a term often discussed with reference to the Light Verse (U. Rubin, "*Nūr Muḥammadī* in *The Encyclopedia of Islam*, new ed.).

55 Al-Ḥallāj, *Diwān al-Ḥallāj*, Kohn: Al-Kamel Verlag, 1997, pp. 119–22.

56 Quoted in al-Sulamī, *Ziyādāt ḥaqā'iq al-tafsīr* (*The Minor Commentary*), Beirut: Dār al-Mashriq, 1986, p. 105.

57 Ibid., p. 106.

58 Al-Ḥallāj quoted in al-Sulamī, *Ḥaqā'iq al-tafsīr*, vol. 2, p. 49; L. Massignon, *Essai sur les origins du lexique technique de la Mystique Musulmane*, Paris: J. Vrin, 1968, p. 385; and Rūzbihān, *'Arā'is al-bayān*, vol. 2, p. 85.

59 Al-Sulamī, *Ḥaqā'iq al-tafsīr*, vol. 2, p. 49; Massignon, *Essai*, p. 385.

60 Al-Sulamī, *Ḥaqā'iq al-tafsīr*, vol. 2, p. 50; Massignon, *Essai*, pp. 385–6; and al-Maybudī, *Kashf al-asrār*, vol. 6, pp. 546–7.

61 Quoted in al-Sulamī, *Ḥaqā'iq al-tafsīr*, vol. 2, p. 45 and Rūzbihān, *'Arā'is al-bayān*, vol. 2, p. 83.

62 Al-Sulamī *Ḥaqā'iq al-tafsīr*, vol. 2, p. 49 and Rūzbihān, *'Arā'is al-bayān*, vol. 2, p. 85.

63 Al-Ghazālī, *The Niche of Lights*, p. 31.

64 Ibid., p. 25.

65 Ibid.

66 Ibid., pp. 36–7.

67 Ibid., pp. 45–50. See H. Landolt's article "Ghazālī and '*Religionswissenschaft*': Some Notes on the *Mishkāt al-anwār* for Professor Charles J. Adams" (*Asiatische*

Studien, 45, 1991, 19–72) for his suggestions for the identification of the various groups al-Ghazālī refers to in the Veils of Light passage.

68 Al-Ghazālī, *The Niche of Lights*, pp. 50–1.

69 Ibid., p. 51.

70 Ibid.

71 The state of annihilation (*fanā'*) described in Part I of the *Mishkāt al-anwār*.

72 Al-Ghazālī, *The Niche of Lights*, pp. 51–2. The issue of whether al-Ghazālī is accepting here the very philosophical theories which he criticized elsewhere has been discussed by such Arab philosophers as Ibn Tufayl (d. 1185) and Ibn Rushd (d. 1198) and modern Western scholars such as W.H.T. Gairdner and M. Watt. Based on the Neoplatonic content of the third section of al-Ghazālī's work, Watt doubted its authenticity. For an excellent summary of and references to previous studies of the *Mishkāt*, studies which have primarily focused on the problems of this third section, see Buchman's Introduction to *The Niche of Lights*, pp. xxvii–xxxii.

73 Ibn Sīnā, *Al-ishārāt wa'l-tanbīhāt*, Tehran: Matba'at al-Haydarī, 1958, vol. 2, pp. 353–4. An English translation of this can be found in M. Ha'iri Yazdi's *The Principles of Epistemology in Islamic Philosophy: Knowledge by Presence*, Albany, NY: SUNY Press, 1992, pp. 193–4, n. 16.

74 In the first section of the *Mishkāt al-anwār* al-Ghazāli uses the term "intellect" (*'aql*) which is the term common to all five elements of Ibn Sīnā's interpretation of the niche, but then switches to the term "spirit" (*rūḥ*) in the second section when presenting his own interpretation of the niche. The term "spirit" is one which Ibn Sīnā uses more generally to refer to either the vegetable, animal, or human souls within man, as opposed to the "intellect" (*'aql*) which is reserved for humans alone.

75 Al-Kāshānī, *Ta'wīlāt*, published as *Tafsīr al-Qur'ān al-karīm* and attributed incorrectly to Ibn 'Arabī, Beirut: Dār al-Yaqẓat al-'Arabiyya, 1968, vol. 2, p. 140. In his *Iṣṭilāḥāt al-ṣufiyya* (*A Glossary of Sufi Technical Terms*, London: Octagon Press, 1991), Kāshānī writes that the "heart" is what is meant by the philosophical term "rational soul" (*al-nafs al-nāṭiqa*), p. 141.

76 Al-Kāshānī, *Ta'wīlāt*, vol. 2, p. 141.

77 Al-Nīsābūrī, *Gharā'ib al-Qur'ān wa raghā'ib al-furqān*, vol. 18, Cairo: Muṣṭafā al-Bābī al-Ḥalabī, 1962–70, p. 199. The reference is to Qur'ān 41:53, which was used by al-Simnānī as well to describe the correspondences between the macrocosm and the microcosm, as detailed in Part I of this study.

78 Al-Nīsābūrī, *Gharā'ib al-Qur'ān*, vol. 18, pp. 199–20. The last line is a reference to Qur'ān 20:5–6: *The Merciful sat upon the throne. To Him belongs what is in the heavens and the earth, and what is between them, and what is under the earth.*

79 The *ḥadīth*, which appears in al-Bukhārī, Riqāq 38, is translated in full by W.A. Graham in his *Divine Word and Prophetic Word in Early Islam: A Reconsideration of the Sources, with Special Reference to the Divine Saying or* Ḥadīth Qudsī (The Hague: Mouton and Co., 1977):

> God said, "Whoever treats a friend of Mine as an enemy, on him I declare war. My servant draws near to Me by means of nothing dearer to Me than that which I have established as a duty for him. And my servant continues drawing nearer to Me through supererogatory acts until I love him; and when I love him, I become his ear with which he hears, his eye with which he sees, his hand with which he grasps, and his foot with which he walks. And if he asks Me [for something], I give it to him. If indeed he seeks My help, I help him. I have never hesitated to do anything as I hesitate [to take] the soul of the man of faith who hates death, for I hate to harm him."
>
> (p. 173)

Graham provides numerous references for Ṣūfī works which cite this *ḥadith*, pp. 173–4.

80 Presumably al-Nīsābūrī is referring to a previous discussion in his commentary.

81 Al-Nīsābūrī, *Gharā'ib al-Qur'ān*, vol. 18, p. 120.

82 Al-Sulamī, *Ḥaqā'iq al-tafsīr*, vol. 2, p. 45 and Ja'far al-Ṣādiq, "Le Tafsir Mystique," p. 212.

83 Al-Qushayrī, *Laṭā'if al-ishārāt*, vol. 4, p. 284.

84 Ibid., pp. 285–6.

85 Al-Maybudī, *Kashf al-asrār*, vol. 6, pp. 542–3.

86 Ibid., p. 546.

87 A Companion of the Prophet who died *c*.682–3.

88 Al-Maybudī, *Kashf al-asrār*, vol. 6, p. 543.

89 Al-Ghazālī refers to this *ḥadīth* in a passage from his autobiography explaining the experience which led him to Ṣūfīsm:

> At length God Most High cured me of that sickness. My soul regained its health and equilibrium and once again I accepted the self-evident data of reason and relied on them with safety and certainty. But that was not achieved by constructing a proof or putting together an argument. On the contrary, it was the effect of a light which God Most High cast into my breast. And that light is the key to most knowledge... And it is this of which the apostle – God's blessing and peace be upon him – said: "God Most High created men in darkness, then sprinkled on them some of His light. From that light then, the unveiling of truth must be sought."
>
> (trans. by R.J. McCarthy, *Freedom and Fulfillment*, Boston, MA: Twayne, 1980, p. 66)

90 In a similar passage of his commentary al-Maybudī writes,

> A shaykh was asked, "What is the sign of that light?" He replied, "Its sign is that through that light the servant knows God without finding Him, loves Him without seeing Him, turns away from being occupied with and remembering himself through being occupied with and remembering Him. He finds ease and rest in His lane, he tells secrets to His friends and asks favors from them. By day he is busy with religion's work, by night intoxicated with certainty's tidings. By day he dwells with creatures of good character, by night with the Real, fixed in sincerity."
>
> (*Kashf al-asrār*, vol. 7, p. 455; English translation here by S. Murata, *Tao of Islam, A Sourcebook of Gender Relationships in Islamic Thought*, Albany, NY: SUNY Press, 1992 p. 27)

91 Al-Maybūdī, *Kashf al-asrār*, vol. 6, pp. 543–4.

92 The *zunnār* was a belt or girdle worn about the waist by Eastern Christians.

93 Al-Maybūdī, *Kashf al-asrār*, vol. 6, p. 545.

94 Ibid., p. 546.

95 T. Izutsu, *Creation and the Timeless Order of Things*, Ashland, OR: White Cloud Press, 1994.

CONCLUSION

1 I use the term "subjectivity" here, following B. Weiss in his article "Exotericism and Objectivity in Islamic Jurisprudence" in *Islamic Law and Jurisprudence*, ed. N. Heer, Seattle: University of Washington Press, 1990. Weiss points out the public nature of

rational argument and transmitted material in Islamic theology and law as compared to the private world of experience upon which Ṣūfism is based.

2 Ibn al-Jawzī, *Muktasar kitāb talbīs Ilbīs*, Beirut: Mu'assasāt al-Risāla, 1992, p. 150.

APPENDIX: COMMENTATORS ON THE QUR'ĀN

1 Information on the life and works of al-Ṭabarī can be found in C. Bosworth, "Al-Ṭabarī" in *The Encyclopedia of Islam*, new ed.; J. McAuliffe, *Qur'ānic Christians: An Analysis of Classical and Modern Exegesis*, Cambridge: Cambridge University Press, 1991, pp. 38–45; and F. Rosenthal's General Introduction to *The History of al-Ṭabarī*, vol. 1 Albany, NY: SUNY Press, 1989, pp. 5–134.

2 Al-Ṭabarī, *Jāmi' al-bayān 'an ta'wīl āy Qur'ān*, Egypt: Muṣṭafā al-Bābi al-Ḥalabi, 1954–7.

3 Bosworth notes that sources introduced by words such as *ḥaddathanā*, *akhbaranā*, or *kataba* indicate that al-Ṭabarī had the recognized license (*ijāza*) to transmit those sources. Where he had no such authority, he used words such as *qāla*, *dhakara*, *rawā*, and *ḥuddithtu*, "Al-Ṭabarī," *Encyclopedia of Islam*.

4 Information on the life and works of al-Zamakhsharī can be found in C. Brockelmann, "Al-Zamakhsharī" in *The Encyclopedia of Islam*, new ed. and McAuliffe, *Qur'ānic Christians*, pp. 49–54.

5 Y. Ceylan, *Theology and Tafsīr in the Major Works of Fakhr al-Dīn al-Rāzī*, Kuala Lumpur: International Institute of Islamic Thought and Civilization, 1996, pp. 16, 19–20 and A.H. Johns, "Solomon and the Queen of Sheba: Fakhr al-Dīn al-Rāzī's Treatment of the Qur'ānic Telling of the Story," *Abr-Nahrain*, 24, 1986, 76–80.

6 M. Ayoub, *The Qur'an and its Interpreters*, vol. 1, Albany, NY: SUNY Press, 1984, p. 6.

7 Al-Zamakhsharī, *Al-Kashshāf 'an ḥaqā'iq al-tanzīl*, Egypt, 1966.

8 Johns, "Solomon and the Queen of Sheba," p. 77.

9 Because few of their works remain, the views of the Karrāmiyya are known primarily through their opponents, who accused them of literalism and anthropomorphism. Al-Rāzī's polemical writings concerning them constitute the last traces of them before their disappearance after the Mongol invasions. See C. Bosworth, "Karrāmiyya" in *The Encyclopedia of Islam*, new ed.

10 Biographical information on al-Rāzī can be found in G. Anawati, "Al-Rāzī" in *The Encyclopedia of Islam*, new ed.; Ceylan, *Theology and Tafsīr* pp. 1–13; F. Kholeif, *A Study on al-Rāzī and His Controversies in Transoxiana*, Beirut: Dar El-Machreq, 1966, pp. 9–25; and McAuliffe, *Qur'ānic Christians*, pp. 63–76.

11 W. Chittick translates a portion of this letter in *The Self-Disclosure of God: Principles of Ibn al-'Arabī's Cosmology*, Albany, NY: SUNY Press, 1998, p. 124.

12 Ceylon, *Theology and Tafsīr*, pp. 16, 19–20; Johns, "Solomon and the Queen of Sheba," pp. 76–80. Although he abridges al-Zamakhsharī, grammatical and linguistic issues still represent the largest part of his comments, according to M. Lagarde, *Index du Grand Commentaire de Fakhr al-Dīn al-Rāzī*, Leiden: E.J. Brill, 1996, p. 3.

13 See McAuliffe, *Qur'ānic Christians*, p. 69.

14 Information on the life and works of al-Qurṭubī can be found in R. Arnaldez's "Al-Ḳurṭubī" in *The Encyclopedia of Islam*, new ed.

15 Al-Qurṭubī, *Al-Jāmi' li-aḥkām al-Qur'ān wa'l-mubayyin li-mā taḍammana min al-sunna wa-āyāt al-furqān*, Beirut: Dār al-Kutub al-'Abrabī, 1980.

16 Al-Qurṭubī shows himself to be aware of these controversies by sometimes offering critical comments relating to *isrā'īliyyāt* material. But, as M. Mashīnī demonstrates, al-Qurṭubī is inconsistent in his methodology, sometimes rejecting the narratives after assessing their source, sometimes including them without comment (*Madrasāt al-tafsīr fī al-Andalus*, Beirut: Mu'assasāt al-Risāla, 1986, pp. 101, 560–78, 826).

R. Arnaldez states that al-Qurṭubī makes very little use of this material (5:531b), but the index to *Al-Jāmiʿ li-aḥkām al-Qurʾān* (*Fahāris al-Jāmiʿ li-aḥkām al-Qurʾān*) lists something like 250 citations from al-Thaʿlabi (Beirut: Dār al-Kutub al-ʿIlmiyya, 1988).

17 N. Calder, "Tafsīr from Ṭabarī to Ibn Kathīr: Problems in the description of a genre, illustrated with reference to the story of Abraham," in *Approaches to the Qurʾān*, eds G.R. Hawting and A.A. Shareef, London: Routledge, 1992, pp. 109–10.

18 Information on the life and works of Ibn Taymiyya can be found in H. Laoust's article "Ibn Taymiyya" in *The Encyclopedia of Islam*, new ed.

19 See G. Makdisi in "The Hanbali School of Sufism," *Humaniora Islamica*, 2, 1974, 61–72 and "Ibn Taimīya: A Ṣūfī of the Qādiriya Order," *American Journal of Arabic Studies*, 1, 1973, 118–29.

20 Makdisi, "Ibn Taimīya," pp. 126–7 and T. Michel, *A Muslim Theologian's Response to Christianity: Ibn Taymiyya's Al-Jawab al-Sahih*, Delmar: Caravan, 1984, pp. 27–8.

21 See T. Homerin, "Ibn Taymīya's *Al-Ṣūfiyah wa-al-fuqarāʾ*," *Arabica*, 32, 1985, 219–44; A. Knysh, *Ibn ʿArabī in the Later Islamic Tradition: The Making of a Polemical Image In Medieval Islam*, Albany, NY: SUNY Press, 1999, pp. 87–111; and T. Michel, "Ibn Taymiyya's *Sharḥ* on the *Futūḥ al-Ghayb* of ʿAbd al-Qādir al-Jīlānī," *Hamdard Islamicus*, 4, 1982, 3–12; and Michel, *A Muslim's Theologian's Response to Christianity*, pp. 27–8.

22 See D. Syafruddin's analysis of this commentary in his "The Principles of Ibn Taymiyya's Qurʾānic Interpretation," M.A. Thesis, Institute of Islamic Studies, McGill University, Montreal, 1994, pp. 78–97.

23 See R. Curtis, "Authentic Interpretation of Classical Islamic Texts: An analysis of the introduction to Ibn Kathīr's 'Tafsīr al-Qurʾān al-ʿAẓīm," Ph.D. dissertation, University of Michigan, 1989, pp. 76–87 and Syaffruddin, "The Principles of Ibn Taymiyya's Qurʾānic Interpretation," pp. 122–3.

WORKS CITED

Primary sources

Abū Ṭālib al-Makkī, Muḥammad. *Qūt al-qulūb*. Cairo: Dār al-Rashād, 1991.

Ash'arī, Abū'l-Ḥasan 'Alī, al-. *Al-Ibāna 'an uṣūl al-diyāna*. Beirut: Dār al-Nafā'is 1994.

Ghazālī, Abū Ḥāmid Muḥammad, al-. *Fayṣal al-tafriqa bayna'l-Islām wa'l-zandaqa*. Casablanca: Dār al-Nashr al-Maghrabiyya, 1983.

—— *Iḥyā' 'ulūm al-dīn*. With commentary by Muḥammad b. Muḥammad Murtada' al-Zabīdī in *Itḥaf al-sāda al-muttaqīn bi-sharḥ*. Beirut: Al-Dār al-Kutub al-'Ilmiyya, 1989.

—— *Iljām al-'awāmm 'an 'ilm al-kalām*. Ed. Muḥammad al-Baghdādī. Beirut: Dār al-Kitāb al-'Arabī, 1985.

—— *Jawāhir al-Qur'ān wa duraruh*. Beirut: Dār al-Afāq al-Jadīda, 1983.

—— *Mishkāt al-anwār wa-miṣfāt al-asrār*. See Translations.

—— *Al-Mustaṣfā min 'ilm al-uṣūl*. Ed. Muḥammad al-Ashqār. Beirut: Mu'assasāt al-Risāla, 1997.

—— *Al-Risālat al-laduniyya*. Cairo, n.d.

Ḥallāj, Al-Ḥusayn b. Manṣūr, al-. *Dīwān al-Ḥallāj*. Koln: Al-Kamel Verlag, 1997.

Ibn Ḥibbān, Abū Bakr Muḥammad. *Al-Musnad al-ṣaḥīḥ 'alā'l-taqāsīm wa'l-anwā'*. Beirut: Mu'assasāt al-Risālā, 1984–91.

Ibn al-Jawzī, Abū'l-Faraj. *Mukhtaṣar kitāb talbīs Iblīs*. Beirut: Mu'assasāt al-Risāla, 1992.

Ibn Qudāma. See translations.

Ibn Sīnā, Abū 'Alī al-Ḥusayn. *Fī ithbāt al-nubuwwāt li-Ibn Sīnā*. Ed. Michael E. Marmura. Beirut: Dār al-Nahār li'l-Nashr, 1968.

—— *Al-Ishārāt wa'l-tanbīhāt*. Tehran: Matba'at al-Haydarī, 1958–9.

Ibn Taymiyya, Aḥmad Taqī al-Dīn. *Muqaddima fī uṣūl al-tafsīr*. Cairo: Maktaba al-Turāth al-Islamiyya, 1988.

—— *Majmū' fatāwā Ibn Taymiyya: al-ḥadīth*, Vol. 18, Beirut, 198–.

—— *Al-radd 'alā al-mantiqiyyīn*. Bombay: Al-Maṭba'at al-Qayyima, 1949.

—— *Al-tafsīr al-kabīr*. Beirut: Dār al-Kutub al-'Ilmiyya, 1988.

Ja'far al-Ṣādiq. "Le Tafsir Mystique attribue a Ga'far Sadiq" (recension al-Sulamī). Ed. Paul Nwyia. *Melanges De L'Universite Saint Joseph*, 43, 1968, 179–230.

Kāshānī, 'Abd al-Razzāq al-. *Iṣṭilāḥāt al-ṣūfiyya*. See Translations: A Glossary of Sufi Technical Terms.

—— *Ta'wīlāt* (*Ta'wīl al-Qur'ān*), published as *Tafsīr al-Qur'ān al-karīm* and attributed incorrectly to Ibn 'Arabī. Beirut: Dār al-Yaqẓat al-'Arabiyya, 1968.

Maybudī, Rashīd al-Dīn al-. *Kashf al-asrār wa 'uddat al-abrār*. Ed. 'A. A. Hikmat. Tehran: Amīr Kabīr, 1982–3.
Nīsābūrī, Niẓām al-Dīn al-. *Gharā'ib al-Qur'ān wa raghā'ib al-furqān*. Ed. Ibrāhīm 'Aṭwah 'Iwaḍ. Cairo: Muṣṭafā al-Bābī al-Ḥalabī, 1962–70.
Qāshānī. See Kāshānī.
Qurṭubī, Muḥammad b. Aḥmad 'Abd Allāh al-Anṣārī al-. *Al-Jāmi' li-aḥkām al-Qur'ān wa'l-mubayyin li-mā taḍammana min al-sunna wa-āyāt al-furqān*. Beirut: Dār al-Kutub al-'Arabī, 1980.
Qushayrī, Abū'l-Qāsim al-. *Laṭā'if al-ishārāt*. Introduction and editing by Ibrāhīm Basyūnī. Cairo: Dār al-Kutub al-'Arabī, 1968–71.
Rāzī, Muḥammad b. 'Umar Fakhr al-Dīn al-. *Sharḥ asmā' Allāh ta'āla wa'l-ṣifāt*. Cairo: Maktaba al-Kulliyāt al-Azhariyya, 1976.
—— *Al-Tafsīr al-kabīr*. Beirut, 1980.
Rūzbihān al-Baqlī, Abū Muḥammad b. Abī Naṣr. *'Arā'is al-bayān fī ḥaqā'iq al-Qur'ān*. Lucknow, 1898.
Sarrāj Abū Naṣr al-. *Kitāb al-luma' fī'l-taṣawwuf*. Ed. Reynold A. Nicholson. Gibb Memorial Series, no. 22. London: Luzac, 1963.
Simnānī, 'Alā' al-Dawla al-. "Muqaddima tafsīr al-Qur'ān li-'Alā' al-dawla al-Simnānī." Ed. Paul Nwyia. *Al-Abḥāth*, 26, 1973–77, 141–57.
Sulamī, Abū 'Abd Al-Raḥmān Muḥammad b. al-Ḥusayn al-. *Ḥaqā'iq al-tafsīr*. Ed. Sayyid 'Umrān, Beirut: Dār al-Kutub al-'Ilmiyya, 2001.
—— *Ziyādāt ḥaqā'iq al-tafsīr* (*The Minor Commentary*). Ed. Gerhard Böwering. Beirut: Dār al-Mashriq, 1986.
Suyūṭī, Jalāl al-Dīn al-. *Al-Itqān fī 'ulūm al-Qur'ān*. Lahore: Suhail Academy, 1980.
Ṭabarī, Abū Ja'far al-. *Jāmi' al-bayān 'an ta'wīl āy al-Qur'ān*. Egypt: Maṣṭafā al-Bābi al-Ḥalabī, 1954–7.
Tha'labī, Ibn Isḥāq Aḥmad b. Muḥammad Ibrāhīm, al. *Qiṣaṣ al-anbiyā': Musammā bi'l-'Arā'is al-majālis*). Egypt: Maktabat al-Jumhūriyya al-'Arabiyya, 195–.
—— *Qatlā'l-Qur'ān*. See translations.
Tustarī, Abū Muḥammad Sahl b. 'Abd Allāh, al. *Tafsīr al-Tustarī*. Ed. Muḥammad Bāsil 'Uyūn al-Sūd, Beirut: Dār al-Kutub al-'Ilmiyya, 2002.
Zamakhsharī, Maḥmūd b. 'Umar Abū'l-Qāsim, al. *Al-Kashshāf 'an ḥaqā'iq al-tanzīl*. Egypt: Mustafā al-Bābī al-Ḥalabī, 1966.

Al-Qur'ān translations

The Holy Quran. Text, translation and commentary by A.Yusuf Ali. New York: Haftner Publication, 1946.
The Koran Interpreted. Trans. Arthur J. Arberry. New York: Macmillan, 1955.
The Message of the Qur'ān. Translation and explanation by Muhammad Asad. Gibraltar: Dar al-Andalus, 1980.

Translations

Abū Ṭālib al-Makkī. *Die Nahrung der Herzen*. Trans. Richard Gramlich. Stuttgart: Franz Steiner Verlag, 1992–5.
Ash'arī, Abū'l-Ḥasan 'Alī, al-. *Al-Ash'arī's Al-Ibānah 'an uṣūl ad-diyānah* (*The Elucidation of Islam's Foundations*). Trans. Walter C. Klein. New Haven, CT: American Oriental Society, 1940.

Ghazālī, Abū Ḥāmid Muḥammad al-. "The Canons of Ta'wil" (*Qānūn al-ta'wīl*). Trans. Nicholas Heer. *Windows on the House of Islam: Muslim Sources of Spirituality and Religious Life*. Ed. John Renard. Berkeley, CA: University of California Press, 1998.

—— *Freedom and Fulfillment: An Annotated Translation of Al-Ghazālī's al-Munqidh min al-Ḍalāl and Other Relevant Works of al-Ghazālī*. Trans. Richard Joseph McCarthy. Boston, MA: Twayne, 1980.

—— *Al-Ghazālī: The Niche of Lights. A parallel English-Arabic text translated, introduced, and annotated* by David Buchman. Provo, UT: Brigham Young University Press, 1998.

—— *Al-Ghazzali's Mishkat al-anwar*. Trans. W.H.T. Gairdner. Lahore: Sh. Muhammad Ashraf, 1991.

—— *The Jewels of the Qur'ān: Al-Ghazālī 's Theory. A Translation, with an introduction and annotation, of al-Ghazālī's Kitāb Jawāhir al-Qur'ān* by Muhammad Abul Quasem. London: Kegan Paul International, 1983.

—— *The Recitation and Interpretation of the Qur'an: Al-Ghazali's Theory*. Trans. Muhammad Abul Quasem. London and Boston: Kegan Paul International, 1982.

—— "Al-Risālat Al-Laduniyya. By Abū Ḥāmid Muḥammad al-Ghazālī (450/1059–505/1111)." Trans. Margaret Smith. *Journal of the Royal Asiatic Society*, 1938, 177–200, 353–74.

Ḥallāj, Al-Ḥusayn b. Manṣūr al-. *The Tawasin of Mansur al-Hallaj: The Great Sufic Text on the Unity of Reality*. Trans. Aisha Abd ar-Rahman at-Tarjumana. Berkeley, CA: Diwan Press, 1974.

Ibn al-Jawzī, Abū'l-Faraj. "The Devil's Delusion." Trans. D.S. Margoliouth. *Islamic Culture*, 10, 1936, 339–68; 11, 1937, 393–403.

Ibn Qudāma, Muwaffaq al-Dīn 'Abd Allāh. *Censure of Speculative Theology: An edition and translation of Ibn Qudāma's Taḥrīm an-naẓar fi kutub ahl al-kalām* by George Makdisi. London: Luzac, 1962.

Ibn Sīnā, Abū 'Alī al-Ḥusayn. "*Avicenna*: On the Proof of Prophecies and the Interpretation of the Prophet's Symbols and Metaphors." Trans. Michael E. Marmura. *Medieval Political Philosophy: A Sourcebook*. Eds Ralph Lerner and Mushin Mahdi. Ithaca, NY: Cornell University Press, 1963, 112–21.

Ibn Taymiyya, Aḥmad b. 'Abd al-Ḥālim. *A Muslim Theologian's Response to Christianity: Ibn Taymiyya's Al-Jawab al-Sahih*. Trans. Thomas Michel. Delmar: Caravan, 1984.

—— *Muqaddima fi uṣūl al-tafsīr: An Introduction to the Principles of Tafseer*. Trans. Muhammad 'Abdul Haq Ansari. Birmingham, UK: Al-Hidaayah Publishing, 1993.

—— "Ibn Taymiyya's *Sharḥ* on the *Futūḥ al-Ghayb* of 'Abd al-Qādir al-Jīlānī." Trans. Thomas Michel. *Hamdard Islamicus*, 4, 1981, 3–12.

—— "Ibn Taimīya's *Al-Ṣūfiyah wa-al-fuqarā'*." Trans. Th. E. Homerin. *Arabica*, 32, 1985, 219–44.

—— "Ibn Taymiyya: Treatise on the Principles of Tafsīr" (excerpt). Trans. Jane Dammen McAuliffe. *Windows on the House of Islam: Muslim Sources on Spirituality and Religious Life*. Ed. John Renard. Berkeley, CA: University of California Press, 1998, pp. 35–43.

Kalābādhī, Abū Bakr al-. *The Doctrine of the Sufis (Kitāb al-ta'arruf li-madhhab ahl al-taṣawwuf)*. Translated by A.J. Arberry. Cambridge: Cambridge University Press, 1977 (first published 1935).

Kāshānī, 'Abd al-Razzāq al-. *A Glossary of Sufi Technical Terms* (*Iṣṭilāḥāt al-ṣūfiyya*). Arabic text with trans. by Nabi Safwat, revised and edited by David Pendlebury. London: Octagon Press, 1991.

Kisā'ī, Muḥammad b. 'Abd Allāh al-. *The Tales of the Prophets of al-Kisa'i*. Translated with notes by W.M. Thackston. Boston, MA: Twayne Publishers, 1978.

Qushayrī, Abū'l-Qāsim al-. *Principles of Sufism*. Trans. B.R. von Schlegell. Berkeley, CA: Mizan Press, 1992.

Rūzbihān al-Baqlī. Le Jasmin des Fideles d'amour (Kitab-e 'Abhar al-'ashiqin). Introduction and translation by Henry Corbin and Mohsin Mo'in. Teheran: L'Institute Franco-Iranien, 1958.

Rūzbihān al-Baqlī. *The Unveiling of Secrets: Diary of a Sufi Master*. Trans. Carl W. Ernst. Chapel Hill, NC: Parvardigar Press, 1997.

Sarrāj Abū Naṣr al-. Schlaglichter über das Sufitums. Trans. Richard Gramlich. Stuttgart: Franz Steiner Verlag, 1990.

Ṭabarī, Abū Ja'far Muḥammad b. Jarīr, al-. *The Commentary on the Qur'ān*. Vol. 1. Trans. J. Cooper. Oxford: Oxford University Press, 1987.

—— *The History of al-Ṭabarī (Ta'rīkh al-rusul wa'l-mulūk)*. Vol. 1. Translation and General Introduction by Franz Rosenthal. Albany, NY: SUNY Press, 1989.

—— *The History of al-Ṭabarī (Ta'rīkh al-rusul wa'l-mulūk)*. Vol. 3. Trans. William Brinner. Albany, NY: SUNY Press, 1991.

Tha'labī, Abū Isḥāq Aḥmad b. Muḥammad Ibrāhīm, al. *'Arā 'is al-majālis fī qiṣaṣ al-anbiyā' Or, "Lives of the Prophets"*. Trans. William M. Brinner. Leiden: E.J. Brill, 2002.

—— *Die vom Koran Getöten: Aṭ-Ṯha'labīs* Qatlā l-Qur'ān *nach der Istanbuler und den Leidener Handschriften*. Edition, commentary and translation by Beate Wiesmüller. Würzburg: Ergon Verlag, 2002.

Secondary works

Abrahamov, Binyamin. "Ibn Taymiyya on the Agreement of Reason with Tradition." *Muslim World*, 82, 1992, 256–72.

Afnan, Soheil M. *Avicenna: His Life and Works*. London: George Allen and Unwin, 1958.

Ahmad, Rashid (Jullandri). "Abu al-Qasim al-Qushairi as a Theologian and Commentator." *The Islamic Quarterly*, 13, 1969, 16–69.

—— "Qur'anic Exegesis and Classical Tafsir." *The Islamic Quarterly*, 12, 1968, 71–119.

Amir-Moezzi, Mohammad Ali. *The Divine Guide in Early Shi'ism: The Sources of Esotericism in Islam*. Trans. David Streight. Albany, NY: SUNY, 1994.

Anawati, G.C. *Mu'allafāt Ibn Sīnā*. Cairo: Dār al-Ma'ārif, 1950.

Arberry, A.J. *Shiraz: Persian City of Saints and Poets*. Norman: University of Oklahoma Press, 1960.

Asad, Muhammad. See Translations: Qur'ān.

'Āṣī, Ḥasan. *Al-tafsīr al-Qur'ānī wa'l-lughat al-ṣūfiyya fī falsafa Ibn Sīnā*. Beirut: Al-Mu'assasāt al-Jāmi'iyya li'l-Dirāsāt wa'l-Nashr wa'l-Tawzī', 1983.

Ayoub, Mahmoud M. *The Qur'an and Its Interpreters*. Vol. 1. Albany, NY: SUNY Press, 1984.

—— *The Qur'an and Its Interpreters: The House of 'Imran*. Vol. 2. Albany, NY: SUNY Press, 1992.

Badawī, 'Abd al-Raḥmān. *Mu'allafāt al-Ghazālī*. Cairo: Al-Majlis al-A'lā liRi'āyat al-Funūn wa'l-ādāb wa'l 'ulūm al-Ijtimā'iyya, 1961.

Bello, Iysa A. *The Medieval Islamic Controversy Between Philosophy and Orthodoxy: Ijma' and Ta'wil in the Conflict Between Al-Ghazali and Ibn Rushd*. Leiden: E.J. Brill, 1989.

Böwering, Gerhard. "The *Adab* Literature of Classical Islam: Anṣārī's Code of Conduct." *Moral Conduct and Authority: The Place of Adab in South Asian Islam*. Ed. Barbara Daly Metcalf. Berkeley, CA: University of California Press, 1984.
—— "Ibn al-'Arabī's Concept of Time." *God is Beautiful and He Loves Beauty*. Eds Alma Giese and J. Christoph Bürgel. Bern: Peter Lang, 1994.
—— "The Major Sources of Sulamī's Minor Qur'ān Commentary." *Oriens*, 35, 1996, 35–56.
—— *The Mystical Vision of Existence in Classical Islam: The Qur'ānic Hermeneutics of the Ṣūfī Sahl at-Tustarī*. Berlin: Walter De Gruyter, 1980.
—— "The Qur'ān Commentary of Al-Sulamī." *Islamic Studies Presented to Charles J. Adams*. Eds Wael B. Hallaq and Donald P. Little. Leiden: E.J. Brill, 1991, pp. 41–56.
Bürgel, Johann Christoph. *The Feather of Simurgh: The "Licit Magic" of the Arts in Medieval Islam*. New York: New York University Press, 1988.
—— "'Symbols and Hints: Some Considerations Concerning the Meaning of Ibn Ṭufayl's *Ḥayy ibn Yaqẓān*." *The World of Ibn Ṭufayl: Interdisciplinary Perspectives on Ḥayy ibn Yaqẓān*. Ed. Lawrence I. Conrad. Leiden: E.J. Brill, 1996, pp. 114–32.
Calder, Norman. "Tafsīr from Ṭabarī to Ibn Kathīr: Problems in the description of a genre, illustrated with reference to the story of Abraham." *Approaches to the Qur'ān*. Ed. G.R. Hawting and Abdul-Kader A. Shareef. London: Routledge, 1993, pp. 101–40.
Ceylan, Yasin. *Theology and Tafsīr in the Major Works of Fakhr al-Dīn al-Rāzī*. Kuala Lumpur: International Institute of Islamic Thought and Civilization, 1996.
Chittick, William. "The Five Divine Presences: From Al-Qūnawī to Al-Qayṣarī." *The Muslim World*, 72, 1982, 107–28.
—— *Imaginal Worlds: Ibn al-'Arabi and the Problem of Religious Diversity*. Albany, NY: SUNY Press, 1994.
—— "Rūmī and *waḥdat al-wujūd*." *Poetry and Mysticism in Islam: The Heritage of Rūmī*. Eds Amin Banani, Richard Hovannisian, and George Sabagh. Cambridge: Cambridge University Press, 1984, pp. 70–111.
—— "The School of Ibn 'Arabī." *History of Islamic Philosophy*. Eds Seyyed Hossein Nasr and Oliver Leaman. Vol. 1. London: Routledge, 1996, pp. 510–23.
—— *The Self-Disclosure of God: Principles of Ibn al-'Arabī's Cosmology*. Albany, NY: SUNY Press, 1998.
—— *The Sufi Path of Knowledge: Ibn al-'Arabi's Metaphysics of Imagination*. Albany, NY: SUNY Press, 1989.
Chodkiewicz, Michel. *An Ocean Without Shore: Ibn Arabi, the Book, and the Law*. Albany, NY: SUNY Press, 1993.
Corbin, Henry. *Creative Imagination in the Sufism of Ibn 'Arabi*. Trans. Ralph Manheim. Princeton, NY: Princeton University Press, 1969.
—— *En Islam Iranien*. Paris: Gallimard, 1972.
—— *The Man of Light in Iranian Sufism*. Trans. Nancy Pearson. Boulder, CO: Shambhala, 1978.
—— *Spiritual Body and Celestial Earth: From Mazdean Iran to Shi'ite Iran*. Trans. Nancy Pearson. Princeton, NY: Princeton University Press, 1977.
Curtis, Roy Young Mukhtar. "Authentic Interpretation of Classical Islamic Texts: An analysis of the introduction of Ibn Kathīr's "Tafsīr al-Qur'ān al-'Aẓīm." PhD Dissertation, The University of Michigan, Ann Arbor, MI, 1989.
Dabashi, Hamid. "Historical Conditions of Persian Sufism during the Seljuk Period." *Classical Persian Sufism: From its Origins to Rumi*. Ed. Leonard Lewisohn London: Khaniqahi Nimatullahi Publications, 1993, pp. 137–74.

Davidson, Herbert A. *Alfarabi, Avicenna, and Averroes, on Intellect: Their Cosmologies, Theories of the Active Intellect, and Theories of Human Intellect.* Oxford: Oxford University Press, 1992.

Dhahabī, Muḥammad Ḥusayn al-. *Al-tafsīr wa'l-mufassirūn*, 2 vols, Cairo: Dār al-kutub al-ḥadītha, 1967.

Elias, Jamal J. *The Throne Carrier of God: The Life and Thought of 'Ala' ad-dawla as-Simnani.* Albany, NY: SUNY Press, 1995.

The Encyclopedia of Islam. Eds C.E. Bosworth, E. van Donzel, W.P. Heinrichs, and G. Lecomte. Leiden: E.J. Brill, 1960–2002.

The Encyclopedia of Religion. Ed. Mircea Eliade. New York: Macmillan, 1987.

Ernst, Carl W. *Ruzbihan Baqli: Mysticism and the Rhetoric of Sainthood in Persian Sufism.* Richmond: Curzon Press, 1995.

—— *The Shambhala Guide to Sufism.* Boston, MA: Shambhala, 1997.

—— "The Symbolism of Birds and Flight in the Writings of Ruzbihan Baqli." *The Legacy of Mediaeval Persian Sufism.* Ed. Leonard Lewisohn. London: Khaniqahi Nimatullahi, 1992, pp. 353–66.

—— *Words of Ecstasy in Sufism.* Albany, NY: SUNY Press, 1985.

Fahāris al-Jāmi' li-aḥkām al-Qur'ān. Beirut: Dār al-Kutub al-'Ilmiyya, 1988.

Gatje, Helmut. *The Qur'an and its Exegesis: Selected Texts with Classical and Modern Muslim Interpretations.* Trans. and ed. by Alford T. Welch. Berkeley, CA: University of California Press, 1976.

Glassé, Cyril. *The Concise Encyclopedia of Islam.* San Francisco, CA: Harper and Row, 1989.

Godlas, Alan A. "Psychology and Self-Transformation in the Sufi Qur'ān Commentary of Rūzbihān al-Baqlī." *Sufi Illuminations*, 1, 1996, 31–62.

—— "Sufi Koran Commentary: A Survey of the Genre." Web-based version of forthcoming article "al-Tafsir al-Sufi" to be published by the *Encyclopedia Iranica.* <www.arches.uga.edu/~godlas/suftaf/oldtafsuftoc.html> (accessed August 10, 2003).

Goldziher, Ignaz. *Die Richtungen der islamischen Koranauslegung.* Leiden: E.J. Brill 1952 (first published 1920).

Graham, William A. *Divine Word and Prophet Word in Early Islam: A Reconsideration of the Sources, with Special Reference to the Divine Saying or* Ḥadīth Qudsī. The Hague: Mouton and Co., 1977.

Habil, Abdurrahman. "Traditional Esoteric Commentaries on the Qur'an." *Islamic Spirituality: Foundations.* Ed. Seyyed Hossein Nasr. New York: Crossroad, 1987, pp. 24–47.

Ha'iri Yazdi, Mehdi. *The Principles of Epistemology in Islamic Philosophy: Knowledge by Presence.* Albany, NY: SUNY Press, 1992.

Halkin, A. S. "The Ḥashawiyya." *Journal of the American Oriental Society*, 54, 1934, 1–28.

Hawting, G.R. and A.K.A. Shareef, Eds. *Approaches to the Qur'an.* London: Routledge, 1993.

Heath, Peter. *Allegory and Philosophy in Avicenna (Ibn Sina): With a Translation of the Book of the Prophet Muḥammad's Ascent to Heaven.* Philadelphia, PA: University of Pennsylvania Press, 1992.

—— "Creative Hermeneutics: A Comparative Analysis of Three Islamic Approaches." *Arabica*, 36, 1989, 173–210.

Heer, Nicholas. "Abū Ḥāmid al-Ghazālī's Esoteric Exegesis of the Koran." *Classical Persian Sufism: From its Origins to Rumi.* Ed. Leonard Lewisohn. London: Khaneqahi Nimatullahi Publications, 1993, pp. 235–57.

Heinrichs, Wolfhart. "Contacts Between Scriptural Hermeneutics and Literary Theory in Islam: The Case of *Majāz*." *Zeitschrift für Geschichte der Arabisch-Islamischen Wissenschaften*, 7, 1991/2, 253–84.

—— "On the Genesis of the *Ḥaqīqa-Majāz* Dichotomy." *Studia Islamica*, 59, 1984, 111–40.

—— "Takhyīl and its Traditions." *God is beautiful and He loves beauty*. Eds Alma Giese and J. Christoph Bürgel. Bern: Peter Lang, 1994, pp. 227–47.

Homerin, Th.E. See translations: Ibn Taymiyya.

Hourani, George F. "The Chronology of Ghazālī's Writings." *Journal of the American Oriental Society*, 79, 1959, 225–33.

Izutsu, Toshihiko. *Creation and the Timeless Order of Things*. Ashland, OR: White Cloud Press, 1994.

Johns, A.H. "Solomon and the Queen of Sheba: Fakhr al-Dīn al-Rāzī's Treatment of the Qur'anic Telling of the Story," *Abr-Nahrain*, 24, 1986, 58–82.

Kassis, Hanna E. *A Concordance of the Qur'an*. Berkeley, CA: University of California Press, 1983.

Kermani, Navid. *Gott ist schön: Das ästhetische Erleben des Koran*. München: Verlag C.H. Beck, 1999.

Kholeif, Fathalla. *A Study on Fakhr al-Dīn al-Rāzī and His Controversies in Transoxiana*. Beirut: Dar El-Machreq, 1966.

Kinberg, Leah. "*Muḥkamāt* and *Mutashābihāt* (Koran 3/7): Implication of a Koranic Pair of Terms in Medieval Exegesis." *Arabica*, 35, 1988, 143–72.

Knysh, Alexander D. *Ibn 'Arabi in the Later Islamic Tradition: The Making of a Polemical Image in Medieval Islam*. Albany, NY: SUNY Press, 1999.

Lagarde, Michel. *Index du Grand Commentaire de Fakhr al-Dīn al-Rāzī*. Leiden: E.J. Brill, 1996.

Landolt, Hermann. "Ghazālī and '*Religionswissenschaft*': Some Notes on the *Mishkāt al-anwār* for Professor Charles J. Adams." *Asiatische Studien*, 45, 1991, 19–72.

Lane, E.W. *Arabic-English Lexicon*. 2 vols Cambridge: The Islamic Texts Society, 1984. (First published 1863–93).

Lewisohn, Leonard. *Beyond Faith and Infidelity: The Sufi Poetry and Teachings of Maḥmūd Shabistarī*. Richmond: Curzon Press, 1995.

Lory, Pierre. *Les Commentaires ésotériques du Coran d'après 'Abd ar-Razzāq al- Qāshānī*. Paris: Les Deux Oceans, 1980.

McAuliffe, Jane Dammen. *Qur'ānic Christians: An Analysis of Classical and Modern Exegesis*. Cambridge: Cambridge University Press, 1991.

—— "Qur'ānic Hermeneutics: The Views of al-Ṭabarī and Ibn Kathīr." *Approaches to the History of the Interpretation of the Qur'ān*. Ed. Andrew Rippin. Oxford: Clarendon Press, 1988, pp. 46–62.

Makdisi, George. "The Hanbali School and Sufism." *Humaniora Islamica*, 2, 1974, 61–72.

—— "Ibn Taimīya: A Ṣūfī of the Qādiriya Order." *American Journal of Arabic Studies*, 1, 1973, 118–29.

Mashīnī, Muṣṭafā Ibrāhīm. *Madrasāt al-tafsīr fī'l-Andalus*. Beirut: Mu'assasāt al-Risāla 1986.

Massignon, Louis. "Elie et son rôle transhistorique, Khadiriya, en Islam." *Opera Minora*, Ed. Y. Moubarac. Vol. 1. Beirut: Dār al-Ma'ārif, 1963, pp. 142–61.

—— *Essai sur les origines du lexique technique de la Mystique Musulmane*. 2nd ed. Paris: J. Vrin, 1968 (1st ed. Paris, 1922).

Massignon, Louis. "La Vie et les oeuvres de Ruzbehan Baqli." *Opera Minora*. Ed. Y. Moubarac. Vol. 2. Beirut: Dār al-Ma'ārif, 1963, pp. 451–65.

Michel, Thomas. See translations: Ibn Taymiyya.

Morris, James Winston. "Ibn Arabi and His Interpreters. Part II (Conclusion): Influences and Interpretations." *Journal of the American Oriental Society* 107, 1987, 101–19.

Murata, Sachiko. *The Tao of Islam: A Sourcebook of Gender Relationships in Islamic Thought*. Albany, NY: SUNY Press 1992.

Muṣṭafā, Aḥmad Amīn. *Takhrīj abyāt laṭā'if al-ishārāt l-imām al-Qushayrī wa dirāsat al-minhaj al-Qushayrī fī'l-istashād al-adabī*. Cairo: Al-Sa'āda, 1986.

Newby, Gordon. "Tafsir Isra'iliyat." *Journal of the American Academy of Religion*, 47, 1979, 685–97.

Nwyia, Paul. *Exégèse Coranique et Language Mystique: Nouvel essai sur le lexique technique des mystiques musulmans*. Beirut: Dar El-Masreq, 1970.

Pavlin, James. "The Medieval Debate over Quranic Hermeneutics: Ibn Taymiyyah's Discussion of al-Ghazali's Metaphysics in the *Bughtat al-Murtadd*." Paper presented at the American Academy of Religion Annual Meeting, Atlanta, GA, Nov. 22–25, 2003.

—— "The *Salafi*-ization of the *Fanā'*: Ibn Taymiyyah and the Annihilation of Self." Paper presented at the Middle East Studies Association Annual Meeting, Washington, DC, Nov. 19–22, 1999.

Rahman, Fazlur. "Dream, Imagination and *'Alam al-mithal*" in *The Dream and Human Societies*. Eds G.E. Grunebaum and Roger Caillois. Berkeley, CA: University of California Press, 1966, pp. 409–19.

Riddell, Peter G. "The Transmission of Narrative-Based Exegesis in Islam." *Islam: Essays on Scripture, Thought and Society*. Eds Riddell and Tony Street. Leiden: E.J. Brill, 1997, pp. 57–80.

Rippin, Andrew, Ed. *Approaches to the History of the Interpretation of the Qur'ān*. Oxford: Clarendon Press, 1988.

—— "The Present Status of *Tafsīr* Studies." *The Muslim World*, 72, 1982, 224–38.

Rokni, M. Mahdi. *Laṭāyif-i az Qur'ān-i karīm*. Mashhad: Mu'assasah-i chāp va intisharāt-i āstān-i quds-i raẓavi, 1996.

Rosenthal, Franz. *Knowledge Triumphant: The Concept of Knowledge in Medieval Islam*. Leiden: E.J. Brill, 1970.

—— *The Muslim Concept of Freedom Prior to the Nineteenth Century*. Leiden: E.J. Brill, 1960.

Sands, Kristin Zahra. "On the Popularity of Husayn Va'iz-i Kashifi's *Mavāhib-i 'aliyya*: A Persian Commentary on the Qur'an." *Iranian Studies*, 36, 2003, 469–83.

Schimmel, Annemarie. *Mystical Dimensions of Islam*. Chapel Hill, NC: University of North Carolina Press, 1975.

Sells, Michael A. "Bewildered Tongue: The Semantics of Mystical Union in Islam." *Mystical Union in Judaism, Christianity, and Islam*. Ed. Moshe Idel and Bernard McGinn. New York: Continuum, 1996.

—— *Early Islamic Mysticism: Sufi, Qur'an, Mi'raj, Poetic and Theological Writings*. New York: Paulist Press, 1996.

Sharī'at, Muḥammad Javād. *Fihrist-i tafsīr-i kashf al-asrār va 'uddat al-abrār ma'rūf bih tafsīr-i Khvājah 'Abd Allāh Anṣārī*. Tehran: Amīr Kabīr, 1363/1984.

Shorter Encyclopaedia of Islam, Eds H.A.R. Gibb and J.H. Kramers. Karachi: South Asian Publishers, 1981.

Smith, Jane I. and Yvonne Y. Haddad. "The Virgin Mary in Islam's Tradition and Commentary." *The Muslim World*, 79, 1989, 161–87.

Syafruddin, Didin, "The Principles of Ibn Taymiyya's Quranic Interpretation." M.A.Thesis, Institute of Islamic Studies, McGill University, Montreal, 1994.

Tabatabai, Allamah. "The Concept of *Al-Ta'wil* in the Qur'an." *Message of Thaqalayn*, 2, 1995, 21–40.

Thackston, W. M. See Translations: *The Tales of the Prophets of al-Kisa'i*.

Watt, W. Montgomery. "The Authenticity of the Works Attributed to al-Ghazālī." *Journal of the Royal Asiatic Society*, 1952, 24–45.

Weiss, Bernard. "Exotericism and Objectivity in Islamic Jurisprudence." *Islamic Law and Jurisprudence*. Ed. Nicholas Heer. Seattle: University of Washington Press, 1990.

Wensinck, A.J. *Concordance et indices de la tradition musulmane*, 2nd ed., 8 vols. Leiden: E.J. Brill, 1992.

—— *The Muslim Creed: Its Genesis and Historical Development*. New York: Barnes and Noble, 1965 (first published 1932).

Wheeler, Brannon M. "The Jewish Origins of Qur'ān 18:65–82? Reexamining Arent Jan Wensinck's Theory." *Journal of the American Oriental Society*, 118, 1998 153–71.

—— *Moses in the Quran and Islamic Exegesis*. London: RoutledgeCurzon, 2002.

Wolfson, Harry. "The Terms *Taṣawwur and Taṣdīq* in Arabic Philosophy and Their Greek, Latin and Hebrew Equivalents." *Muslim World*, 33, 1943, 114–28.

INDEX OF QUR'ĀNIC VERSES

INDEX OF *AḤĀDĪTH* AND SAYINGS

INDEX OF SELECTED NAMES AND TERMS